NEW PENGUIN SHAKESPEARE

GENERAL EDITOR: T. J. B. SPENCER

ASSOCIATE EDITOR: STANLEY WELLS

WILLIAM SHAKESPEARE

＊

THE LIFE OF
TIMON OF ATHENS

EDITED BY
G. R. HIBBARD

PENGUIN BOOKS

PENGUIN BOOKS

Published by the Penguin Group
Penguin Books Ltd, 27 Wrights Lane, London W8 5TZ, England
Penguin Books USA Inc., 375 Hudson Street, New York, New York 10014, USA
Penguin Books Australia Ltd, Ringwood, Victoria, Australia
Penguin Books Canada Ltd, 10 Alcorn Avenue, Toronto, Ontario, Canada M4V 3B2
Penguin Books (NZ) Ltd, 182–190 Wairau Road, Auckland 10, New Zealand

Penguin Books Ltd, Registered Offices: Harmondsworth, Middlesex, England

This edition first published in Penguin Books 1970
7 9 10 8

Printed in England by Clays Ltd, St Ives plc
Set in Monotype Ehrhardt

CONTENTS

INTRODUCTION

Timon of Athens is the bitterest and most negative of all Shakespeare's tragedies. The death of the hero is quite unlike the death of any other of his tragic protagonists. Timon does not die on stage, nor does he leave it fighting as Macbeth does. Instead of being borne off as a corpse, he makes his final exit on his own two feet, combining, as he goes, a malediction on humanity and its devotion to profit with a plea to nature for the sympathy that he neither expects nor desires from his fellow-men. His last words are:

> *Lips, let four words go by, and language end:*
> *What is amiss, plague and infection mend!*
> *Graves only be men's works, and death their gain!*
> *Sun, hide thy beams. Timon hath done his reign.*
>
> V.1.218–21

He is never seen again. Some twenty lines later, a soldier, who has been sent to seek for him, finds his tomb by the sea-shore. On it is an inscription, saying that Timon is dead, and an epitaph written in a language that the soldier does not know. Exactly how he died, or, indeed, how his body has come to be in the tomb, we are not told; his end remains a mystery. Yet we do not resent this lack of explicitness, or feel it as an artistic defect. On the contrary, it seems right and appropriate, for Shakespeare, at this point in the play, is dealing with a form of experience that cannot, by its very nature, be rendered through any grand heroic gesture, such as that with which Othello quits the scene of life. Since the end of Act III, Timon has

7

been cursing a world that has treated him abominably yet which refuses to leave him alone. Nauseated by the ingratitude and duplicity of the Athenians, he has vainly sought to isolate himself from them, and has even found some consolation in the spontaneity and simplicity of the natural world. But this is not enough to give him the will to live. He has now reached the stage at which there is nothing further to be done and nothing more to be said. Only death can grant him the total isolation from men and the absorption into the processes of the universe that he craves for. He recognizes that he has come to a dead-end, and he acts in accordance with what he has realized by disappearing into his cave, the dark hole in the earth from which he will emerge no more. In effect, he buries himself alive. It is the ultimate act of protest against the conditions of existence, and it is wholly negative. There is no affirmation of values here, for the assertion of his own royalty of nature that Timon makes in his final sentence is cancelled out by his action in abdicating his role as a man. Nevertheless, there is something admirable in the resolution, bleak, bitter, and disillusioned though it is, with which he accepts the grim logic of his situation. Whatever one may think about the attitude he has taken up, he has at least the virtue of holding to it and abiding by it with absolute consistency.

It is not only Timon's last exit, however, that sets him apart from Shakespeare's other tragic heroes, and that makes his tragedy unlike theirs; the way in which he is presented is also exceptional. Different from each other though they are, the rest all have this much in common, that they exist in a firmly defined context of close personal relationships, where ties of blood are of central importance. They have wives, or parents, or children, who are deeply involved in the tragic situation, and usually help to create it. Timon, on the other hand, appears before us in the state that Coriolanus aspires to but cannot possibly attain, since he has mother, wife, and child:

> *As if a man were author of himself*
> *And knew no other kin.*
>
> *Coriolanus*, V.3.36–7

Nor is it merely his lack of kindred that is strange; there seems to be no one with whom he is on truly intimate terms; and, strangest of all, women play no part whatever in his life.

Moreover, although the play is entitled *The Life of Timon of Athens*, it is, paradoxically, the most remote from biography of all the tragedies. Shakespeare, in his work generally, has a remarkable capacity for investing his characters with a past and for giving them a background by little touches, often widely dispersed over a play, that ultimately come together and cohere in the mind, creating the impression that these figures of the imagination have led an independent existence of their own before becoming caught up in the business of the play to which they belong. We know, for example, that Hamlet, when young, was much attached to Yorick the jester and was a great favourite with him; that he has been a student at the University of Wittenberg; that he was once 'The glass of fashion and the mould of form'; even that there was a time in his life when, in order to be in the fashion, he deliberately sought not to write the legible hand that he had been taught. Falstaff almost seems to have the needs of his biographer in mind when he tells the Lord Chief Justice: 'My lord, I was born about three of the clock in the afternoon, with a white head and something a round belly. For my voice – I have lost it with hallooing and singing of anthems' (2 *Henry IV*, I.2.176–9). There is nothing like this in Shakespeare's treatment of Timon. We are never told how he acquired his wealth, whether by inheritance or as a reward for some kind of service, or how long he has been giving it away, as we see him doing so generously at the play's opening. Even his age is left quite uncertain. He is not only a man without a family and without close personal relationships of any description, but also a man who is substantially without a past. He is, by far and away, the most generalized of all the tragic heroes.

This same generalized quality is also apparent in the other characters and in the design of the play as a whole, which has all the appearance of a radical experiment. The main outlines of the action are unusually simple and diagrammatic. What happens in this tragedy can be stated, without doing violence to it, in a few sentences. At the beginning Timon, who is the embodiment of philanthropy, is giving lavishly to the men he thinks of as his friends. He looks on his wealth as unlimited, but he has, in fact, given away so much already that he is on the verge of bankruptcy. The appearance of a number of servants, sent by his creditors to demand the repayment of the loans they have made to him, forces him to see his financial position as it really is. At first the knowledge does not depress him. Holding extremely idealistic views about the goodness of human nature and the solidarity of Athenian society, he regards his own necessitous state as a golden opportunity for proving the validity of his conviction that all men are brothers, only too eager to do benefits to each other. He therefore dispatches his servants to his various friends, requesting them for money. In each case the servant is met with a blank refusal. The shock produced by this cynical betrayal of his trust in human nature causes a transformation in Timon. His love for humanity turns into hatred of humanity; the philanthropist becomes the misanthropist.

Summoning his friends to a feast, he offers them dishes filled with lukewarm water, utters a scathing speech denouncing their hypocrisy and self-seeking, and finally drives them out of his house with blows. Then, disgusted with Athens and with human society, he retires to the woods, where he lives on roots and berries, voicing his disillusioned loathing of mankind in long searing curses of quite extraordinary power and virulence. Eventually, when the impulse to curse is exhausted, he makes his tomb by the sea, and there he dies.

In this sequence of events there has been no element of intrigue; and the fluctuations of fortune that make the other tragedies so exciting to witness or to read have had no place in it. *Timon of Athens* offers no conflict of 'mighty opposites' locked in a life-and-death struggle over an issue that is of supreme importance to both. The strenuousness that is so characteristic of Shakespearian tragedy in general is notably lacking from it. In so far as Timon has an antagonist at all, that antagonist is not another character but Athenian society as a whole and the naked self-interest by which that society is dominated. Even so, however, there is little justification for using the word 'conflict' in this connexion, since all that happens at the level of action is that Timon's friends milk him dry before he realizes that they are doing it, and then forget about him. He, for his part, gives them no cause to remember him, because his response to their treatment of him is to banish himself from Athens. It is the logical step for him to take, deriving from his perception of the fact that it is impossible to do battle against total indifference.

The play comes much closer to fable and parable than does any other of the tragedies. The course that the action will take has already been established and mapped out before Timon himself appears. The tragedy begins quietly with four of the hero's clients waiting to see their patron. As they talk, interest is focused on the account the Poet is giving the Painter of a composition that he has recently roughed out. It is an allegorical poem, designed as a warning to the hero. It depicts the goddess Fortune enthroned on the summit of 'a high and pleasant hill'. Down below men of all kinds wait eagerly for her favours, and, when she picks out Timon and summons him to her, they immediately become his sycophants, following close at his heels as he makes his way up the steep slope. But, as soon as the fickle goddess changes her mind and spurns Timon from her, his erstwhile adorers disregard him completely and allow him to fall, 'Not one accompanying his declining foot' (I.1.91). As well as forecasting how the action will develop, the Poet has announced some of the central themes of the play. Its concern is to be with certain basic human failings: the universal worship of fortune, in the sense of wealth; the readiness with which men resort to flattery, in order to ingratiate themselves with the wealthy; and, above all, the ingratitude they show to their benefactors, as soon as those benefactors cease to be of use to them. The audience, at this stage, has, of course, no means of deciding how far the Poet's preliminary sketch of what it is about to see is either accurate or complete, but it has been given a lead as to where its attention is to be focused up to the point where Timon is ruined.

The story of Alcibiades, which is obviously meant to serve as both a parallel and a contrast to that of Timon, is much less of a fable. Here there is a real conflict of characters and attitudes that takes the form of action. By trying to intervene with the Athenian Senate on behalf of a fellow-soldier of his who has killed another man in what appears to have been a duel, Alcibiades incurs the wrath of the Senate, which condemns him to banishment for his contumacy in daring to question its decree that the soldier be executed. His reaction is to gather an army together and march on the ungrateful city. But his anger against Athens, unlike Timon's hatred of mankind, is neither implacable nor undiscriminating. With the city lying at his mercy, he is met by two of the senators who assure him that not all of them were a party to his banishment, and that the men who were his and Timon's enemies are now dead. On these grounds they plead with him to spare the city; and, after listening to them, he eventually accedes to their request, on condition that the guilty shall be punished. By acting in this way and tempering justice with mercy, he brings the play to the normal conclusion of a Shakespearian tragedy, producing some kind of order and assurance of a continuity of government out of what would otherwise have been total chaos.

*

While the main function of Alcibiades in the play is clear enough, however, the manner in which his story is incorporated into the general design is far from satisfactory. In *King Lear*, the other tragedy that makes use of a double plot, Gloucester is introduced at the very beginning of the play, before Lear himself appears, and from then onwards he is never allowed to drop out of sight. Alcibiades, on the other hand, though he appears in the first scene, does nothing of any significance and seems no more than a minor character until the opening of III.5. At this point he suddenly and quite unexpectedly assumes a major role as he confronts the Senate and pleads passionately for the life of his friend. Viewed in isolation, the scene is highly dramatic, quite the most exciting thing in the play so far, but it loses some of the impact that it ought to make, because it has not been prepared for. There has been no mention hitherto of the friend, or of his crime; he is never seen on the stage, he is not even given a name. The senators describe him as 'a sworn rioter' and a thoroughly dissolute and subversive character, whereas Alcibiades regards him as a good soldier and a man of honour. It is never made clear which view of him is the right one, and there is no indication whether the sentence of death passed on him is actually carried out or not. It has been suggested that he is Timon himself, but there is no evidence whatever to support this idea. The whole incident remains tantalizing and obscure when it ought to be explicit, for it is of considerable structural importance. In the first place, it demonstrates that there is nothing anomalous about the ingratitude that the rulers of Athens show towards Timon, since they treat Alcibiades in exactly the same way, setting no more by the blood that he has shed for the state than they do by the benefactions that Timon has conferred on it; and, secondly, it has consequences that lead directly to the conclusion of the drama. The scene is a pivotal one, yet it has not been properly built into the action.

By comparison with the part of the play devoted to Alcibiades, that concerning Timon is far more coherent, though here too there are problems. The main one arises from the fact that we are not told enough, or told soon enough, about the nature of the hero's services to the state. The first hint we have of them is when Timon, now aware that he is bankrupt, says to Flavius:

> Go you, sir, to the senators,
> Of whom, even to the state's best health, I have
> Deserved this hearing. Bid 'em send o'th'instant
> A thousand talents to me.   II.2.201-4

The lines indicate that what Timon did must have been of great importance to justify the request for such a monstrous sum, but they leave the nature of his action un-specified. After this we hear no more of the matter until IV.3.93–6, when Alcibiades, having met the self-banished Timon in the woods, says to him:

> *I have heard, and grieved,*
> *How cursèd Athens, mindless of thy worth,*
> *Forgetting thy great deeds, when neighbour states,*
> *But for thy sword and fortune, trod upon them. . . .*

Here, at last, we seem to be about to learn just what it was that Timon did for the city; but again we are disappointed. The sentence is never completed. Timon cuts Alcibiades short; and all we know is that the hero played some vital part in saving the state at some unspecified time. Later it becomes clear that he has a great reputation as a soldier, since the Athenians, faced with Alcibiades and his aveng-ing army, seek desperately to persuade Timon to return to the city and organize its defence, plainly regarding him as the one man capable of leading an effective resistance. But by the time this happens, in the latter half of V.1, the play is nearly over, and, before the end of the scene, Timon has left the stage for good. Had we known from somewhere near the play's beginning about his achievements as a soldier, our sense of the ingratitude of Athens towards him would have been enormously increased, and so would our awareness of the parallel between his situation and that of Alcibiades. As it is, however, the arrival of the two senators to ask Timon for his help merely causes surprise and bewilderment. Like the scene between Alcibiades and the Senate, this should have been prepared for but has not been.

Something odd is happening when in a play by Shake-speare, who in the rest of his work is such a master in the art of plotting, it is possible to point to inadequacies in this respect that badly blunt the impact of what should have been two of the most significant scenes in the play. Odder still, while some of the material needed to make *Timon of Athens* a coherent and satisfactory drama appears to be missing, it contains other matter that seems to be otiose and irrelevant. The Fool, who turns up with Apemantus at II.2.49, is a case in point. He is on the stage for about seventy lines, during the course of which we learn that his mistress keeps a brothel, and that he perceives a close connexion between her trade and that of a usurer. But, after this scene is over, he never appears again, and even while it is taking place he says nothing that could not equally well have been said by Apemantus. It is hard to resist the conclusion that the Fool must be a false start, the vestige of some idea that Shakespeare had but then discarded.

Furthermore, the writing of the play is uneven. Much of it, and especially almost everything that is said by Timon from his entry '*in a rage*' towards the end of III.4, is in Shakespeare's mature manner, cogent in thought, supple in movement, impassioned in utterance, and rich in imagery. It leaves one in no doubt that this tragedy must be roughly contemporary with *King Lear* and *Coriolanus*, the two plays with which it has so many other things in common. But there are other passages where the writing seems comparatively thin. There is an abrupt drop in temperature, as it were, when Apemantus makes his first entry at I.1.177, and proceeds to rail against Athens and against Timon's guests; the scoffs and witticisms that Apemantus and the Fool direct at the usurers' men in II.2 look distinctly threadbare; and even in IV.3, which is the very heart of the play, it is difficult not to feel that the exchanges between Timon and Apemantus go on too long, and that the opprobrious epithets they hurl at each other do not do much credit to the inventiveness of either of them.

The conclusion that these strange features – the gaps in the plotting, the false start with the Fool, and the unevenness of the writing – point to is that *Timon of Athens* is not, at least in the form in which it has survived, a completely finished play. Parts of it are in their final shape, but other parts remain as first rough sketches for scenes that were left to be tidied up and tightened up; and it looks very much as though some scenes, or at any rate some essential pieces of information, still needed to be fitted in when Shakespeare laid the draft by. Further evidence that this is indeed the case is furnished by the state of the text. There are passages in which regular blank verse, what appears to be highly irregular blank verse, and what can most easily be read as prose, are found mixed with each other in an erratic and unpredictable manner. The exchanges that follow on the first entry of Apemantus are a good example. The first four lines of the dialogue between him and Timon (I.1.182–237) are in normal Shakespearian blank verse. Then follow four brief speeches that have a pronounced rhythm but that certainly do not fall into blank verse of any recognizable sort; and these are succeeded by a perfect line of verse (line 190). More irregular verse appears for the next nine lines, but eventually, at line 200, prose takes over, though even here one indisputable line of blank verse breaks in when Timon says: 'How dost thou like this jewel, Apemantus?' (line 213). The scene between Alcibiades and the Senate, III.5, though written in verse throughout, also has some unusual qualities. A high proportion of the lines are short lines, and the transitions from one idea to another are strangely abrupt. The firm yet flexible control of the complex verse paragraph which is one of the most impressive characteristics of Shakespeare's mature writing is absent from this scene. There is broken music where one would expect complicated harmonies. Most modern critics are agreed that these lines represent a first draft, left to be perfected in the process of revision, a process that was not completed in the text available to the printers of the Folio. The manner in which the tragedy found its way into the Folio, the numerous confusions about the names of characters, about entries, and about sums of money, together with the indefinite and impractical nature of many of the stage directions – more fully discussed in An Account of the Text (pages 255–62) – all lend support to the theory that the text, as we have it, must be an incomplete revision of a first draft, as does the number of passages in the play that yield no ready or satisfactory sense.

*

In many of Shakespeare's plays difficulties of reading and meaning can often be illuminated, and even cleared up, by a reference to his source or sources. In *Coriolanus*, for instance, a gap in the sense at II.3.242–4 can be made good by supplying the missing words from Plutarch's biography of the hero. But in the case of *Timon of Athens* the sources are of little assistance in such matters, because, for the greater part of the play, Shakespeare's dependence on them seems to have been of a general rather than a close and specific nature. He took the rough outlines of his sub-plot from Plutarch's *Life of Alcibiades*, the parallel life to that of Coriolanus; but Plutarch's account of the reasons that led to the banishment of Alcibiades from Athens is entirely different from Shakespeare's, and says nothing whatever about the mysterious friend condemned by the Senate. There is a brief mention of Timon in this biography, where he is called 'Timon, surnamed Misanthropus (as who would say, Loup-garou, or the manhater)', but this does not take one very far. Much more important is the short passage about Timon in Plutarch's *Life of Antony* – it is printed in *Shakespeare's Plutarch*, edited by T. J. B. Spencer (1964), pages 263–6 – from which Shakespeare derived the two epitaphs inscribed on Timon's tomb (V.4.70–73). This refers to the friendship between Timon and Alcibiades; it states that Timon sometimes made Apemantus of his company, because they were similar in character and behaviour; and it begins with the following description of Antony's actions on his return to Egypt after his defeat at the battle of Actium:

> *he forsook the city [Alexandria] and company of his friends, and built him a house in the sea, by the isle of Pharos, upon certain forced mounts which he caused to be cast into the sea, and dwelt there, as a man that banished himself from all men's company, saying that he would lead Timon's life, because he had the like wrong offered him that was before offered unto Timon; and that for the unthankfulness of those he had done good unto and whom he took to be his friends he was angry with all men and would trust no man.*
> (*Shakespeare's Plutarch*, page 263)

Here it is clearly suggested that Timon became a misanthrope because of the ingratitude of those he had helped, but there is nothing about his having once been extremely wealthy. Moreover, he is not completely antisocial, since he still lives in Athens and has some kind of relationship with Alcibiades and Apemantus. In short, while Plutarch provided Shakespeare with an idea and a few isolated incidents, he offered him nothing that could be called a plot.

The ultimate source of the plot in *Timon of Athens* is the dialogue *Timon, or the Misanthrope*, written in Greek by

Lucian of Samosata, who lived from about A.D. 125 to 180. The form in which Shakespeare knew this work is not clear. Lucian enjoyed great popularity in the sixteenth and seventeenth centuries; and though there was no English translation of this dialogue available to Shakespeare he could have read it in Latin, French, or Italian. It is also possible that he may have known of it from some intermediate writer, or even from conversation. An outline of the dialogue will establish its connexion with his play. It opens with Timon, now working as a farm-labourer in the field of Poverty, appealing to Zeus to punish his ungrateful friends, who flattered and fleeced him when he was rich but neglect and despise him since he became poor. Zeus eventually listens, and sends Plutus (Wealth) down to Timon. At first Timon is reluctant to receive Plutus, seeing him merely as a source of care and trouble, but, realizing that it is useless to struggle against the will of the gods, he finally plunges his spade into the soil and digs up gold. The news of his lucky strike spreads quickly, and he is soon besieged by his old friends, seeking to win his new-found wealth from him by flattery once more. But Timon is not to be taken in this time. He has made up his mind to keep his riches to himself, to live as a solitary, and to hate and mistrust all men. He allows each of the 'friends' to expose himself for the hypocritical sycophant that he really is, and then drives him away with blows from a mattock and with showers of stones.

The dialogue contains the essential matter of the play. Lucian explains, as Plutarch does not, precisely why Timon has become a misanthropist. He also provides the main motive for the later half of the tragedy, where Timon's discovery of gold in the woods brings his flatterers flocking back to him, so that they can be exposed to the full force of his irony and contempt. Even the basic pattern of the two works is the same, for Shakespeare begins his play by dramatizing the earlier part of Timon's life which is described in narrative form in the dialogue. There are no convincing verbal parallels between Lucian's dialogue and Shakespeare's play, but the dialogue does contain the material out of which come the incidents of Timon's freeing of Ventidius from gaol (I.1.98–112) and of his giving his servant Lucilius the money that will enable him to marry the daughter of the Old Athenian (I.1.114–55). Moreover, there are certain similarities of ideas. Hermes, speaking to Zeus about Timon's case, puts forward two alternative explanations to account for Timon's losing his wealth to his false friends, and he also equates the friends with birds and beasts of prey. He says:

Why, if you like to put it so, it was kindness and generosity and universal compassion that ruined him; but it would be nearer the truth to call him a fool and a simpleton and a blunderer; he did not realize that his protégés were carrion crows and wolves; vultures were feeding on his unfortunate liver, and he took them for friends and good comrades, showing a fine appetite just to please him.

(*The Works of Lucian of Samosata*, translated by H. W. Fowler and F. G. Fowler (Oxford, 1905), Volume I, pages 33–4)

Both of Lucian's explanations find their way into the play, and the notion of the flatterers as animals is enormously expanded in it, as is the complementary idea of parasites feeding on their host.

The most obvious difference between the play and the dialogue is that Shakespeare's Timon, unlike Lucian's, does not keep the gold that he finds and use it to go on living. He advises Flavius to do what Lucian's Timon expresses the intention of doing (IV.3.528–36), but he himself rejects both gold and life. The dialogue is a sardonic comedy, because disillusionment with society makes Lucian's Timon hard-bitten, cynical, and capable of coping with ungrateful men on their own terms. Shakespeare's play is tragic, because his Timon is, and remains, a man of feeling, rendered more vulnerable, not less so, by the disillusionment he undergoes.

*

Puzzling yet compelling, *Timon of Athens* has aroused reactions of the most widely divergent kind. Dr Johnson was favourably impressed by what he saw as its pronounced cautionary and didactic tendencies, writing of it:

> *The play of* Timon *is a domestic tragedy and therefore strongly fastens on the attention of the reader. In the plan there is not much art, but the incidents are natural, and the characters various and exact. The catastrophe affords a very powerful warning against that ostentatious liberality which scatters bounty but confers no benefits, and buys flattery but not friendship.*
>
> (*Dr Johnson on Shakespeare*, edited by
> W. K. Wimsatt (1969), pages 127–8)

In Johnson's eyes Timon is something of a fool. His behaviour is dictated by the desire to cut a figure; and he has no proper understanding of the nature of human relationships. There is much in the play to support this view. Time after time in the first Act, where Timon is giving so lavishly, Apemantus warns him that he is surrounded by flatterers, not friends, and that they are, in effect, eating him alive. He says, for example: 'O you gods! What a number of men eats Timon, and he sees 'em not! It grieves me to see so many dip their meat in one man's blood. And all the madness is he cheers them up to't' (I.2.38–41). The idea of cannibalism, of men preying on Timon, is, in fact, one of the leading themes of the tragedy, endorsed repeatedly by reiterated images. Timon, however, pays no heed to the surly cautions of the philosopher, dismissing them as the angry railings of a discontented man who is unfit for human society. Yet he is so naïve that he still makes Apemantus welcome on the sole grounds that he is an Athenian, saying to him: 'Th' art an Athenian, therefore welcome' (I.2.34–5). The assumption that all Athenians are good is plainly stupid, but it is in keeping with the sentiments that Timon voices in the affirmation of his faith in humanity and in the solidarity of society which he makes in the same scene, when he declares: 'We are born to do benefits. And what better or properer can we call our own than the riches of our friends?' (I.2.99–101). The trust and the idealism expressed here have their attractiveness, but there is no escaping the unrealistic quality of the attitude to mankind that Timon adopts; and the excessive emotionalism of the lines that follow as he bursts into tears suggests that there is a considerable element of self-indulgence about it all.

The first Act also makes it plain that Timon's behaviour is not of the kind that creates true friendship, since it is entirely lacking in reciprocity. His response to a gift is to regard it as a challenge, and to make it look trifling by repaying it with a much larger gift. The Second Lord is in the right when he remarks, near the end of the first scene:

> No meed but he repays
> Sevenfold above itself; no gift to him
> But breeds the giver a return exceeding
> All use of quittance.   I.1.282–5

A man who acts like this is positively asking to be exploited. Moreover, Timon's generosity cannot be called charity, since the main recipients of it are not those in true need but those who already have enough, and more than enough. He is, in fact, the prodigal, wasting his substance on show and vanity, as Apemantus tells him at the end of the first Act. The account that Flavius gives his master of the scenes of riot and drunkenness that have accompanied his great banquets leaves us in no doubt on this score. He speaks of occasions

When all our offices have been oppressed
With riotous feeders, when our vaults have wept
With drunken spilth of wine, when every room
Hath blazed with lights and brayed with minstrelsy. . . .

II.2.163–6

It is also made clear in these opening scenes that the money Timon is giving away so carelessly is not really his to give, since it is borrowed. His bankruptcy comes as a surprise to no one but himself, and it does not abate his naïveté, for he still believes that his friends will rally to his aid. Nor does he come to terms with things as they are when the true nature of his friends is revealed to him in a manner that admits of no evasion. All that he does is to swing from one extreme of folly to another. His ardent faith in the goodness of men is replaced by an equally undiscriminating conviction of the badness of men. Leaving his native city, he calls on the gods to destroy it, because it is wholly given over to wickedness. Oblivious of his previous assertion that all Athenians are welcome to him, he now cries out:

The gods confound – hear me, you good gods all –
Th' Athenians both within and out that wall.

IV.1.37–8

And, having taken up this attitude, he adheres to it in the face of the incontrovertible proof of its inadequacy and wrongheadedness that is brought by the appearance of Flavius in IV.3, come to comfort him and to offer all the help that is in his power. Confronted with the disturbing fact that men can be loyal, generous, and self-sacrificing, Timon makes Flavius an exception from the general curse that he has pronounced on humanity, but then gives him gold on condition that he becomes as much a misanthrope as his master. The rejection of the steward and all that he stands for is sheer perversity; Timon prefers to ignore facts rather than to abandon the negative stance that he has taken up.

When all this is taken into account, it looks as though Apemantus is in the right, and is giving a lead to the audience, when he tells Timon at their last meeting: 'Thou art the cap of all the fools alive' (IV.3.360). It does so until one turns to the play to see what the word 'fool' means in it. The opposite of 'foolish' is 'wise'; and a clear indication of the ironical significance that 'wise' takes on in this tragedy is provided by what Timon says to Flavius when the latter has finally convinced him that no motive other than pure disinterested goodness has brought him to seek his master. Comparing the conduct of Flavius with that of the rest of the world, Timon says:

> Methinks thou art more honest now than wise.
> For by oppressing and betraying me
> Thou mightst have sooner got another service. . . .
>
> IV.3.505–7

'Wise' here means 'worldly-wise, unprincipled and self-seeking', and it is opposed to 'honest', which thus becomes equated with 'foolish'. To dismiss Timon as a fool is to adopt the standards of his friends. Indeed, one of them, Lucullus, actually says of Timon: 'Every man has his fault, and honesty is his' (III.1.28), and then goes

25

on to try to bribe Timon's servant Flaminius into telling his master that he has been unable to see Lucullus, saying to him: 'Thy lord's a bountiful gentleman; but thou art wise. . . . Here's three solidares for thee. Good boy, wink at me, and say thou sawest me not'. The answer of Flaminius is to fling the coins back, whereupon Lucullus remarks: 'Ha! Now I see thou art a fool, and fit for thy master' (III.1.39–50).

Nor is it safe to take everything that Apemantus says at its face value. There is something of the choric figure about him, but he is certainly not an impartial and detached observer. His cynicism is an attitude that he has adopted in order to vent a grudge against the world and to make himself appear distinguished. In his own way he is ostentatious. He deals in the sweeping generalization that calls attention to itself by looking clever or outrageous. He has no sooner entered the play than he refers to all Timon's guests as knaves, and, on being asked why, retorts 'Are they not Athenians?', as though that proved the matter. Words like 'fool' and 'knave' are part of his stock in trade. That he is so often right about the Athenians is due to no particular insight on his part, but to the fact that Athens is a corrupt society with which Apemantus, a product of it, is very much in tune. The first thing we hear about him, before he has actually appeared on the stage at all, is that he too, though he abhors himself, is, nevertheless, a sycophant where Timon is concerned. The Poet tells us:

> *even he drops down*
> *The knee before him, and returns in peace*
> *Most rich in Timon's nod.*   I.1.62–4

The difference between Apemantus and Timon's friends is that they use others and feed on them for the sake of material profit, whereas he uses them in order to inflate his own ego and to feed his sense of superiority which is a sort of envy.

*

The true chorus in the first part of *Timon of Athens* is the three Strangers who appear in III.2. They have not been seen before, and they will not be seen again. They come from the world outside the play; they are not involved in the action in any way; they have no connexion with any of the other characters; their sole function is to offer a detached unbiased interpretation of what they witness; and they speak with a unanimous voice. They are, in fact, the representatives of true humanity and of religion. What they say, therefore, carries a peculiar weight and authority. The scene in which they take part is carefully chosen. It is the middle scene of the three consecutive scenes in which Timon's friends, one after the other, deny him in his need. In the course of it Lucius exposes himself completely for what he is, base, mercenary, and deceitful. After he has left the stage, the Strangers remain behind to comment on what they have seen. They are shocked and horrified. The First, with a clear allusion to the betrayal of Christ by Judas Iscariot, says:

> Who can call him his friend
> That dips in the same dish? III.2.67–8

The Third indicts the behaviour of Lucius in one telling sentence: 'Religion groans at it'; and the First concludes the scene by giving his version of Timon's character. There is not a word of criticism in it; Timon is given unstinted praise

> For his right noble mind, illustrious virtue,
> And honourable carriage. . . . III.2.82–3

27

What the scene depicts is the act of betrayal, already predicted by Apemantus in I.2, where, as he sits by himself at the great feast Timon is giving, he says: 'The fellow that sits next him, now parts bread with him, pledges the breath of him in a divided draught, is the readiest man to kill him' (I.2.45–8). Timon lives in a society where Judas is supreme. His fundamental error is that he is too trusting; he takes it for granted that men mean what they say. In one sense he has every reason to do so, because an absolute identity of promise and performance is the basis of his own life. The first thing we see him doing in the play is promising to pay the debt owed by Ventidius, thus freeing him from gaol. That promise is carried out; in the next scene, I.2, Ventidius appears as a free man. And, because promise and performance are synonymous for Timon, he makes the generous though foolish assumption that the two things are equally synonymous for others. It is not the loss of his wealth that disillusions him with mankind, but the proof that loss brings with it of the impossibility of reconciling what men do with what they say. When Alcibiades comes upon him in his self-imposed exile, and asks what he can do to show his friendship for him, Timon is completely sceptical. The dialogue between them runs thus:

ALCIBIADES *Noble Timon,*
  What friendship may I do thee?
TIMON *None, but to*
  Maintain my opinion.
ALCIBIADES *What is it, Timon?*
TIMON
  Promise me friendship, but perform none.
  If thou wilt promise, the gods plague thee, for
  Thou art a man. If thou dost not perform,
  Confound thee, for thou art a man. IV.3.70–76

Final confirmation of the deliberate divorce that Athens has made between saying and doing is provided by the arrival of the Poet and the Painter at Timon's cave in V.1. They have come because they have heard that he still has gold. Not knowing that he is overhearing them, they speak of their plans to fool him with promises they have no intention of keeping; and the Painter states their creed in all its cynicism by saying:

> *Promising is the very air o'th'time; it opens the eyes of*
> *expectation. Performance is ever the duller for his act, and*
> *but in the plainer and simpler kind of people the deed of*
> *saying is quite out of use. To promise is most courtly and*
> *fashionable. Performance is a kind of will or testament*
> *which argues a great sickness in his judgement that makes it.*
>
> V.1.22–8

This deliberate rejection of plain-dealing results in the finest piece of sustained irony in the whole play as Timon, taking advantage of what he has overheard, uses the word 'honest' time and again to and about the two prostitute artists while leading them on to the point where he at last shows them openly, in a manner which even they cannot mistake, what he really thinks of them.

For Timon, the inseparability of promise and performance is the foundation of human society. It is not his view alone, but one that he shares with Aristotle, Cicero, and the humanists of the sixteenth century. Sir Thomas Elyot, for example, in his book *The Governor* (1531), quotes Cicero as saying that 'nothing keepeth so together a public weal as faith [the honouring of covenants and agreements] doth' (Everyman edition, pages 222–3). It therefore follows that in Timon's eyes a society in which there is no trust among men is a contradiction in terms. He thus arrives at much the same position as that which

Jonathan Swift was to take up in his *Gulliver's Travels*. There, Gulliver, among the Houyhnhnms, has the greatest difficulty in making the horse who is his master understand what a lie is, because to say 'the thing which is not' is, to the horse, a total perversion of the function of language. Furthermore, it is this same perversion of speech that Gulliver concentrates on when describing the activities of a politician in terms that apply equally well to Timon's flatterers. He says:

> *I told him [the horse] that a first or chief minister of state, whom I intended to describe, was a creature wholly exempt from joy and grief, love and hatred, pity and anger; at least makes use of no other passions but a violent desire of wealth, power, and titles; that he applies his words to all uses, except to the indication of his mind; that he never tells a truth, but with an intent that you should take it for a lie; nor a lie, but with a design that you should take it for a truth. . . . The worst mark you can receive is a promise, especially when it is confirmed with an oath; after which every wise man retires, and gives over all hopes.*
>
> (*Gulliver's Travels*, Part IV, Chapter 6)

There are other similarities between the two works; for, just as Gulliver comes to prefer the company of the horses to that of human beings, so Timon comes to see his fellow-men as worse than the animal creation. There are good reasons why he should. For Shakespeare and his age, it was the gift of speech, the organ of rational thought and the instrument of society, that differentiated man from the beasts. His great contemporary Richard Hooker writes:

> *Between man and beasts there is no possibility of sociable communion, because the well-spring of that communion is a natural delight which man hath to transfuse from himself*

into others, and to receive from others into himself especially those things wherein the excellency of his kind doth most consist. The chiefest instrument of human communion therefore is speech, because thereby we impart mutually one to another the conceits of our understanding.... Civil society doth more content the nature of a man than any private kind of solitary living, because in society this good of mutual participation is so much larger than otherwise.
(*Of the Laws of Ecclesiastical Polity*, Book I,
Section X, Subsection 12)

It is 'this good of mutual participation' that Timon thinks he is pursuing in the first part of the play. What he is driven to realize by the pressure of experience is that those among whom he lives set no value by it, and that they consistently debase the currency of language, so that 'sociable communion' with them becomes impossible. Because, in the words of Apemantus, 'The commonwealth of Athens is become a forest of beasts' (IV.3.349–50), Timon leaves it, and goes off to the woods. The accusation that he shows no sense of the importance of reciprocity in friendship is true; but it does need to be balanced by a recognition that his honesty in word and deed, which is one of his most positive characteristics, meets with no reciprocal honesty from the world he moves in. Shakespeare underlines this fact in Act I. The main function of Apemantus at the beginning is to alert the audience to the hollowness of what Timon's 'friends' say. His deflating comments culminate in a specific and concrete reference to the idea of debasement. At the end of Timon's confession of faith in the brotherhood of man, which is the central speech in the second scene, the Second Lord says:

> *Joy had the like conception in our eyes,*
> *And at that instant like a babe sprung up.*

Apemantus promptly brings out the spurious nature of these sentiments by remarking:

> *Ho, ho! I laugh to think that babe a bastard.*
>
> I.2.107–9

*

The Painter, in his cynical justification of 'promise' as opposed to 'performance', makes an exception of 'the plainer and simpler kind of people', because they are so far behind the fashion as still to think of a man's word as his bond. This section of society is represented in the play by Flavius and the rest of Timon's servants, who remain true to him in his poverty and misfortune. Dr Johnson is emphatic that their behaviour reflects most favourably on the character of their master; he writes:

> *Nothing contributes more to the exaltation of Timon's character than the zeal and fidelity of his servants. Nothing but real virtue can be honoured by domestics; nothing but impartial kindness can gain affection from dependants.* (*Dr Johnson on Shakespeare*, page 127)

Johnson is, of course, right. Timon's household has been a genuine community in which the servants have thought of themselves as part of the family; and even when they have to leave it, in IV.2, they still feel that they belong to it in their hearts and that they will remain 'fellows' in spite of being separated from each other. The play is not only about the effect that the loss of his fortune has on Timon, it is also about the destruction of a whole way of life.

Timon's style of living, as it is depicted in the first part of the tragedy, conforms with that which was expected of a great man in the early seventeenth century. He lives in a large house; he is surrounded by masses of servants; he entertains; he hunts; he visits his friends and neighbours;

and, above all, he practises the old custom of 'housekeeping', meaning that he keeps open house for all and sundry in the manner so vividly described by Chaucer in his portrait of the Franklin in the Prologue to *The Canterbury Tales*. It is the fact that he can do so no longer which first brings home to him the nature of the reversal he has suffered. When he enters '*in a rage*' in III.4 it is because he has discovered that his doors, which have hitherto been open to all men, are now locked and barred to keep out his debtors. He says:

> *What, are my doors opposed against my passage?*
> *Have I been ever free, and must my house*
> *Be my retentive enemy, my gaol?*
> *The place which I have feasted, does it now,*
> *Like all mankind, show me an iron heart?*

> III.4.80–84

But as well as living according to the old feudal ideal of generous hospitality, Timon also seeks to live, as many aristocrats of the time were doing, according to the new Renaissance ideals. He is a patron of the arts, and he entertains his friends with a courtly masque as the fitting epilogue to the banquet he has provided for them. In fact, he goes in for the 'conspicuous consumption' which became such a pronounced feature of upper-class life in England during the last twenty years or so of Elizabeth's reign and continued under her successor. There was a passion for building new and elaborate houses; men appeared at court with 'whole manors on their backs' in the form of rich clothes; they put on lavish and spectacular shows for their sovereign; they began to spend part of each year in London; and they went in for the gentlemanly vice of gaming. Seeking to live up to two ideals of conduct, both expensive, at the same time, the great frequently

found themselves short of ready money, and proceeded to
borrow it. The situation of Timon, when he discovers that
his once extensive lands have been sold or mortgaged, was
not uncommon. Many of the Elizabethan aristocracy,
including Shakespeare's own patron the Earl of Southampton, to whom he had dedicated both *Venus and Adonis* and
The Rape of Lucrece, were deeply in debt. According to a
modern economic historian, Southampton's annual income
was well over £3,000, yet, when he took part in Essex's
revolt of 1601, he had raised at least £20,000 during the
previous four years by selling about a third of his estates,
and was still in debt to the tune of nearly £8,000. And he
was by no means an isolated case. (See Lawrence Stone,
The Crisis of the Aristocracy (1965), pages 482–5.)

The general attitude to the extravagance of the nobility
was not a critical one. Generosity was considered the true
mark of the aristocrat, for the original meaning of the
word 'generous', still current in Shakespeare's day, was
'of high birth'. To keep open house was to benefit one's
neighbours; to be lavish in spending was to create a sense
of magnificence, and to bring drama and excitement into
the lives of ordinary people. It is by no means unlikely that
Shakespeare, at the age of eleven, may have seen something of *The Princely Pleasures at Kenilworth*, the rich and
varied series of pageants and shows that the Earl of
Leicester put on to entertain the Queen, and which lasted
for three whole weeks. Moreover, writers generally were
very dependent on the patronage of the great. It was the
curmudgeon, regarded as responsible for 'the decay of
housekeeping', who was the object of satire, and, with
him, the usurer. Seeing the break-up of households such
as Timon's, men in general felt that living communities
were being destroyed to satisfy the greed of money-
lenders or 'covetous cormorants' as they were often

called. Nearly a hundred years before the composition of *Timon of Athens* Sir Thomas More had written: 'where money beareth all the stroke, it is hard and almost impossible that there the weal public may justly be governed, and prosperously flourish' (*Utopia*, Everyman edition, page 50). Since 1516 England had become far wealthier, and the power of money had increased, but men still tended to think along traditional lines. To the moralists, the preachers, the poets, and the playwrights, it seemed that human beings and human values were being sacrificed on the altar of gain.

Judas sold Christ for thirty pieces of silver. There are allusions to him in *Timon of Athens* because it is the same greed for money that turns the hero's friends into flatterers, debasing the currency of words, destroying his image of society, and betraying all that he believes in. In Athens there are, apart from the bond of loyalty and service that unites Timon's servants with their master, no valid human relationships. Their place has been taken by the cash-book and by a cold impersonal legalism. Alcibiades, when he appears before the Senate, makes the same discovery as Timon made in the previous scene. The Senate meets his passionate appeal that mercy should be shown to the condemned man and that his own services to the state should be taken into account with an unrelenting application of the letter of the law. Thwarted in his generous efforts, and banished for making them, he accuses the Senate of valuing nothing but money, saying to them:

> *Banish me?*
> *Banish your dotage. Banish usury*
> *That makes the Senate ugly.*   III.5.98–100

Seen from this point of view, the play is at least as much a social satire as a tragedy, for the destructive power of

35

money continues to obsess Timon after he has left Athens behind him. Alone in the woods, he digs for roots, and, like the Timon of Lucian's dialogue, he finds gold. But, instead of rejoicing over it, he execrates it, seeing it as the great transforming agent in life, turning all things into their opposites and corrupting their natures. It is not surprising that Karl Marx, in a note to his *Das Kapital* (Part I, Chapter III, Section 3a), should have quoted the lines beginning 'Gold? Yellow, glittering, precious gold?' (IV.3.26) in a passage which is concerned with explaining the way in which any commodity can be converted into money, for they are one of the most devastating expressions in literature of the consequences that come from substituting 'the cold cash nexus', as Marx called it, in place of true human relationships. In a series of vivid images, which enact the reversals they depict, Timon describes gold turning men away from religion and morality, leading them to commit murder, making a mockery of justice and authority, and replacing the joyful life-giving ceremony of marriage with a sordid bargain between greed on the one side and impotence and disease on the other.

*

Timon's soliloquy on the destructive power of money says much that is highly relevant to life in the early seventeenth century and, as Marx recognized, at any time since that date, but its primary interest, nonetheless, lies in what it tells us about the hero himself and about his state of mind. In its impassioned manner and in its resort to striking imagery it is unlike anything that he says in the earlier part of the play. It is true that in Act I he creates an impression of generosity and splendour and that he is the indubitable centre of interest, but he is not a figure that fills the mind with an immediate sense of greatness, nor does he speak the kind of poetry that lingers in the memory and that we soon come to recognize as his authentic utterance. A comparison with any of the other tragic heroes will establish this point at once. His main characteristic is that he is essentially a man of feeling, as his repeated references to the heart demonstrate, and it is his vulnerability that we are made most aware of. His part in the second movement of the play, which extends from the opening of Act II to within forty lines of the end of III.4, is confined to a single scene, II.2, where he is at last forced to recognize that he is ruined, and, with misplaced optimism, decides to send to his friends for aid. The centre of interest in this part of the play is Athenian society rather than the hero, and the prevailing tone is one of sardonic comedy as his creditors harry him and his friends let him down. The three parallel scenes at the opening of Act III are one of the great achievements of the play in their contemptuously accurate exposure of the gross ingratitude and the self-righteous hypocrisy that men are capable of when they feel their pockets threatened by the demand that they should put into practice the principles they have hitherto found it highly profitable to profess. Here Timon is acted on. We are kept aware of him, but we do not see what is happening to him.

Then, at III.4.79, Timon enters '*in a rage*' (to quote the original stage direction). The third and final movement has begun. He is a changed man, speaking a new language. It has acquired a sharp cutting-edge, such as it has never had before. He quibbles on the word 'bills', and bids the usurers' men, who are importuning him for payment, to 'Knock me down with 'em; cleave me to the girdle' (III.4.91), because he now realizes that in Athens a piece of paper acknowledging a debt is a deadly weapon. Moreover, when he speaks to Flavius at the end of this scene, giving orders that his friends be invited to yet another banquet, he has gained a new kind of confidence; there is something almost sinister in the assurance with which he makes his wishes known without revealing their purpose. From this point onwards he dominates the play by virtue of what he says.

The new attitude and the new language correspond to a new insight into things. The difference between Act I and the third movement, which has now started, is like the difference between William Blake's *Songs of Innocence* and his *Songs of Experience*. Practically everything that happens in this third movement – and it is this more than anything else that gives the play its unique design – is either a reversal or a repetition of what happened in Act I. The magnificent banquet of I.2, where Timon expressed his faith in the reality and value of friendship, becomes the mock-banquet of III.6, where he proclaims the villainy of mankind and denounces his false friends, describing them as animals endowed with the specific and universal human quality of hypocrisy. Instead of being the splendidly dressed centre of a throng of admirers, he is now, by deliberate choice, a naked solitary. In Athens he lost his wealth by giving it away to help and pleasure others; in the woods he finds gold, but he gives it now to thieves and whores, so that they may use it to destroy and infect others. The characters who appeared in Act I reappear. They have not changed, but Timon has, and he therefore sees them in another light, finding a bitter ironical satisfaction in turning them inside out, as it were, to reveal the seamy reality beneath the smooth exterior.

The tragedy of Timon is the tragedy of innocence betrayed. When he enters in a rage, he has undergone the shattering experience of having learnt that those he has loved and trusted have been using him as a mere instrument for furthering their own ends; that he himself, for what he is in himself as a unique personality, has meant nothing to them; and that the code of values he has lived by has no validity for society. For a man like Timon, who has believed implicitly in what Keats calls 'the holiness of the Heart's affections', the result of this discovery of chaos in the world outside him is an emotional chaos in himself. Yet, to his credit, he makes no attempt to get even with his betrayers by adopting their standards and tactics. Apemantus, coming to him in the woods, suggests that he should, telling him:

> *Be thou a flatterer now, and seek to thrive*
> *By that which has undone thee.*   IV.3.211–12

But Timon rejects any such course. In fact, he has rejected it – if he has ever given it a thought – before Apemantus appears to tempt him to it. There is a clear and pointed contrast in this respect between him and Alcibiades. In seeking vengeance on Athens the soldier is, in a sense, merely acting towards the Athenians as they have acted towards him; and, because his attitude is at bottom not really different from that of the Senate, he is ultimately able to reach an accommodation with them. Timon is, however – and it is the quality in him that endows him with tragic grandeur – an absolutist, not a temporizer. Apemantus is quite right when he tells Timon: 'The middle of humanity thou never knewest, but the extremity of both ends' (IV.3.302–3), but the judgement is also irrelevant, for, had Timon been a man of moderation, there would have been no tragic action. For him there can be no compromise; since Athens has betrayed him, since no one in it shares his convictions about the nature and purpose of human life, and since these convictions are too deeply held to be lightly abandoned, he does the only thing possible; he leaves Athens and attempts to live by himself.

Timon's original error – the typical error of the innocent man – was to mistake the iron age in which he was really living for the golden age of brotherly love. He now seeks to go back to the true golden age of myth when there was no money, no trade, and when men were supposed to have lived on the natural fruits of the earth. The most positive thing in the last part of the play, even though it is applied in the end to satirical purposes, is the marvellous feeling that Timon shows for the bountifulness of nature and for the richness and fertility of the good earth, the common mother of all living things. The lines that he addresses to the Bandits seem to anticipate Caliban's description of the fruitfulness of the magical island in *The Tempest*. He tells them:

> *Why should you want? Behold, the earth hath roots;*
> *Within this mile break forth a hundred springs;*
> *The oaks bear mast, the briars scarlet hips;*
> *The bounteous housewife Nature on each bush*
> *Lays her full mess before you. Want? Why want?*

IV.3.419–23

But Timon is not a sub-human creature like Caliban, to whom solitude is the normal condition of existence. To him a society of one is no society. His body may be in the woods, but his heart and mind are still in Athens. Whether he has an audience or not, he has to go on speaking. The impulse to use the 'chiefest instrument of human communion' is irrepressible in him. The great curses that he utters, filled with bitterness and loathing, are the expressions of a thwarted love for man that feeds upon itself. It is not cynicism that leads him to pray in IV.1 that all the normal arrangements of society should be overturned and destroyed. His speech is the words of a man who has believed deeply and whole-heartedly in the ideal of an ordered civilized state, but who has been driven to the conclusion that order in Athens is a mockery of the real thing, masking a chaotic conflict of appetites. He therefore asks that the true state of affairs be recognized, saying:

> *Piety and fear,*
> *Religion to the gods, peace, justice, truth,*
> *Domestic awe, night-rest, and neighbourhood,*
> *Instruction, manners, mysteries, and trades,*
> *Degrees, observances, customs, and laws,*
> *Decline to your confounding contraries,*
> *And yet confusion live.*   IV.1.15–21

Yet the very terms in which the curse is phrased, together with its orderly progression, bear witness to the profound reverence and affection that Timon has for these principles of civilized living. It is the perversion of them that he hates, not the principles themselves.

The puzzling and powerfully disturbing feature in the curses is their intense and obsessive concern with sex and with sexual disease. Timon has shown no interest in this side of life hitherto; in fact, the absence of women from the first part of the play is one of its strangest characteristics. But, as soon as he leaves Athens, sex becomes a major preoccupation with him. How does it come about? There are two possible answers. First, there is an obvious link – it is also present in *Measure for Measure* – between the practice of usury and that of prostitution. In both cases advantage is taken of other people's needs in order to treat them as mere instruments to be exploited for gain and pleasure. Moreover, the idea of money as a bawd or a whore was a commonplace of the time, since money is used promiscuously by one man after another. Timon actually addresses the gold he finds as 'Thou common whore of mankind' (IV.3.43). The second and more important reason for the prevalence of sexual ideas and images in this part of the play is that Timon clearly hates himself for having bestowed his own love on the undeserving who have thrown it back in his face.

All the same, the violence, the intensity, and the hysteria of these curses do convey the impression that there is something radically wrong with Timon himself. This sense is increased and endorsed by the fact that his anger and his criticism are directed outwards, not at himself. The comparison with King Lear, who also curses on a gigantic scale, is instructive. Though Timon's wrongs are great, they are as nothing by the side of those that Lear endures. Yet Lear passes beyond the stage of self-pity to a full recognition of his own responsibility for what has happened. As a result he grows in stature. This does not happen to Timon. He pities himself, and comes close to asking for pity from Apemantus at the very moment that he reviles the philosopher most bitterly. Speaking of the way in which his friends have treated him, he says that they

> left me open, bare,
> For every storm that blows

and then he adds:

> I to bear this,
> That never knew but better, is some burden.
> IV.3.266–8

Instead of coming to terms with himself and growing in spiritual stature as a consequence of his experience, Timon remains immobilized, as it were, in the fixed posture of the much wronged man. And he persists in that posture after Flavius has proved to him that his original vision of society was not altogether wrong. There is about him something of the obstinacy of the man who is weak and unsure of himself. In the last analysis he is, as a tragic hero, inadequate, because he lacks that inner core of resolution that enables a man to look at himself as he really is.

Nevertheless, we prefer him to Apemantus because, unlike the professional cynic, Timon always cares. The very force with which he denounces man shows that man's estate remains a matter of passionate concern to him, though the concern is an inverted one. Nor must it be overlooked that those who visit him in the woods, with the single exception of Flavius, do nothing and say nothing that can affect the attitude he has adopted. They merely serve to harden him in it. Indeed the conversation between the Poet and the Painter which he overhears might have been designed for that purpose; and the way in which the two Senators speak about the city's love for him in terms of entries in a ledger, when they come to ask for his aid in V.i, shows conclusively that Athens has not changed in the least.

Furthermore, something does happen to Timon himself. By uttering his rage he gains a greater control over it – the subtle and restrained irony with which he exposes the two artists is another sort of thing from the invective that he hurls at Apemantus – and finally exhausts it. Gradually a new kind of music begins to make itself heard, as his thoughts move from the injustice of the world to the constant movement of the sea that is bitter and desolate but also neutral and indifferent. For him the sea becomes associated with death and release. Both the exhaustion and the fresh direction of the thought are evident for the first time as he turns away wearily from his railing-match with Apemantus, and, addressing himself, says:

> *Then, Timon, presently prepare thy grave.*
> *Lie where the light foam of the sea may beat*
> *Thy grave-stone daily.*   IV.3.379–81

Here the note is one of defeat, but something more positive emerges when, in the course of his meeting with the two Senators, Timon becomes abstracted for a time from the immediate business in hand, and, again speaking as though to himself, says:

> *My long sickness*
> *Of health and living now begins to mend,*
> *And nothing brings me all things.*   V.1.184–6

The lines suggest not merely that he has resigned himself to the fact of death, but also that in a manner he cannot properly grasp or define his experience of destitution has brought some kind of understanding. The sentiment certainly has much in common with the medieval *contemptus mundi*, the conception of life as an inevitable but painful period during which the soul is incarcerated in the prison of the body from which it longs to escape, through the door of death, into its own true home, which is outside this world altogether. But this new insight is never developed or made more explicit. In the end we are left with the lonely grave 'Upon the beachèd verge of the salt flood' (V.1.214), and with the unrelenting epitaphs inscribed upon it. The hint that Timon may have learnt something of vital importance from what has happened to him remains as nothing more than a tantalizing possibility. Characteristically the play offers no assurance.

FURTHER READING

Editions and Editorial Problems

THE most recent scholarly editions of the play, to both of which the present edition is much indebted, are by J. C. Maxwell in the New Cambridge Shakespeare (1957), and by H. J. Oliver in the new Arden Shakespeare (1959). There is a concise statement of the textual peculiarities of *Timon of Athens* in W. W. Greg's *The Shakespeare First Folio* (Oxford, 1955); and the case for its being an unfinished work is well put by Una Ellis-Fermor in her essay '*Timon of Athens*: An Unfinished Play', published originally in the *Review of English Studies* 18 (1942), and now available in her *Shakespeare the Dramatist*, edited by Kenneth Muir (1961). E. A. J. Honigmann makes some excellent suggestions about the nature of the text in his *The Stability of Shakespeare's Text* (1965); and C. J. Sisson's *New Readings in Shakespeare* (Cambridge, 1956) is helpful on some of the detail. The most comprehensive account of the circumstances in which the play was printed and of the way in which the text was set up is by Charlton Hinman in his monumental work *The Printing and Proof-Reading of the First Folio of Shakespeare* (Oxford, 1963).

Sources

The fullest collection of sources and analogues, together with an introductory essay on them, is in Geoffrey Bullough's *Narrative and Dramatic Sources of Shakespeare*, Volume 6 (1966). The passage about Timon in Plutarch's *Life of Antony* is also to be found in *Shakespeare's Plutarch*, edited by T. J. B. Spencer (Penguin Shakespeare Library, 1964), pages 263–6. There is a thorough review of the source material in the chapter on the play in Willard Farnham's *Shakespeare's Tragic Frontier*

(Berkeley and Los Angeles, 1950); and some interesting ideas about the possibility of the Timon story having been affected by oriental tales in G. A. Bonnard's 'Note sur les sources de *Timon of Athens*', *Études Anglaises* 7 (1954), pages 39–69. The relationship between Shakespeare's tragedy and the academic play *The Comedy of Timon*, which she regards as a burlesque of it, is examined by M. C. Bradbrook in her essay '*The Comedy of Timon*: A Reveling Play of the Inner Temple', *Renaissance Drama* 9 (1966), pages 83–103.

Criticism

The critical disagreement that *Timon of Athens* has given rise to over the last three centuries is recorded and studied by Francelia Butler in her book *The Strange Critical Fortunes of Shakespeare's 'Timon of Athens'* (Ames, Iowa, 1966). In the eighteenth century there was little controversy over what the play was about; it was seen, as Dr Johnson saw it (*Dr Johnson on Shakespeare*, edited by W. K. Wimsatt, Penguin Shakespeare Library, 1969, pages 127–8), as a moral play, showing the dangers of ostentatious liberality. This line of approach was most fully developed by William Richardson in the relevant section of his *Essays on Shakespeare's Dramatic Characters* (1783). The romantics, however, viewed it in a different light. William Hazlitt thought highly of it, seeing Timon as the idealist in conflict with the world, and describing it in his *Characters of Shakespeare's Plays* (1817) as one of the few plays by Shakespeare in which 'he seems to be in earnest throughout, never to trifle nor to go out of his way'. Algernon Swinburne goes much further than Hazlitt; for him Timon is a Christ-like figure of the pre-Christian era whose main characteristic is his nobility (*A Study of Shakespeare*, 1880).

Broadly speaking, criticism of the tragedy in the twentieth century has followed either the romantic line of approach in regarding Timon as the idealist and much wronged man, or the eighteenth-century view that Shakespeare's attitude to him is a critical one and that he is presented as an inadequate human being, if not a foolish one. The most enthusiastic and distinguished exponent of the romantic reading of the play is G. Wilson Knight, whose essay on it in his book *The Wheel of Fire* (1930) has done more to stimulate interest in *Timon of Athens* than any other interpretation of it. Knight, who has played the part of Timon, describes the tragic movement of this drama as being 'more precipitous and unimpeded than any other in Shakespeare; one which is conceived on a scale even more tremendous than that of *Macbeth* and *King Lear*; and whose universal tragic significance is of all most clearly apparent'. The rhetorical manner in which the essay is written engenders mistrust in many, including the present editor, but, despite its excesses, this study does offer a reading of the play which cannot be ignored. Peter Alexander is much more concise than Wilson Knight, but his comments in his *Shakespeare's Life and Art* (1939) leave one in no doubt that he is in agreement with Knight about Timon's essential nobility of spirit, and he adds the telling *caveat*: 'To say that Timon took his trouble too much to heart is just what the senators said of the soldier [condemned to death in III.5]; and the criticism that finds in his untimely death a judgment on his "kindly self-indulgence" or "easy generosity" is exactly in the senatorial vein' (page 184). Further support for this position is provided by A. S. Collins who finds the central theme of the play in the conflict between the ideal of friendship and a commercial society ('*Timon of Athens*: A Reconsideration', *Review of English Studies* 22 (1946), pages 96–108), and by E. C. Pettet, whose essay '*Timon of Athens*: The Disruption of Feudal Morality', published in the *Review of English Studies* 23 (1947), pages 321–36, relates the action of the tragedy to the controversy over usury and sees the work as 'a tract for the times'. Harold S. Wilson is largely on the same side in his book *On the Design of Shakespearian Tragedy* (Toronto, 1957), but he thinks of the play as essentially a poem, and admits that it is very difficult to stage satisfactorily.

The complete antithesis to the attitude of the critics mentioned above is to be found in O. J. Campbell's *Shakespeare's Satire* (New York, 1943), where the play is presented as a 'tragical satire' in the manner of Ben Jonson, with Timon himself as a fool and an object of scorn. A much more judicious account is given by Willard Farnham, in his *Shakespeare's Tragic Frontier*. He considers Timon to be 'a deeply flawed hero', draws attention to the use of beast imagery in the play, and concludes that the final note is one of pity for the hero, despite his faults. This is substantially the verdict of J. C. Maxwell and H. J. Oliver in the pithy introductions to their respective editions of the tragedy, listed under *Editions and Editorial Problems* (page 45). Derek Traversi takes much the same line in his chapter on the play in the third, revised and enlarged, edition of his *An Approach to Shakespeare* (1969); and it has been further reinforced by a distinguished essay from L. C. Knights, '*Timon of Athens*', published in *The Morality of Art*, edited by D. W. Jefferson (1969).

The imagery of the play, which is one of its most striking characteristics, excited interest as long ago as the eighteenth century when Walter Whiter had some excellent things to say about it in his *A Specimen of a Commentary on Shakespeare* (1794), now available in an edition by Alan Over and Mary Bell (1967). The fullest treatment of the matter is in W. H. Clemen's *The Development of Shakespeare's Imagery* (1951).

Some fresh thinking about the structure of the tragedy, and especially about the use of parallels and contrasts in it, is to be found in E. A. J. Honigmann's essay '*Timon of Athens*', published in *Shakespeare Quarterly* 12 (1961), pages 3–20; and T. J. B. Spencer has dealt with the confusion over the talents in a learned and entertaining fashion in his 'Shakespeare Learns the Value of Money', *Shakespeare Survey* 6 (1953), pages 128–35.

A radically new analysis, both of the structure and of the meaning of the drama, is given by M. C. Bradbrook in her lecture *The Tragic Pageant of 'Timon of Athens'*, which is now available in her book *Shakespeare the Craftsman* (1969). Relating the play to the shows and pageants of the time, as well as to the court masque, she argues that it is an experiment in a new mode.

Those who are interested in the relationship between *Timon of Athens* and the other late tragedies cannot do better than consult G. K. Hunter's essay 'The Last Tragic Heroes', published in *Later Shakespeare* (Stratford-upon-Avon Studies 8), edited by J. R. Brown and B. Harris (1966); and those who find Shakespeare's picture of classical Athens bizarre and disconcerting will find some excellent reasons for revising this view if they will turn to ' "Greeks" and "Merrygreeks": A Background to *Timon of Athens* and *Troilus and Cressida*', by T. J. B. Spencer, published in *Essays on Shakespeare and Elizabethan Drama*, edited by Richard Hosley (1963).

The last decade has seen no slackening of interest in the tragedy. It is treated at length by Rolf Soellner in his '*Timon of Athens* : *Shakespeare's Pessimistic Tragedy*' (Columbus, Ohio, 1979), which also contains an account of the play's stage history by Gary Jay Williams. Maurice Charney provides a compact and judicious review of critical opinion over the years in his contribution to *Shakespeare: Select Bibliographical Guides*, edited by Stanley Wells (Oxford, 1973). The possible connection between Shakespeare's play and the anonymous comedy *Timon* has been further explored by James C. Bulman, Jr. in two articles: 'The Date and Production of "Timon" Reconsidered', *Shakespeare Survey 27* (1974), and 'Shakespeare's Use of the *Timon* Comedy', *Shakespeare Survey 29* (1976). As the latter title shows, he is firmly of the opinion that the comedy preceded *Timon of Athens* and that Shakespeare made considerable use of it. Bertrand Evans, in his *Shakespeare's Tragic Practice* (Oxford, 1979), more interested than most critics are in the conduct of the tragic action, links *Timon* with *Coriolanus* because, as he puts it, the two protagonists are, of all the tragic heroes, 'least equipped to survive in their worlds'; and Harry Levin emphasizes what he sees as the play's limitations and inadequacies in his 'Shakespeare's Misanthrope', *Shakespeare Survey 26* (1973).

G.R.H.
April 1980

THE LIFE OF TIMON OF ATHENS

THE CHARACTERS IN THE PLAY

TIMON, a noble Athenian
FLAVIUS, Timon's steward
FLAMINIUS ⎫
LUCILIUS ⎬ servants of Timon
SERVILIUS ⎪
and others ⎭
ALCIBIADES, an Athenian captain
PHRYNIA ⎫ mistresses of Alcibiades
TIMANDRA ⎭

APEMANTUS, a churlish philosopher
A Fool
A Page
Three Strangers

LUCIUS ⎫
LUCULLUS ⎬ flattering lords
SEMPRONIUS ⎭
VENTIDIUS, one of Timon's false friends
Other Lords
CAPHIS ⎫
PHILOTUS ⎪ servants of the flattering lords and of
TITUS ⎬ Timon's creditors
HORTENSIUS ⎪
and others ⎭
A Poet
A Painter
A Jeweller

A Merchant
An Old Athenian
Seven Senators
Three Bandits
Soldier
Two Messengers
Cupid and Amazons in the masque
Other Soldiers, Officers, and Attendants

Enter Poet and Painter, Jeweller and Merchant, at **I.1**
several doors

POET

  Good day, sir.

PAINTER   I am glad y'are well.

POET

  I have not seen you long. How goes the world?

PAINTER

  It wears, sir, as it grows.

POET   Ay, that's well known.
  But what particular rarity? What strange,
  Which manifold record not matches? See,
  Magic of bounty, all these spirits thy power
  Hath conjured to attend! I know the merchant.

PAINTER

  I know them both; th'other's a jeweller.

MERCHANT

  O, 'tis a worthy lord!

JEWELLER   Nay, that's most fixed.

MERCHANT

  A most incomparable man, breathed, as it were,   10
  To an untirable and continuate goodness.
  He passes.

JEWELLER I have a jewel here –

MERCHANT

  O pray, let's see't. For the Lord Timon, sir?

JEWELLER

  If he will touch the estimate. But for that –

POET (*reciting to himself*)
  'When we for recompense have praised the vile,
  It stains the glory in that happy verse
  Which aptly sings the good.'
MERCHANT (*looking at the jewel*) 'Tis a good form.
JEWELLER
  And rich. Here is a water, look ye.
PAINTER
  You are rapt, sir, in some work, some dedication
20 To the great lord.
POET   A thing slipped idly from me.
  Our poesy is as a gum which oozes
  From whence 'tis nourished. The fire i'th'flint
  Shows not till it be struck. Our gentle flame
  Provokes itself, and like the current flies
  Each bound it chafes. What have you there?
PAINTER
  A picture, sir. When comes your book forth?
POET
  Upon the heels of my presentment, sir.
  Let's see your piece.
PAINTER
  'Tis a good piece.
POET
30 So 'tis. This comes off well and excellent.
PAINTER
  Indifferent.
POET   Admirable. How this grace
  Speaks his own standing! What a mental power
  This eye shoots forth! How big imagination
  Moves in this lip! To th'dumbness of the gesture
  One might interpret.
PAINTER
  It is a pretty mocking of the life.

56

Here is a touch. Is't good?
POET   I will say of it,
   It tutors nature. Artificial strife
   Lives in these touches livelier than life.
        Enter certain senators, and pass over the stage
PAINTER
   How this lord is followed!   40
POET
   The senators of Athens – happy man!
PAINTER
   Look, more!
POET
   You see this confluence, this great flood of visitors.
   I have in this rough work shaped out a man
   Whom this beneath world doth embrace and hug
   With amplest entertainment. My free drift
   Halts not particularly, but moves itself
   In a wide sea of tax. No levelled malice
   Infects one comma in the course I hold,
   But flies an eagle flight, bold and forth on,   50
   Leaving no tract behind.
PAINTER
   How shall I understand you?
POET
   I will unbolt to you.
   You see how all conditions, how all minds,
   As well of glib and slipp'ry creatures as
   Of grave and austere quality, tender down
   Their services to Lord Timon. His large fortune,
   Upon his good and gracious nature hanging,
   Subdues and properties to his love and tendance
   All sorts of hearts; yea, from the glass-faced flatterer 60
   To Apemantus, that few things loves better
   Than to abhor himself – even he drops down

57

The knee before him, and returns in peace
Most rich in Timon's nod.

PAINTER

I saw them speak together.

POET   Sir,
I have upon a high and pleasant hill
Feigned Fortune to be throned. The base o'th'mount
Is ranked with all deserts, all kind of natures,
That labour on the bosom of this sphere
70 To propagate their states. Amongst them all
Whose eyes are on this sovereign lady fixed
One do I personate of Lord Timon's frame,
Whom Fortune with her ivory hand wafts to her,
Whose present grace to present slaves and servants
Translates his rivals.

PAINTER   'Tis conceived to scope.
This throne, this Fortune, and this hill, methinks,
With one man beckoned from the rest below,
Bowing his head against the steepy mount
To climb his happiness, would be well expressed
80 In our condition.

POET   Nay, sir, but hear me on.
All those which were his fellows but of late –
Some better than his value – on the moment
Follow his strides, his lobbies fill with tendance,
Rain sacrificial whisperings in his ear,
Make sacred even his stirrup, and through him
Drink the free air.

PAINTER   Ay, marry, what of these?

POET

When Fortune in her shift and change of mood
Spurns down her late beloved, all his dependants,
Which laboured after him to the mountain's top
90 Even on their knees and hands, let him fall down,

58

Not one accompanying his declining foot.

PAINTER

'Tis common.
A thousand moral paintings I can show
That shall demonstrate these quick blows of Fortune's
More pregnantly than words. Yet you do well
To show Lord Timon that mean eyes have seen
The foot above the head.

> *Trumpets sound. Enter Lord Timon, addressing him-*
> *self courteously to every suitor; a Messenger from*
> *Ventidius talking with him; Lucilius and other*
> *servants following*

TIMON

Imprisoned is he, say you?

MESSENGER

Ay, my good lord. Five talents is his debt,
His means most short, his creditors most strait.   100
Your honourable letter he desires
To those have shut him up, which failing
Periods his comfort.

TIMON   Noble Ventidius! Well,
I am not of that feather to shake off
My friend when he must need me. I do know him
A gentleman that well deserves a help,
Which he shall have. I'll pay the debt, and free him.

MESSENGER

Your lordship ever binds him.

TIMON

Commend me to him. I will send his ransom;
And, being enfranchised, bid him come to me.   110
'Tis not enough to help the feeble up,
But to support him after. Fare you well.

MESSENGER

All happiness to your honour!   *Exit*

Enter an Old Athenian

OLD ATHENIAN
Lord Timon, hear me speak.

TIMON   Freely, good father.

OLD ATHENIAN
Thou hast a servant named Lucilius.

TIMON
I have so. What of him?

OLD ATHENIAN
Most noble Timon, call the man before thee.

TIMON
Attends he here, or no? Lucilius!

LUCILIUS
Here, at your lordship's service.

OLD ATHENIAN
120 This fellow here, Lord Timon, this thy creature,
By night frequents my house. I am a man
That from my first have been inclined to thrift,
And my estate deserves an heir more raised
Than one which holds a trencher.

TIMON   Well, what further?

OLD ATHENIAN
One only daughter have I, no kin else,
On whom I may confer what I have got.
The maid is fair, o'th'youngest for a bride,
And I have bred her at my dearest cost
In qualities of the best. This man of thine
130 Attempts her love. I prithee, noble lord,
Join with me to forbid him her resort;
Myself have spoke in vain.

TIMON   The man is honest.

OLD ATHENIAN
Therefore he will be, Timon.
His honesty rewards him in itself;

It must not bear my daughter.

TIMON   Does she love him?

OLD ATHENIAN

She is young and apt.
Our own precedent passions do instruct us
What levity's in youth.

TIMON (*to Lucilius*)   Love you the maid?

LUCILIUS

Ay, my good lord, and she accepts of it.

OLD ATHENIAN

If in her marriage my consent be missing,   140
I call the gods to witness, I will choose
Mine heir from forth the beggars of the world,
And dispossess her all.

TIMON   How shall she be endowed
If she be mated with an equal husband?

OLD ATHENIAN

Three talents on the present; in future, all.

TIMON

This gentleman of mine hath served me long.
To build his fortune I will strain a little,
For 'tis a bond in men. Give him thy daughter.
What you bestow, in him I'll counterpoise,
And make him weigh with her.

OLD ATHENIAN   Most noble lord,   150
Pawn me to this your honour, she is his.

TIMON

My hand to thee; mine honour on my promise.

LUCILIUS

Humbly I thank your lordship. Never may
That state or fortune fall into my keeping
Which is not owed to you.
                              Exeunt Lucilius and Old Athenian

POET (*presenting a poem*)
Vouchsafe my labour, and long live your lordship!

TIMON
I thank you; you shall hear from me anon.
Go not away. (*To Painter*) What have you there, my
friend?

PAINTER
A piece of painting, which I do beseech
160   Your lordship to accept.

TIMON   Painting is welcome.
The painting is almost the natural man;
For since dishonour traffics with man's nature,
He is but outside; these pencilled figures are
Even such as they give out. I like your work,
And you shall find I like it. Wait attendance
Till you hear further from me.

PAINTER   The gods preserve ye!

TIMON
Well fare you, gentleman. Give me your hand.
We must needs dine together. (*To Jeweller*) Sir, your
jewel
Hath suffered under praise.

JEWELLER   What, my lord, dispraise?

TIMON
170   A mere satiety of commendations.
If I should pay you for't as 'tis extolled,
It would unclew me quite.

JEWELLER   My lord, 'tis rated
As those which sell would give. But you well know
Things of like value, differing in the owners,
Are prizèd by their masters. Believe't, dear lord,
You mend the jewel by the wearing it.

TIMON
Well mocked.

Enter Apemantus

MERCHANT

No, my good lord; he speaks the common tongue
Which all men speak with him.

TIMON

Look who comes here. Will you be chid? 180

JEWELLER

We'll bear, with your lordship.

MERCHANT   He'll spare none.

TIMON

Good morrow to thee, gentle Apemantus.

APEMANTUS

Till I be gentle, stay thou for thy good morrow,
When thou art Timon's dog, and these knaves honest.

TIMON

Why dost thou call them knaves? Thou knowest them
         not.

APEMANTUS

Are they not Athenians?

TIMON

Yes.

APEMANTUS

Then I repent not.

JEWELLER

You know me, Apemantus?

APEMANTUS

Thou knowest I do. I called thee by thy name. 190

TIMON

Thou art proud, Apemantus.

APEMANTUS

Of nothing so much as that I am not like Timon.

TIMON

Whither art going?

APEMANTUS
  To knock out an honest Athenian's brains.

TIMON
  That's a deed thou'lt die for.

APEMANTUS
  Right, if doing nothing be death by th'law.

TIMON
  How likest thou this picture, Apemantus?

APEMANTUS
  The best, for the innocence.

TIMON
  Wrought he not well that painted it?

200 APEMANTUS He wrought better that made the painter, and yet he's but a filthy piece of work.

PAINTER Y'are a dog.

APEMANTUS Thy mother's of my generation. What's she, if I be a dog?

TIMON Wilt dine with me, Apemantus?

APEMANTUS No. I eat not lords.

TIMON An thou shouldst, thou'dst anger ladies.

APEMANTUS O, they eat lords. So they come by great bellies.

210 TIMON That's a lascivious apprehension.

APEMANTUS So thou apprehendest it. Take it for thy labour.

TIMON
  How dost thou like this jewel, Apemantus?

APEMANTUS Not so well as plain-dealing, which will not cost a man a doit.

TIMON What dost thou think 'tis worth?

APEMANTUS Not worth my thinking. How now, poet!

POET How now, philosopher!

APEMANTUS Thou liest.

220 POET Art not one?

APEMANTUS Yes.

POET Then I lie not.

APEMANTUS Art not a poet?

POET Yes.

APEMANTUS Then thou liest. Look in thy last work,
where thou hast feigned him a worthy fellow.

POET That's not feigned – he is so.

APEMANTUS Yes, he is worthy of thee, and to pay thee
for thy labour. He that loves to be flattered is worthy
o'th'flatterer. Heavens, that I were a lord!   230

TIMON What wouldst do then, Apemantus?

APEMANTUS E'en as Apemantus does now: hate a lord
with my heart.

TIMON What, thyself?

APEMANTUS Ay.

TIMON Wherefore?

APEMANTUS That I had no angry wit to be a lord. – Art
not thou a merchant?

MERCHANT Ay, Apemantus.

APEMANTUS Traffic confound thee, if the gods will not! 240

MERCHANT If traffic do it, the gods do it.

APEMANTUS Traffic's thy god, and thy god confound
thee!

Trumpet sounds. Enter a Messenger

TIMON

What trumpet's that?

MESSENGER

'Tis Alcibiades, and some twenty horse,
All of companionship.

TIMON

Pray entertain them, give them guide to us.

Exeunt some attendants

You must needs dine with me. Go not you hence
Till I have thanked you. When dinner's done,

250 Show me this piece. I am joyful of your sights.
    Enter Alcibiades, with the rest
    Most welcome, sir!
APEMANTUS   So, so, there!
    Aches contract and starve your supple joints!
    That there should be small love amongst these sweet
        knaves,
    And all this courtesy! The strain of man's bred out
    Into baboon and monkey.
ALCIBIADES
    Sir, you have saved my longing, and I feed
    Most hungerly on your sight.
TIMON   Right welcome, sir!
    Ere we depart we'll share a bounteous time
    In different pleasures. Pray you, let us in.
                    Exeunt all but Apemantus
    Enter two Lords
260 FIRST LORD What time o'day is't, Apemantus?
APEMANTUS Time to be honest.
FIRST LORD That time serves still.
APEMANTUS
    The more accursèd thou that still omittest it.
SECOND LORD
    Thou art going to Lord Timon's feast?
APEMANTUS
    Ay, to see meat fill knaves and wine heat fools.
SECOND LORD
    Fare thee well, fare thee well.
APEMANTUS
    Thou art a fool to bid me farewell twice.
SECOND LORD Why, Apemantus?
APEMANTUS Shouldst have kept one to thyself, for I
270 mean to give thee none.
FIRST LORD Hang thyself.

APEMANTUS No, I will do nothing at thy bidding. Make
thy requests to thy friend.

SECOND LORD Away, unpeaceable dog, or I'll spurn thee
hence.

APEMANTUS I will fly, like a dog, the heels o'th'ass. *Exit*

FIRST LORD

He's opposite to humanity.
Come, shall we in
And taste Lord Timon's bounty? He outgoes
The very heart of kindness. 280

SECOND LORD

He pours it out. Plutus, the god of gold,
Is but his steward. No meed but he repays
Sevenfold above itself; no gift to him
But breeds the giver a return exceeding
All use of quittance.

FIRST LORD   The noblest mind he carries
That ever governed man.

SECOND LORD

Long may he live in fortunes. Shall we in?

FIRST LORD

I'll keep you company.   *Exeunt*

Hautboys playing loud music. A great banquet served I.2
*in; Flavius and others attending; and then enter
Lord Timon, Alcibiades, the States, the Athenian
Lords, and Ventidius which Timon redeemed from
prison. Then comes, dropping after all, Apemantus,
discontentedly, like himself*

VENTIDIUS

Most honoured Timon, it hath pleased the gods
To remember my father's age, and call him to long
peace.

He is gone happy, and has left me rich.
Then, as in grateful virtue I am bound
To your free heart, I do return those talents,
Doubled with thanks and service, from whose help
I derived liberty.

TIMON   O, by no means,
Honest Ventidius. You mistake my love.
I gave it freely ever, and there's none
10   Can truly say he gives, if he receives.
If our betters play at that game, we must not dare
To imitate them; faults that are rich are fair.

VENTIDIUS
A noble spirit!

TIMON   Nay, my lords,
Ceremony was but devised at first
To set a gloss on faint deeds, hollow welcomes,
Recanting goodness, sorry ere 'tis shown;
But where there is true friendship there needs none.
Pray, sit. More welcome are ye to my fortunes
Than my fortunes to me.
        They sit

FIRST LORD
20   My lord, we always have confessed it.

APEMANTUS
Ho, ho, confessed it? Hanged it, have you not?

TIMON
O, Apemantus, you are welcome.

APEMANTUS   No,
You shall not make me welcome.
I come to have thee thrust me out of doors.

TIMON
Fie, th' art a churl. Y'have got a humour there
Does not become a man; 'tis much too blame.
They say, my lords, *Ira furor brevis est*;

But yond man is ever angry.
Go, let him have a table by himself;
For he does neither affect company,   30
Nor is he fit for't, indeed.

APEMANTUS
Let me stay at thine apperil, Timon.
I come to observe, I give thee warning on't.

TIMON I take no heed of thee. Th' art an Athenian,
therefore welcome. I myself would have no power –
prithee let my meat make thee silent.

APEMANTUS I scorn thy meat. 'Twould choke me, for I
should ne'er flatter thee. O you gods! What a number of
men eats Timon, and he sees 'em not! It grieves me to
see so many dip their meat in one man's blood. And all   40
the madness is he cheers them up to't.
I wonder men dare trust themselves with men.
Methinks they should invite them without knives:
Good for their meat, and safer for their lives.
There's much example for't. The fellow that sits next
him, now parts bread with him, pledges the breath of
him in a divided draught, is the readiest man to kill
him. 'T has been proved. If I were a huge man, I should
fear to drink at meals,
Lest they should spy my windpipe's dangerous notes.   50
Great men should drink with harness on their throats.

TIMON
My lord, in heart! And let the health go round.

SECOND LORD
Let it flow this way, my good lord.

APEMANTUS Flow this way? A brave fellow. He keeps
his tides well. Those healths will make thee and thy
state look ill, Timon.
Here's that which is too weak to be a sinner,
Honest water, which ne'er left man i'th'mire.

This and my food are equals, there's no odds.

60 Feasts are too proud to give thanks to the gods.

APEMANTUS'S GRACE

Immortal gods, I crave no pelf,
I pray for no man but myself.
Grant I may never prove so fond
To trust man on his oath or bond,
Or a harlot for her weeping,
Or a dog that seems a-sleeping,
Or a keeper with my freedom,
Or my friends if I should need 'em.
Amen. So fall to't.

70 Rich men sin, and I eat root.

(*He eats and drinks*)

Much good dich thy good heart, Apemantus.

TIMON Captain Alcibiades, your heart's in the field now.

ALCIBIADES My heart is ever at your service, my lord.

TIMON You had rather be at a breakfast of enemies than a dinner of friends.

ALCIBIADES So they were bleeding new, my lord. There's no meat like 'em. I could wish my best friend at such a feast.

APEMANTUS Would all those flatterers were thine
80 enemies then, that then thou mightst kill 'em – and bid me to 'em.

FIRST LORD Might we but have that happiness, my lord, that you would once use our hearts, whereby we might express some part of our zeals, we should think ourselves for ever perfect.

TIMON O, no doubt, my good friends, but the gods themselves have provided that I shall have much help from you. How had you been my friends else? Why have you that charitable title from thousands, did not
90 you chiefly belong to my heart? I have told more of you

to myself than you can with modesty speak in your own behalf; and thus far I confirm you. O you gods, think I, what need we have any friends if we should ne'er have need of 'em? They were the most needless creatures living should we ne'er have use for 'em, and would most resemble sweet instruments hung up in cases, that keeps their sounds to themselves. Why, I have often wished myself poorer that I might come nearer to you. We are born to do benefits. And what better or properer can we call our own than the riches of 100 our friends? O, what a precious comfort 'tis to have so many like brothers commanding one another's fortunes! O, joy's e'en made away ere't can be born! Mine eyes cannot hold out water, methinks. To forget their faults, I drink to you.

APEMANTUS Thou weepest to make them drink, Timon.

SECOND LORD
Joy had the like conception in our eyes,
And at that instant like a babe sprung up.

APEMANTUS
Ho, ho! I laugh to think that babe a bastard.

THIRD LORD
I promise you, my lord, you moved me much. 110

APEMANTUS Much!
          Sound tucket

TIMON What means that trump?
          Enter a Servant
How now?

SERVANT Please you, my lord, there are certain ladies most desirous of admittance.

TIMON Ladies? What are their wills?

SERVANT There comes with them a forerunner, my lord, which bears that office to signify their pleasures.

TIMON I pray let them be admitted.

Enter Cupid

CUPID

120   Hail to thee, worthy Timon, and to all
       That of his bounties taste! The five best senses
       Acknowledge thee their patron, and come freely
       To gratulate thy plenteous bosom. Th'ear,
       Taste, touch, smell, all pleased from thy table rise;
       They only now come but to feast thine eyes.

TIMON

       They're welcome all; let 'em have kind admittance.

                                          Exit Cupid

       Music make their welcome.

FIRST LORD

       You see, my lord, how ample y'are beloved.

           *Music. Enter Cupid with a Masque of Ladies as
           Amazons, with lutes in their hands, dancing and
           playing*

APEMANTUS

       Hoy-day, what a sweep of vanity comes this way!
130   They dance? They are madwomen.
       Like madness is the glory of this life
       As this pomp shows to a little oil and root.
       We make ourselves fools to disport ourselves,
       And spend our flatteries to drink those men
       Upon whose age we void it up again
       With poisonous spite and envy.
       Who lives that's not depravèd or depraves?
       Who dies that bears not one spurn to their graves
       Of their friends' gift?
140   I should fear those that dance before me now
       Would one day stamp upon me. 'T has been done.
       Men shut their doors against a setting sun.

           *The Lords rise from table, with much adoring of
           Timon, and to show their loves each single out an*

72

Amazon, and all dance, men with women, a lofty
strain or two to the hautboys, and cease

TIMON

You have done our pleasures much grace, fair ladies,
Set a fair fashion on our entertainment,
Which was not half so beautiful and kind.
You have added worth unto't and lustre,
And entertained me with mine own device.
I am to thank you for't.

FIRST LADY

My lord, you take us even at the best.

APEMANTUS Faith, for the worst is filthy, and would not 150
hold taking, I doubt me.

TIMON

Ladies, there is an idle banquet attends you,
Please you to dispose yourselves.

ALL THE LADIES

Most thankfully, my lord.

Exeunt Cupid and Ladies

TIMON   Flavius!

FLAVIUS

My lord?

TIMON   The little casket bring me hither.

FLAVIUS

Yes, my lord. (*Aside*) More jewels yet!
There is no crossing him in's humour,
Else I should tell him well, i'faith I should,
When all's spent, he'd be crossed then, an he could.
'Tis pity bounty had not eyes behind,   160
That man might ne'er be wretched for his mind. *Exit*

FIRST LORD Where be our men?

SERVANT Here, my lord, in readiness.

SECOND LORD Our horses!

Enter Flavius, with the casket

73

TIMON

O my friends,
I have one word to say to you. Look you, my good lord,
I must entreat you honour me so much
As to advance this jewel. Accept it and wear it,
Kind my lord.

FIRST LORD

170 I am so far already in your gifts.

ALL

So are we all.
Enter a Servant

FIRST SERVANT My lord, there are certain nobles of the
Senate newly alighted and come to visit you.

TIMON They are fairly welcome.

Exit Servant

FLAVIUS I beseech your honour, vouchsafe me a word.
It does concern you near.

TIMON Near? Why then, another time I'll hear thee. I
prithee let's be provided to show them entertainment.

FLAVIUS (*aside*) I scarce know how.
Enter another Servant

SECOND SERVANT

180 May it please your honour, Lord Lucius,
Out of his free love, hath presented to you
Four milk-white horses, trapped in silver.

TIMON

I shall accept them fairly. Let the presents
Be worthily entertained.   *Exit Servant*
Enter a third Servant
                    How now? What news?

THIRD SERVANT Please you, my lord, that honourable
gentleman Lord Lucullus entreats your company tomorrow to hunt with him, and has sent your honour
two brace of greyhounds.

74

TIMON

    I'll hunt with him; and let them be received,

    Not without fair reward.   *Exit Servant*

FLAVIUS (*aside*)   What will this come to?   190

    He commands us to provide and give great gifts,

    And all out of an empty coffer;

    Nor will he know his purse, or yield me this,

    To show him what a beggar his heart is,

    Being of no power to make his wishes good.

    His promises fly so beyond his state

    That what he speaks is all in debt. He owes

    For every word. He is so kind that he now

    Pays interest for't. His land's put to their books.

    Well, would I were gently put out of office   200

    Before I were forced out!

    Happier is he that has no friend to feed

    Than such that do e'en enemies exceed.

    I bleed inwardly for my lord.   *Exit*

TIMON

    You do yourselves much wrong.

    You bate too much of your own merits.

    Here, my lord, a trifle of our love.

SECOND LORD

    With more than common thanks I will receive it.

THIRD LORD O, he's the very soul of bounty.

TIMON And now I remember, my lord, you gave good   210
    words the other day of a bay courser I rode on. 'Tis
    yours because you liked it.

THIRD LORD O, I beseech you pardon me, my lord, in
    that.

TIMON You may take my word, my lord. I know no man
    can justly praise but what he does affect. I weigh my
    friend's affection with mine own. I'll tell you true, I'll
    call to you.

ALL THE LORDS O, none so welcome.

TIMON

220   I take all and your several visitations
So kind to heart, 'tis not enough to give.
Methinks I could deal kingdoms to my friends,
And ne'er be weary. Alcibiades,
Thou art a soldier, therefore seldom rich.
It comes in charity to thee; for all thy living
Is 'mongst the dead, and all the lands thou hast
Lie in a pitched field.

ALCIBIADES Ay, defiled land, my lord.

FIRST LORD We are so virtuously bound –

230 TIMON And so am I to you.

SECOND LORD So infinitely endeared –

TIMON All to you. Lights, more lights!

FIRST LORD

The best of happiness, honour, and fortunes
Keep with you, Lord Timon!

TIMON

Ready for his friends.

                  Exeunt all but Apemantus and Timon

APEMANTUS   What a coil's here,
Serving of becks and jutting-out of bums!
I doubt whether their legs be worth the sums
That are given for 'em. Friendship's full of dregs.
Methinks false hearts should never have sound legs.

240   Thus honest fools lay out their wealth on curtsies.

TIMON Now, Apemantus, if thou wert not sullen, I
would be good to thee.

APEMANTUS No, I'll nothing. For if I should be bribed
too, there would be none left to rail upon thee, and then
thou wouldst sin the faster. Thou givest so long, Timon,
I fear me thou wilt give away thyself in paper shortly.
What needs these feasts, pomps, and vainglories?

TIMON Nay, an you begin to rail on society once, I am
sworn not to give regard to you. Farewell, and come
with better music.   *Exit* 250
APEMANTUS So. Thou wilt not hear me now; thou shalt
not then. I'll lock thy heaven from thee.
O, that men's ears should be
To counsel deaf, but not to flattery.   *Exit*

Enter a Senator   II.1
SENATOR
And late five thousand. To Varro and to Isidore
He owes nine thousand, besides my former sum,
Which makes it five and twenty. Still in motion
Of raging waste? It cannot hold, it will not.
If I want gold, steal but a beggar's dog
And give it Timon, why, the dog coins gold.
If I would sell my horse and buy twenty more
Better than he, why, give my horse to Timon,
Ask nothing, give it him, it foals me straight,
And able horses. No porter at his gate,   10
But rather one that smiles and still invites
All that pass by. It cannot hold. No reason
Can sound his state in safety. Caphis, ho!
Caphis, I say!
Enter Caphis
CAPHIS   Here, sir. What is your pleasure?
SENATOR
Get on your cloak, and haste you to Lord Timon.
Importune him for my moneys. Be not ceased
With slight denial, nor then silenced when
'Commend me to your master' and the cap
Plays in the right hand, thus. But tell him
My uses cry to me, I must serve my turn   20

77

Out of mine own. His days and times are past,
And my reliances on his fracted dates
Have smit my credit. I love and honour him,
But must not break my back to heal his finger.
Immediate are my needs, and my relief
Must not be tossed and turned to me in words,
But find supply immediate. Get you gone.
Put on a most importunate aspect,
A visage of demand. For I do fear,
30 When every feather sticks in his own wing,
Lord Timon will be left a naked gull,
Which flashes now a phoenix. Get you gone.

CAPHIS
I go, sir.

SENATOR
I go, sir? Take the bonds along with you,
And have the dates in. Come.
                He gives the bonds to Caphis

CAPHIS   I will, sir.

SENATOR   Go.   *Exeunt*

II.2   *Enter Flavius, Timon's steward, with many bills in
            his hand*

FLAVIUS
No care, no stop, so senseless of expense
That he will neither know how to maintain it,
Nor cease his flow of riot. Takes no account
How things go from him, nor resumes no care
Of what is to continue. Never mind
Was to be so unwise, to be so kind.
What shall be done? He will not hear till feel.
I must be round with him. Now he comes from hunting.
Fie, fie, fie, fie!

Enter Caphis, with the Servants of Isidore and Varro

CAPHIS

  Good even, Varro. What, you come for money?   10

VARRO'S SERVANT Is't not your business too?

CAPHIS It is. And yours too, Isidore?

ISIDORE'S SERVANT It is so.

CAPHIS Would we were all discharged!

VARRO'S SERVANT I fear it.

CAPHIS Here comes the lord.

    Enter Timon and his train, with Alcibiades

TIMON

  So soon as dinner's done, we'll forth again,

  My Alcibiades. (*To Caphis*) With me? What is your will?

CAPHIS

  My lord, here is a note of certain dues.

TIMON

  Dues? Whence are you?

CAPHIS   Of Athens here, my lord.   20

TIMON

  Go to my steward.

CAPHIS

  Please it your lordship, he hath put me off

  To the succession of new days this month.

  My master is awaked by great occasion

  To call upon his own, and humbly prays you

  That with your other noble parts you'll suit

  In giving him his right.

TIMON -   Mine honest friend,

  I prithee but repair to me next morning.

CAPHIS

  Nay, good my lord –

TIMON   Contain thyself, good friend.

VARRO'S SERVANT

  One Varro's servant, my good lord –   30

ISIDORE'S SERVANT From Isidore. He humbly prays
your speedy payment.

CAPHIS
If you did know, my lord, my master's wants –

VARRO'S SERVANT 'Twas due on forfeiture, my lord,
six weeks and past.

ISIDORE'S SERVANT
Your steward puts me off, my lord, and I
Am sent expressly to your lordship.

TIMON
Give me breath.
I do beseech you, good my lords, keep on.

40 I'll wait upon you instantly. *Exeunt Alcibiades and Lords*
                    (*To Flavius*) Come hither. Pray you,
How goes the world that I am thus encountered
With clamorous demands of broken bonds,
And the detention of long-since-due debts
Against my honour?

FLAVIUS (*to Caphis and the other Servants*)
                          Please you, gentlemen,
The time is unagreeable to this business.
Your importunacy cease till after dinner,
That I may make his lordship understand
Wherefore you are not paid.

TIMON   Do so, my friends.
See them well entertained.   *Exit*

FLAVIUS   Pray draw near.   *Exit*
        Enter Apemantus and the Fool

50 CAPHIS Stay, stay, here comes the fool with Apemantus.
Let's ha' some sport with 'em.

VARRO'S SERVANT Hang him, he'll abuse us!

ISIDORE'S SERVANT A plague upon him, dog!

VARRO'S SERVANT How dost, fool?

APEMANTUS Dost dialogue with thy shadow?

VARRO'S SERVANT I speak not to thee.

APEMANTUS No, 'tis to thyself. (*To the Fool*) Come away.

ISIDORE'S SERVANT (*to Varro's Servant*) There's the fool hangs on your back already.

APEMANTUS No, thou standest single, th' art not on him yet. 60

CAPHIS Where's the fool now?

APEMANTUS He last asked the question. Poor rogues and usurers' men, bawds between gold and want!

ALL THE SERVANTS What are we, Apemantus?

APEMANTUS Asses.

ALL THE SERVANTS Why?

APEMANTUS That you ask me what you are, and do not know yourselves. Speak to 'em, fool.

FOOL How do you, gentlemen? 70

ALL THE SERVANTS Gramercies, good fool. How does your mistress?

FOOL She's e'en setting on water to scald such chickens as you are. Would we could see you at Corinth!

APEMANTUS Good, gramercy.

Enter Page

FOOL Look you, here comes my mistress' page.

PAGE (*to the Fool*) Why, how now, captain? What do you in this wise company? How dost thou, Apemantus?

APEMANTUS Would I had a rod in my mouth, that I might answer thee profitably. 80

PAGE Prithee, Apemantus, read me the superscription of these letters. I know not which is which.

APEMANTUS Canst not read?

PAGE No.

APEMANTUS There will little learning die then, that day thou art hanged. This is to Lord Timon; this to Alcibiades. Go, thou wast born a bastard, and thou'lt die a bawd.

PAGE Thou wast whelped a dog, and thou shalt famish a
90   dog's death. Answer not, I am gone.   *Exit*

APEMANTUS E'en so. Thou outrunnest grace. Fool, I
will go with you to Lord Timon's.

FOOL Will you leave me there?

APEMANTUS If Timon stay at home. – You three serve
three usurers?

ALL THE SERVANTS Ay. Would they served us!

APEMANTUS So would I – as good a trick as ever hang-
man served thief.

FOOL Are you three usurers' men?

100 ALL THE SERVANTS Ay, fool.

FOOL I think no usurer but has a fool to his servant. My
mistress is one, and I am her fool. When men come to
borrow of your masters, they approach sadly and go
away merry. But they enter my mistress' house merrily
and go away sadly. The reason of this?

VARRO'S SERVANT I could render one.

APEMANTUS Do it then, that we may account thee a
whoremaster and a knave; which notwithstanding, thou
shalt be no less esteemed.

110 VARRO'S SERVANT What is a whoremaster, fool?

FOOL A fool in good clothes, and something like thee.
'Tis a spirit. Sometime 't appears like a lord, sometime
like a lawyer, sometime like a philosopher, with two
stones more than's artificial one. He is very often like a
knight. And, generally, in all shapes that man goes up
and down in, from fourscore to thirteen, this spirit
walks in.

VARRO'S SERVANT Thou art not altogether a fool.

FOOL Nor thou altogether a wise man. As much foolery
120 as I have, so much wit thou lackest.

APEMANTUS That answer might have become Apemantus.

82

ALL THE SERVANTS *Aside, aside!* Here comes Lord
  Timon.
    Enter Timon and Flavius
APEMANTUS Come with me, fool, come.
FOOL I do not always follow lover, elder brother, and
  woman; sometime the philosopher.
                 Exeunt Apemantus and Fool

FLAVIUS
  Pray you, walk near. I'll speak with you anon.
                      Exeunt Servants

TIMON
  You make me marvel wherefore ere this time
  Had you not fully laid my state before me,   130
  That I might so have rated my expense
  As I had leave of means.
FLAVIUS   You would not hear me.
  At many leisures I proposed –
TIMON   Go to.
  Perchance some single vantages you took
  When my indisposition put you back,
  And that unaptness made your minister
  Thus to excuse yourself.
FLAVIUS   O my good lord,
  At many times I brought in my accounts,
  Laid them before you. You would throw them off,
  And say you found them in mine honesty.   140
  When for some trifling present you have bid me
  Return so much, I have shook my head and wept;
  Yea, 'gainst th'authority of manners prayed you
  To hold your hand more close. I did endure
  Not seldom, nor no slight checks, when I have
  Prompted you in the ebb of your estate
  And your great flow of debts. My loved lord –
  Though you hear now too late, yet now's a time –

The greatest of your having lacks a half
150 To pay your present debts.

TIMON   Let all my land be sold.

FLAVIUS

'Tis all engaged, some forfeited and gone,
And what remains will hardly stop the mouth
Of present dues. The future comes apace.
What shall defend the interim? And at length
How goes our reck'ning?

TIMON

To Lacedaemon did my land extend.

FLAVIUS

O my good lord, the world is but a word.
Were it all yours to give it in a breath,
How quickly were it gone!

TIMON   You tell me true.

FLAVIUS

160 If you suspect my husbandry of falsehood,
Call me before th'exactest auditors,
And set me on the proof. So the gods bless me,
When all our offices have been oppressed
With riotous feeders, when our vaults have wept
With drunken spilth of wine, when every room
Hath blazed with lights and brayed with minstrelsy,
I have retired me to a wasteful cock
And set mine eyes at flow.

TIMON   Prithee no more.

FLAVIUS

Heavens, have I said, the bounty of this lord!
170 How many prodigal bits have slaves and peasants
This night englutted! Who is not Timon's?
What heart, head, sword, force, means, but is Lord
          Timon's?
Great Timon, noble, worthy, royal Timon!

Ah, when the means are gone that buy this praise,
The breath is gone whereof this praise is made.
Feast-won, fast-lost. One cloud of winter showers,
These flies are couched.

TIMON   Come, sermon me no further.
No villainous bounty yet hath passed my heart;
Unwisely, not ignobly, have I given.
Why dost thou weep? Canst thou the conscience lack   180
To think I shall lack friends? Secure thy heart.
If I would broach the vessels of my love,
And try the argument of hearts, by borrowing,
Men and men's fortunes could I frankly use
As I can bid thee speak.

FLAVIUS   Assurance bless your thoughts!
TIMON
And in some sort these wants of mine are crowned,
That I account them blessings. For by these
Shall I try friends. You shall perceive
How you mistake my fortunes;
I am wealthy in my friends.   190
Within there! Flaminius! Servilius!

        Enter Flaminius, Servilius, and another Servant
SERVANTS My lord? My lord?
TIMON I will dispatch you severally. You to Lord Lucius,
   to Lord Lucullus you – I hunted with his honour today
   – you to Sempronius. Commend me to their loves. And
   I am proud, say, that my occasions have found time to
   use 'em toward a supply of money. Let the request be
   fifty talents.

FLAMINIUS As you have said, my lord. *Exeunt Servants*
FLAVIUS (*aside*) Lord Lucius and Lucullus? Hum!   200
TIMON
   Go you, sir, to the senators,
   Of whom, even to the state's best health, I have

Deserved this hearing. Bid 'em send o'th'instant
A thousand talents to me.

FLAVIUS   I have been bold,
For that I knew it the most general way,
To them to use your signet and your name.
But they do shake their heads, and I am here
No richer in return.

TIMON   Is't true? Can't be?

FLAVIUS

They answer, in a joint and corporate voice,
210 That now they are at fall, want treasure, cannot
Do what they would, are sorry – you are honourable –
But yet they could have wished – they know not –
Something hath been amiss – a noble nature
May catch a wrench – would all were well – 'tis pity.
And so, intending other serious matters,
After distasteful looks and these hard fractions,
With certain half-caps and cold-moving nods
They froze me into silence.

TIMON   You gods reward them!
Prithee, man, look cheerly. These old fellows
220 Have their ingratitude in them hereditary.
Their blood is caked, 'tis cold, it seldom flows.
'Tis lack of kindly warmth they are not kind.
And nature, as it grows again toward earth,
Is fashioned for the journey, dull and heavy.
Go to Ventidius. Prithee be not sad,
Thou art true and honest. Ingeniously I speak,
No blame belongs to thee. Ventidius lately
Buried his father, by whose death he's stepped
Into a great estate. When he was poor,
230 Imprisoned, and in scarcity of friends,
I cleared him with five talents. Greet him from me.
Bid him suppose some good necessity

Touches his friend, which craves to be remembered
With those five talents. That had, give't these fellows
To whom 'tis instant due. Ne'er speak or think
That Timon's fortunes 'mong his friends can sink.

FLAVIUS
I would I could not think it.
That thought is bounty's foe –
Being free itself, it thinks all others so.   *Exeunt*

          Flaminius waiting to speak with Lucullus from his III.1
          master. Enter a Servant to him

SERVANT I have told my lord of you. He is coming down
to you.

FLAMINIUS I thank you, sir.
          Enter Lucullus

SERVANT Here's my lord.

LUCULLUS (*aside*) One of Lord Timon's men? A gift, I
warrant. Why, this hits right: I dreamt of a silver basin
and ewer tonight. (*To Flaminius*) Flaminius, honest
Flaminius, you are very respectively welcome, sir. (*To
Servant*) Fill me some wine.   *Exit Servant*
And how does that honourable, complete, free-hearted 10
gentleman of Athens, thy very bountiful good lord and
master?

FLAMINIUS His health is well, sir.

LUCULLUS I am right glad that his health is well, sir.
And what hast thou there under thy cloak, pretty
Flaminius?

FLAMINIUS Faith, nothing but an empty box, sir, which,
in my lord's behalf, I come to entreat your honour to
supply; who, having great and instant occasion to use
fifty talents, hath sent to your lordship to furnish him, 20
nothing doubting your present assistance therein.

LUCULLUS La, la, la, la! 'Nothing doubting', says he?
Alas, good lord! A noble gentleman 'tis, if he would not
keep so good a house. Many a time and often I ha' dined
with him and told him on't, and come again to supper to
him of purpose to have him spend less. And yet he
would embrace no counsel, take no warning by my
coming. Every man has his fault, and honesty is his. I
ha' told him on't, but I could ne'er get him from't.

Enter Servant, with wine

30 SERVANT Please your lordship, here is the wine.

LUCULLUS Flaminius, I have noted thee always wise.
Here's to thee.

FLAMINIUS Your lordship speaks your pleasure.

LUCULLUS I have observed thee always for a towardly
prompt spirit, give thee thy due, and one that knows
what belongs to reason, and canst use the time well, if
the time use thee well. Good parts in thee. (*To Servant*)
Get you gone, sirrah. *Exit Servant*
Draw nearer, honest Flaminius. Thy lord's a bountiful
40 gentleman; but thou art wise, and thou knowest well
enough, although thou comest to me, that this is no
time to lend money, especially upon bare friendship
without security. Here's three solidares for thee. Good
boy, wink at me, and say thou sawest me not. Fare thee
well.

FLAMINIUS

Is't possible the world should so much differ,
And we alive that lived? Fly, damnèd baseness,
To him that worships thee!

He throws the money back at Lucullus

LUCULLUS Ha! Now I see thou art a fool, and fit for thy
50 master. *Exit*

FLAMINIUS

May these add to the number that may scald thee!

88

Let molten coin be thy damnation,
Thou disease of a friend and not himself!
Has friendship such a faint and milky heart
It turns in less than two nights? O you gods!
I feel my master's passion. This slave,
Unto this hour, has my lord's meat in him.
Why should it thrive and turn to nutriment
When he is turned to poison?
O, may diseases only work upon't!   60
And when he's sick to death, let not that part of nature
Which my lord paid for be of any power
To expel sickness, but prolong his hour!   *Exit*

Enter Lucius, with three Strangers   III.2

LUCIUS Who, the Lord Timon? He is my very good
friend and an honourable gentleman.

FIRST STRANGER We know him for no less, though we
are but strangers to him. But I can tell you one thing,
my lord, and which I hear from common rumours: now
Lord Timon's happy hours are done and past, and his
estate shrinks from him.

LUCIUS Fie, no, do not believe it. He cannot want for
money.

SECOND STRANGER But believe you this, my lord, that   10
not long ago one of his men was with the Lord Lucullus
to borrow so many talents, nay, urged extremely for't,
and showed what necessity belonged to't, and yet was
denied.

LUCIUS How?

SECOND STRANGER I tell you, denied, my lord.

LUCIUS What a strange case was that! Now, before the
gods, I am ashamed on't. Denied that honourable man?
There was very little honour showed in't. For my own

20   part, I must needs confess, I have received some small
kindnesses from him, as money, plate, jewels, and such-
like trifles, nothing comparing to his. Yet, had he mistook him and sent to me, I should ne'er have denied his
occasion so many talents.

    Enter Servilius

SERVILIUS See, by good hap, yonder's my lord. I have
    sweat to see his honour. My honoured lord!

LUCIUS Servilius? You are kindly met, sir. Fare thee
    well. Commend me to thy honourable virtuous lord, my
    very exquisite friend.

30 SERVILIUS May it please your honour, my lord hath
    sent –

LUCIUS Ha? What has he sent? I am so much endeared
    to that lord; he's ever sending. How shall I thank him,
    thinkest thou? And what has he sent now?

SERVILIUS 'Has only sent his present occasion now, my
    lord, requesting your lordship to supply his instant use
    with so many talents.

LUCIUS

    I know his lordship is but merry with me;

    He cannot want fifty five hundred talents.

SERVILIUS

40   But in the mean time he wants less, my lord.

    If his occasion were not virtuous,

    I should not urge it half so faithfully.

LUCIUS

    Dost thou speak seriously, Servilius?

SERVILIUS Upon my soul, 'tis true, sir.

LUCIUS What a wicked beast was I to disfurnish myself
    against such a good time, when I might ha' shown my-
    self honourable! How unluckily it happened that I
    should purchase the day before for a little part and undo
    a great deal of honour! Servilius, now before the gods,

I am not able to do – the more beast, I say! I was send- 50
ing to use Lord Timon myself, these gentlemen can
witness; but I would not, for the wealth of Athens, I
had done't now. Commend me bountifully to his good
lordship, and I hope his honour will conceive the
fairest of me, because I have no power to be kind. And
tell him this from me, I count it one of my greatest
afflictions, say, that I cannot pleasure such an honourable gentleman. Good Servilius, will you befriend me
so far as to use mine own words to him?

SERVILIUS Yes, sir, I shall. 60

LUCIUS I'll look you out a good turn, Servilius.

Exit Servilius

True, as you said, Timon is shrunk indeed,
And he that's once denied will hardly speed. *Exit*

FIRST STRANGER

Do you observe this, Hostilius?

SECOND STRANGER Ay, too well.

FIRST STRANGER

Why, this is the world's soul,
And just of the same piece
Is every flatterer's spirit. Who can call him his friend
That dips in the same dish? For in my knowing
Timon has been this lord's father,
And kept his credit with his purse, 70
Supported his estate. Nay, Timon's money
Has paid his men their wages. He ne'er drinks
But Timon's silver treads upon his lip.
And yet – O see the monstrousness of man
When he looks out in an ungrateful shape –
He does deny him, in respect of his,
What charitable men afford to beggars.

THIRD STRANGER

Religion groans at it.

FIRST STRANGER   For mine own part,
I never tasted Timon in my life,
80 Nor came any of his bounties over me
To mark me for his friend. Yet I protest,
For his right noble mind, illustrious virtue,
And honourable carriage,
Had his necessity made use of me,
I would have put my wealth into donation,
And the best half should have returned to him,
So much I love his heart. But, I perceive,
Men must learn now with pity to dispense,
For policy sits above conscience.   *Exeunt*

III.3   *Enter a Third Servant of Timon, with Sempronius,*
another of Timon's friends

SEMPRONIUS
Must he needs trouble me in't? Hum! 'Bove all others?
He might have tried Lord Lucius or Lucullus.
And now Ventidius is wealthy too,
Whom he redeemed from prison. All these
Owes their estates unto him.

SERVANT   My lord,
They have all been touched and found base metal,
For they have all denied him.

SEMPRONIUS
How? Have they denied him?
Has Ventidius and Lucullus denied him?
10 And does he send to me? Three? Hum?
It shows but little love or judgement in him.
Must I be his last refuge? His friends, like physicians,
Thrice give him over. Must I take th'cure upon me?
'Has much disgraced me in't. I'm angry at him
That might have known my place. I see no sense for't

But his occasions might have wooed me first;
For, in my conscience, I was the first man
That e'er received gift from him.
And does he think so backwardly of me now
That I'll requite it last? No;   20
So it may prove an argument of laughter
To th'rest, and I 'mongst lords be thought a fool.
I'd rather than the worth of thrice the sum
'Had sent to me first, but for my mind's sake;
I'd such a courage to do him good. But now return,
And with their faint reply this answer join:
Who bates mine honour shall not know my coin. *Exit*
SERVANT Excellent! Your lordship's a goodly villain. The
  devil knew not what he did when he made man politic –
  he crossed himself by't. And I cannot think but in the 30
  end the villainies of man will set him clear. How fairly
  this lord strives to appear foul! Takes virtuous copies to
  be wicked, like those that under hot ardent zeal would
  set whole realms on fire.
Of such a nature is his politic love.
This was my lord's best hope. Now all are fled,
Save only the gods. Now his friends are dead,
Doors that were ne'er acquainted with their wards
Many a bounteous year must be employed
Now to guard sure their master.   40
And this is all a liberal course allows:
Who cannot keep his wealth must keep his house. *Exit*

        Enter two Servants of Varro, and the Servant of III.4
        Lucius, meeting Titus, Hortensius, and other Servants
        of Timon's creditors, waiting for his coming out
FIRST VARRO'S SERVANT
  Well met. Good morrow, Titus and Hortensius.

TITUS
  The like to you, kind Varro.

HORTENSIUS   Lucius!
  What, do we meet together?

LUCIUS'S SERVANT   Ay, and I think
  One business does command us all, for mine
  Is money.

TITUS   So is theirs and ours.

    Enter Philotus

LUCIUS'S SERVANT
  And Sir Philotus too!

PHILOTUS   Good day at once.

LUCIUS'S SERVANT
  Welcome, good brother. What do you think the hour?

PHILOTUS
  Labouring for nine.

LUCIUS'S SERVANT
  So much?

PHILOTUS   Is not my lord seen yet?

LUCIUS'S SERVANT   Not yet.

PHILOTUS
10 I wonder on't. He was wont to shine at seven.

LUCIUS'S SERVANT
  Ay, but the days are waxed shorter with him.
  You must consider that a prodigal course
  Is like the sun's, but not, like his, recoverable.
  I fear
  'Tis deepest winter in Lord Timon's purse;
  That is, one may reach deep enough and yet
  Find little.

PHILOTUS   I am of your fear for that.

TITUS
  I'll show you how t'observe a strange event.
  Your lord sends now for money?

HORTENSIUS Most true, he does.

TITUS

And he wears jewels now of Timon's gift, 20

For which I wait for money.

HORTENSIUS

It is against my heart.

LUCIUS'S SERVANT

Mark how strange it shows

Timon in this should pay more than he owes;

And e'en as if your lord should wear rich jewels

And send for money for 'em.

HORTENSIUS

I'm weary of this charge, the gods can witness;

I know my lord hath spent of Timon's wealth,

And now ingratitude makes it worse than stealth.

FIRST VARRO'S SERVANT

Yes, mine's three thousand crowns. What's yours? 30

LUCIUS'S SERVANT

Five thousand mine.

FIRST VARRO'S SERVANT

'Tis much deep; and it should seem by th'sum

Your master's confidence was above mine,

Else surely his had equalled.

Enter Flaminius

TITUS One of Lord Timon's men.

LUCIUS'S SERVANT Flaminius? Sir, a word. Pray, is my
lord ready to come forth?

FLAMINIUS No, indeed he is not.

TITUS We attend his lordship. Pray signify so much.

FLAMINIUS I need not tell him that; he knows. You are 40
too diligent. *Exit*

Enter Flavius in a cloak, muffled

LUCIUS'S SERVANT

Ha! Is not that his steward muffled so?

He goes away in a cloud. Call him, call him.

TITUS Do you hear, sir?

SECOND VARRO'S SERVANT By your leave, sir.

FLAVIUS What do ye ask of me, my friend?

TITUS

We wait for certain money here, sir.

FLAVIUS   Ay,
If money were as certain as your waiting,
'Twere sure enough.

50 Why then preferred you not your sums and bills
When your false masters eat of my lord's meat?
Then they could smile and fawn upon his debts,
And take down th'interest into their glutt'nous maws.
You do yourselves but wrong to stir me up.
Let me pass quietly.
Believe't, my lord and I have made an end;
I have no more to reckon, he to spend.

LUCIUS'S SERVANT Ay, but this answer will not serve.

FLAVIUS

If 'twill not serve, 'tis not so base as you,
60 For you serve knaves.   *Exit*

FIRST VARRO'S SERVANT How? What does his cashiered worship mutter?

SECOND VARRO'S SERVANT No matter what. He's poor,
and that's revenge enough. Who can speak broader than
he that has no house to put his head in? Such may rail
against great buildings.

Enter Servilius

TITUS O, here's Servilius. Now we shall know some
answer.

SERVILIUS If I might beseech you, gentlemen, to repair
70 some other hour, I should derive much from't. For,
take't of my soul, my lord leans wondrously to discon-

tent. His comfortable temper has forsook him. He's
much out of health and keeps his chamber.

LUCIUS'S SERVANT
　Many do keep their chambers are not sick.
　And if it be so far beyond his health,
　Methinks he should the sooner pay his debts,
　And make a clear way to the gods.

SERVILIUS　　　　　　　　　　Good gods!

TITUS
　We cannot take this for an answer, sir.

FLAMINIUS (*within*)
　Servilius, help! My lord, my lord!
　　　Enter Timon, in a rage

TIMON
　What, are my doors opposed against my passage?　80
　Have I been ever free, and must my house
　Be my retentive enemy, my gaol?
　The place which I have feasted, does it now,
　Like all mankind, show me an iron heart?

LUCIUS'S SERVANT Put in now, Titus.

TITUS My lord, here is my bill.

LUCIUS'S SERVANT Here's mine.

HORTENSIUS And mine, my lord.

BOTH VARRO'S SERVANTS And ours, my lord.

PHILOTUS All our bills.　　　　　　　　　　　90

TIMON
　Knock me down with 'em; cleave me to the girdle.

LUCIUS'S SERVANT Alas, my lord –

TIMON
　Cut my heart in sums.

TITUS Mine, fifty talents.

TIMON
　Tell out my blood.

LUCIUS'S SERVANT Five thousand crowns, my lord.

TIMON

    Five thousand drops pays that. What yours? And yours?

FIRST VARRO'S SERVANT My lord –

SECOND VARRO'S SERVANT My lord –

TIMON

100   Tear me, take me, and the gods fall upon you!   *Exit*

HORTENSIUS Faith, I perceive our masters may throw
    their caps at their money. These debts may well be
    called desperate ones, for a madman owes 'em.

                                  Exeunt

     Enter Timon and Flavius

TIMON

    They have e'en put my breath from me, the slaves.
    Creditors? Devils!

FLAVIUS My dear lord –

TIMON

    What if it should be so?

FLAVIUS My lord –

TIMON

    I'll have it so. My steward!

110 FLAVIUS Here, my lord.

TIMON

    So fitly! Go, bid all my friends again,
    Lucius, Lucullus, and Sempronius – all.
    I'll once more feast the rascals.

FLAVIUS   O my lord,
    You only speak from your distracted soul;
    There is not so much left to furnish out
    A moderate table.

TIMON   Be it not in thy care.
    Go, I charge thee. Invite them all, let in the tide
    Of knaves once more. My cook and I'll provide.

                                  Exeunt

Enter three Senators at one door, Alcibiades meeting
them, with attendants

FIRST SENATOR

My lord, you have my voice to't; the fault's bloody.
'Tis necessary he should die;
Nothing emboldens sin so much as mercy.

SECOND SENATOR

Most true. The law shall bruise him.

ALCIBIADES

Honour, health, and compassion to the Senate!

FIRST SENATOR

Now, captain?

ALCIBIADES

I am an humble suitor to your virtues;
For pity is the virtue of the law,
And none but tyrants use it cruelly.
It pleases time and fortune to lie heavy   10
Upon a friend of mine, who in hot blood
Hath stepped into the law, which is past depth
To those that without heed do plunge into't.
He is a man, setting his fate aside,
Of comely virtues;
Nor did he soil the fact with cowardice –
An honour in him which buys out his fault –
But with a noble fury and fair spirit,
Seeing his reputation touched to death,
He did oppose his foe.   20
And with such sober and unnoted passion
He did behove his anger, ere 'twas spent,
As if he had but proved an argument.

FIRST SENATOR

You undergo toó strict a paradox,
Striving to make an ugly deed look fair.
Your words have took such pains as if they laboured

To bring manslaughter into form, and set quarrelling
Upon the head of valour; which indeed
Is valour misbegot, and came into the world
30 When sects and factions were newly born.
He's truly valiant that can wisely suffer
The worst that man can breathe,
And make his wrongs his outsides,
To wear them, like his raiment, carelessly,
And ne'er prefer his injuries to his heart,
To bring it into danger.
If wrongs be evils and enforce us kill,
What folly 'tis to hazard life for ill!

ALCIBIADES
My lord –

FIRST SENATOR
You cannot make gross sins look clear:
40 To revenge is no valour, but to bear.

ALCIBIADES
My lords, then, under favour – pardon me,
If I speak like a captain –
Why do fond men expose themselves to battle,
And not endure all threats? Sleep upon't,
And let the foes quietly cut their throats
Without repugnancy? If there be
Such valour in the bearing, what make we
Abroad? Why then women are more valiant
That stay at home, if bearing carry it,
50 And the ass more captain than the lion,
The fellow loaden with irons wiser than the judge,
If wisdom be in suffering. O my lords,
As you are great, be pitifully good.
Who cannot condemn rashness in cold blood?
To kill, I grant, is sin's extremest gust,
But in defence, by mercy, 'tis most just.

To be in anger is impiety;
But who is man that is not angry?
Weigh but the crime with this.

SECOND SENATOR
You breathe in vain.

ALCIBIADES   In vain? His service done   60
At Lacedaemon and Byzantium
Were a sufficient briber for his life.

FIRST SENATOR
What's that?

ALCIBIADES
Why, I say, my lords, 'has done fair service,
And slain in fight many of your enemies.
How full of valour did he bear himself
In the last conflict, and made plenteous wounds!

SECOND SENATOR
He has made too much plenty with 'em.
He's a sworn rioter; he has a sin
That often drowns him and takes his valour prisoner.   70
If there were no foes, that were enough
To overcome him. In that beastly fury
He has been known to commit outrages
And cherish factions. 'Tis inferred to us
His days are foul and his drink dangerous.

FIRST SENATOR
He dies.

ALCIBIADES Hard fate! He might have died in war.
My lords, if not for any parts in him –
Though his right arm might purchase his own time
And be in debt to none – yet, more to move you,
Take my deserts to his and join 'em both.   80
And, for I know your reverend ages love
Security, I'll pawn my victories, all
My honour to you, upon his good returns.

If by this crime he owes the law his life,
Why, let the war receive't in valiant gore,
For law is strict, and war is nothing more.

FIRST SENATOR
We are for law. He dies. Urge it no more
On height of our displeasure. Friend or brother,
He forfeits his own blood that spills another.

ALCIBIADES
90   Must it be so? It must not be.
My lords, I do beseech you know me.

SECOND SENATOR   How?

ALCIBIADES
Call me to your remembrances.

THIRD SENATOR   What?

ALCIBIADES
I cannot think but your age has forgot me;
It could not else be I should prove so base
To sue and be denied such common grace.
My wounds ache at you.

FIRST SENATOR   Do you dare our anger?
'Tis in few words, but spacious in effect.
We banish thee for ever.

ALCIBIADES   Banish me?
Banish your dotage. Banish usury
100 That makes the Senate ugly.

FIRST SENATOR
If after two days' shine Athens contain thee,
Attend our weightier judgement.
And, not to swell our spirit,
He shall be executed presently.   *Exeunt Senators*

ALCIBIADES
Now the gods keep you old enough, that you may live
Only in bone, that none may look on you!
I'm worse than mad. I have kept back their foes,

While they have told their money and let out
Their coin upon large interest, I myself
Rich only in large hurts. All those for this?   110
Is this the balsam that the usuring Senate
Pours into captains' wounds? Banishment!
It comes not ill. I hate not to be banished.
It is a cause worthy my spleen and fury,
That I may strike at Athens. I'll cheer up
My discontented troops, and lay for hearts.
'Tis honour with worst lands to be at odds;
Soldiers should brook as little wrongs as gods.   *Exit*

Music. Servants attending. Enter Lucullus and III.6
Lucius, Sempronius and Ventidius, at several doors,
senators and lords

LUCULLUS The good time of day to you, sir.

LUCIUS I also wish it to you. I think this honourable lord
did but try us this other day.

LUCULLUS Upon that were my thoughts tiring when we
encountered. I hope it is not so low with him as he made
it seem in the trial of his several friends.

LUCIUS It should not be, by the persuasion of his new
feasting.

LUCULLUS I should think so. He hath sent me an earnest
inviting, which many my near occasions did urge me to   10
put off. But he hath conjured me beyond them, and I
must needs appear.

LUCIUS In like manner was I in debt to my importunate
business, but he would not hear my excuse. I am sorry,
when he sent to borrow of me, that my provision was
out.

LUCULLUS I am sick of that grief too, as I understand
how all things go.

LUCIUS Every man here's so. What would he have
20   borrowed of you?

LUCULLUS A thousand pieces.

LUCIUS A thousand pieces?

LUCULLUS What of you?

LUCIUS He sent to me, sir –

    Enter Timon and attendants

  Here he comes.

TIMON With all my heart, gentlemen both! And how fare
  you?

LUCULLUS Ever at the best, hearing well of your lordship.

30 LUCIUS The swallow follows not summer more willing
  than we your lordship.

TIMON (*aside*) Nor more willingly leaves winter. Such
  summer birds are men. (*To them*) Gentlemen, our
  dinner will not recompense this long stay. Feast your
  ears with the music awhile, if they will fare so harshly
  o'th'trumpet's sound. We shall to't presently.

LUCULLUS I hope it remains not unkindly with your
  lordship that I returned you an empty messenger.

TIMON O sir, let it not trouble you.

40 LUCIUS My noble lord –

TIMON Ah, my good friend, what cheer?

LUCIUS My most honourable lord, I am e'en sick of
  shame that when your lordship this other day sent to
  me I was so unfortunate a beggar.

TIMON Think not on't, sir.

LUCIUS If you had sent but two hours before –

TIMON Let it not cumber your better remembrance.

    The banquet is brought in

  Come, bring in all together.

LUCIUS All covered dishes.

50 LUCULLUS Royal cheer, I warrant you.

SEMPRONIUS Doubt not that, if money and the season
  can yield it.

LUCULLUS How do you? What's the news?

SEMPRONIUS Alcibiades is banished. Hear you of it?

LUCULLUS *and* LUCIUS Alcibiades banished?

SEMPRONIUS 'Tis so, be sure of it.

LUCULLUS How? How?

LUCIUS I pray you, upon what?

TIMON My worthy friends, will you draw near?

SEMPRONIUS I'll tell you more anon. Here's a noble feast 60
  toward.

LUCIUS This is the old man still.

SEMPRONIUS Will't hold? Will't hold?

LUCIUS It does; but time will – and so –

SEMPRONIUS I do conceive.

TIMON Each man to his stool, with that spur as he would
  to the lip of his mistress. Your diet shall be in all places
  alike. Make not a City feast of it, to let the meat cool ere
  we can agree upon the first place. Sit, sit. The gods
  require our thanks. 70

You great benefactors, sprinkle our society with thankful-
ness. For your own gifts make yourselves praised; but
reserve still to give, lest your deities be despised. Lend to
each man enough, that one need not lend to another; for
were your godheads to borrow of men, men would forsake
the gods. Make the meat be beloved more than the man that
gives it. Let no assembly of twenty be without a score of
villains. If there sit twelve women at the table let a dozen of
them be – as they are. The rest of your fees, O gods – the
Senators of Athens, together with the common leg of people – 80
what is amiss in them, you gods, make suitable for destruc-
tion. For these my present friends, as they are to me
nothing, so in nothing bless them, and to nothing are they
welcome.

Uncover, dogs, and lap.

The dishes are uncovered and seen to be full of warm
water and stones

SOME What does his lordship mean?

OTHERS I know not.

TIMON

May you a better feast never behold,

You knot of mouth-friends! Smoke and lukewarm
water

90 Is your perfection. This is Timon's last,

Who, stuck and spangled with your flatteries,

Washes it off, and sprinkles in your faces

Your reeking villainy.

He throws the water in their faces

Live loathed and long,

Most smiling, smooth, detested parasites,

Courteous destroyers, affable wolves, meek bears,

You fools of fortune, trencher-friends, time's flies,

Cap-and-knee slaves, vapours, and minute-jacks!

Of man and beast the infinite malady

Crust you quite o'er! What, dost thou go?

100 Soft, take thy physic first. Thou too, and thou.

Stay, I will lend thee money, borrow none.

He throws the stones at them, and drives them out

What? All in motion? Henceforth be no feast

Whereat a villain's not a welcome guest.

Burn house! Sink Athens! Henceforth hated be

Of Timon man and all humanity.   *Exit*

Enter lords and senators

LUCULLUS How now, my lords?

LUCIUS Know you the quality of Lord Timon's fury?

SEMPRONIUS Push! Did you see my cap?

VENTIDIUS I have lost my gown.

110 LUCULLUS He's but a mad lord, and naught but humours

sways him. He gave me a jewel th'other day, and now he
has beat it out of my hat. Did you see my jewel?

SEMPRONIUS Did you see my cap?

LUCIUS Here 'tis.

VENTIDIUS Here lies my gown.

LUCULLUS Let's make no stay.

LUCIUS

Lord Timon's mad.

SEMPRONIUS   I feel't upon my bones.

VENTIDIUS

One day he gives us diamonds, next day stones.

                              Exeunt

    Enter Timon   IV.1

TIMON

Let me look back upon thee. O thou wall
That girdles in those wolves, dive in the earth
And fence not Athens. Matrons, turn incontinent.
Obedience fail in children. Slaves and fools
Pluck the grave wrinkled Senate from the bench,
And minister in their steads. To general filths
Convert o'th'instant, green virginity,
Do't in your parents' eyes. Bankrupts, hold fast;
Rather than render back, out with your knives
And cut your trusters' throats. Bound servants, steal.   10
Large-handed robbers your grave masters are,
And pill by law. Maid, to thy master's bed;
Thy mistress is o'th'brothel. Son of sixteen,
Pluck the lined crutch from thy old limping sire,
With it beat out his brains. Piety and fear,
Religion to the gods, peace, justice, truth,
Domestic awe, night-rest, and neighbourhood,
Instruction, manners, mysteries, and trades,

Degrees, observances, customs, and laws,
20 Decline to your confounding contraries,
And yet confusion live. Plagues incident to men,
Your potent and infectious fevers heap
On Athens, ripe for stroke. Thou cold sciatica,
Cripple our senators, that their limbs may halt
As lamely as their manners. Lust and liberty
Creep in the minds and marrows of our youth,
That 'gainst the stream of virtue they may strive,
And drown themselves in riot. Itches, blains,
Sow all th'Athenian bosoms, and their crop
30 Be general leprosy. Breath infect breath,
That their society, as their friendship, may
Be merely poison. Nothing I'll bear from thee
But nakedness, thou detestable town.
Take thou that too, with multiplying bans.
Timon will to the woods, where he shall find
Th'unkindest beast more kinder than mankind.
The gods confound – hear me, you good gods all –
Th'Athenians both within and out that wall.
And grant, as Timon grows, his hate may grow
40 To the whole race of mankind, high and low.
Amen.   *Exit*

IV.2   *Enter Flavius, with two or three Servants*

FIRST SERVANT
Hear you, master steward, where's our master?
Are we undone, cast off, nothing remaining?

FLAVIUS
Alack, my fellows, what should I say to you?
Let me be recorded by the righteous gods,
I am as poor as you.

FIRST SERVANT   Such a house broke!

So noble a master fallen! All gone, and not
One friend to take his fortune by the arm,
And go along with him?

SECOND SERVANT   As we do turn our backs
From our companion thrown into his grave,
So his familiars to his buried fortunes   10
Slink all away, leave their false vows with him,
Like empty purses picked. And his poor self,
A dedicated beggar to the air,
With his disease of all-shunned poverty,
Walks, like contempt, alone. More of our fellows.
          Enter other Servants

FLAVIUS
All broken implements of a ruined house.

THIRD SERVANT
Yet do our hearts wear Timon's livery;
That see I by our faces. We are fellows still,
Serving alike in sorrow. Leaked is our bark,
And we, poor mates, stand on the dying deck,   20
Hearing the surges threat. We must all part
Into this sea of air.

FLAVIUS   Good fellows all,
The latest of my wealth I'll share amongst you.
Wherever we shall meet, for Timon's sake,
Let's yet be fellows. Let's shake our heads and say,
As 'twere a knell unto our master's fortunes,
'We have seen better days'. Let each take some.
          He gives them money
Nay, put out all your hands. Not one word more.
Thus part we rich in sorrow, parting poor.
          Flavius and the Servants embrace each other.
                    Exeunt Servants
O the fierce wretchedness that glory brings us!   30
Who would not wish to be from wealth exempt,

Since riches point to misery and contempt?
Who would be so mocked with glory, or to live
But in a dream of friendship,
To have his pomp and all what state compounds
But only painted, like his varnished friends?
Poor honest lord, brought low by his own heart,
Undone by goodness! Strange, unusual blood,
When man's worst sin is he does too much good.
40 Who then dares to be half so kind again?
For bounty, that makes gods, does still mar men.
My dearest lord, blest to be most accursed,
Rich only to be wretched, thy great fortunes
Are made thy chief afflictions. Alas, kind lord,
He's flung in rage from this ingrateful seat
Of monstrous friends;
Nor has he with him to supply his life,
Or that which can command it.
I'll follow and inquire him out.
50 I'll ever serve his mind with my best will;
Whilst I have gold I'll be his steward still.   *Exit*

IV.3   *Enter Timon in the woods*

TIMON

O blessed breeding sun, draw from the earth
Rotten humidity. Below thy sister's orb
Infect the air. Twinned brothers of one womb,
Whose procreation, residence, and birth,
Scarce is dividant – touch them with several fortunes,
The greater scorns the lesser. Not nature,
To whom all sores lay siege, can bear great fortune
But by contempt of nature.
Raise me this beggar and deject that lord –
10 The senator shall bear contempt hereditary,

The beggar native honour.
It is the pasture lards the wether's sides,
The want that makes him lean. Who dares, who dares,
In purity of manhood stand upright,
And say, 'This man's a flatterer'? If one be,
So are they all, for every grise of fortune
Is smoothed by that below. The learnèd pate
Ducks to the golden fool. All's obliquy;
There's nothing level in our cursèd natures
But direct villainy. Therefore be abhorred   20
All feasts, societies, and throngs of men.
His semblable, yea himself, Timon disdains.
Destruction fang mankind. Earth, yield me roots.

He digs

Who seeks for better of thee, sauce his palate
With thy most operant poison. What is here?
Gold? Yellow, glittering, precious gold?
No, gods, I am no idle votarist.
Roots, you clear heavens! Thus much of this will make
Black white, foul fair, wrong right,
Base noble, old young, coward valiant.   30
Ha, you gods! Why this? What, this, you gods? Why,
     this
Will lug your priests and servants from your sides,
Pluck stout men's pillows from below their heads.
This yellow slave
Will knit and break religions, bless th'accursed,
Make the hoar leprosy adored, place thieves,
And give them title, knee, and approbation,
With senators on the bench. This is it
That makes the wappened widow wed again –
She, whom the spital-house and ulcerous sores   40
Would cast the gorge at, this embalms and spices
To th'April day again. Come, damned earth,

Thou common whore of mankind, that puts odds
Among the rout of nations, I will make thee
Do thy right nature.

March afar off

                    Ha? A drum? Th' art quick,
But yet I'll bury thee. Thou'lt go, strong thief,
When gouty keepers of thee cannot stand.
Nay, stay thou out for earnest.

He keeps some of the gold, and buries the rest
Enter Alcibiades, with drum and fife, in warlike
manner; and Phrynia and Timandra

ALCIBIADES

What art thou there? Speak.

TIMON

50   A beast, as thou art. The canker gnaw thy heart
For showing me again the eyes of man!

ALCIBIADES

What is thy name? Is man so hateful to thee
That art thyself a man?

TIMON

I am Misanthropos, and hate mankind.
For thy part, I do wish thou wert a dog,
That I might love thee something.

ALCIBIADES   I know thee well;
But in thy fortunes am unlearned and strange.

TIMON

I know thee too, and more than that I know thee
I not desire to know. Follow thy drum.

60   With man's blood paint the ground gules, gules.
Religious canons, civil laws are cruel;
Then what should war be? This fell whore of thine
Hath in her more destruction than thy sword,
For all her cherubin look.

PHRYNIA   Thy lips rot off!

TIMON

I will not kiss thee; then the rot returns
To thine own lips again.

ALCIBIADES

How came the noble Timon to this change?

TIMON

As the moon does, by wanting light to give.
But then renew I could not like the moon;
There were no suns to borrow of.

ALCIBIADES   Noble Timon,   70
What friendship may I do thee?

TIMON   None, but to
Maintain my opinion.

ALCIBIADES   What is it, Timon?

TIMON

Promise me friendship, but perform none.
If thou wilt promise, the gods plague thee, for
Thou art a man. If thou dost not perform,
Confound thee, for thou art a man.

ALCIBIADES

I have heard in some sort of thy miseries.

TIMON

Thou sawest them when I had prosperity.

ALCIBIADES

I see them now. Then was a blessed time.

TIMON

As thine is now, held with a brace of harlots.   80

TIMANDRA

Is this th'Athenian minion whom the world
Voiced so regardfully?

TIMON   Art thou Timandra?

TIMANDRA

Yes.

TIMON

Be a whore still. They love thee not that use thee.
Give them diseases, leaving with thee their lust.
Make use of thy salt hours. Season the slaves
For tubs and baths; bring down rose-cheeked youth
To the tub-fast and the diet.

TIMANDRA   Hang thee, monster!

ALCIBIADES

Pardon him, sweet Timandra, for his wits
90 Are drowned and lost in his calamities.
I have but little gold of late, brave Timon,
The want whereof doth daily make revolt
In my penurious band. I have heard, and grieved,
How cursèd Athens, mindless of thy worth,
Forgetting thy great deeds, when neighbour states,
But for thy sword and fortune, trod upon them –

TIMON

I prithee beat thy drum and get thee gone.

ALCIBIADES

I am thy friend, and pity thee, dear Timon.

TIMON

How dost thou pity him whom thou dost trouble?
100 I had rather be alone.

ALCIBIADES   Why, fare thee well.
Here is some gold for thee.

TIMON   Keep it, I cannot eat it.

ALCIBIADES

When I have laid proud Athens on a heap –

TIMON

Warrest thou 'gainst Athens?

ALCIBIADES   Ay, Timon, and have cause.

TIMON

The gods confound them all in thy conquest,

And thee after, when thou hast conquered!

ALCIBIADES

Why me, Timon?

TIMON   That by killing of villains
Thou wast born to conquer my country.
Put up thy gold. Go on. Here's gold. Go on.
Be as a planetary plague, when Jove
Will o'er some high-viced city hang his poison   110
In the sick air. Let not thy sword skip one.
Pity not honoured age for his white beard;
He is an usurer. Strike me the counterfeit matron –
It is her habit only that is honest,
Herself's a bawd. Let not the virgin's cheek
Make soft thy trenchant sword; for those milk-paps
That, through the window, bared, bore at men's eyes
Are not within the leaf of pity writ,
But set them down horrible traitors. Spare not the babe
Whose dimpled smiles from fools exhaust their mercy;   120
Think it a bastard whom the oracle
Hath doubtfully pronounced thy throat shall cut,
And mince it sans remorse. Swear against objects.
Put armour on thine ears and on thine eyes,
Whose proof nor yells of mothers, maids, nor babes,
Nor sight of priests in holy vestments bleeding,
Shall pierce a jot. There's gold to pay thy soldiers.
Make large confusion; and, thy fury spent,
Confounded be thyself. Speak not, be gone.

ALCIBIADES

Hast thou gold yet? I'll take the gold thou givest me,   130
Not all thy counsel.

TIMON

Dost thou or dost thou not, heaven's curse upon thee!

PHRYNIA *and* TIMANDRA

Give us some gold, good Timon. Hast thou more?

TIMON

    Enough to make a whore forswear her trade,
    And to make whores, a bawd. Hold up, you sluts,
    Your aprons mountant. You are not oathable,
    Although I know you'll swear, terribly swear,
    Into strong shudders and to heavenly agues
    Th'immortal gods that hear you. Spare your oaths;
140   I'll trust to your conditions. Be whores still.
    And he whose pious breath seeks to convert you –
    Be strong in whore, allure him, burn him up;
    Let your close fire predominate his smoke,
    And be no turncoats. Yet may your pains, six months,
    Be quite contrary; and thatch
    Your poor thin roofs with burdens of the dead –
    Some that were hanged. No matter.
    Wear them, betray with them, whore still.
    Paint till a horse may mire upon your face.
150   A pox of wrinkles!

PHRYNIA *and* TIMANDRA Well, more gold. What then?
    Believe't that we'll do anything for gold.

TIMON

    Consumptions sow
    In hollow bones of man; strike their sharp shins,
    And mar men's spurring. Crack the lawyer's voice,
    That he may never more false title plead,
    Nor sound his quillets shrilly. Hoar the flamen,
    That scolds against the quality of flesh
    And not believes himself. Down with the nose,
    Down with it flat, take the bridge quite away
160   Of him that, his particular to foresee,
    Smells from the general weal. Make curled-pate ruffians
        bald,
    And let the unscarred braggarts of the war
    Derive some pain from you. Plague all,

That your activity may defeat and quell
The source of all erection. There's more gold.
Do you damn others, and let this damn you,
And ditches grave you all!

PHRYNIA *and* TIMANDRA

More counsel with more money, bounteous Timon.

TIMON

More whore, more mischief first. I have given you
    earnest.

ALCIBIADES

Strike up the drum towards Athens. Farewell, Timon. 170
If I thrive well, I'll visit thee again.

TIMON

If I hope well, I'll never see thee more.

ALCIBIADES

I never did thee harm.

TIMON

Yes, thou spokest well of me.

ALCIBIADES   Callest thou that harm?

TIMON

Men daily find it. Get thee away, and take
Thy beagles with thee.

ALCIBIADES   We but offend him. Strike!
            Drum beats. Exeunt all but Timon

TIMON

That nature, being sick of man's unkindness,
Should yet be hungry! Common mother, thou,
    (*he digs*)
Whose womb unmeasurable and infinite breast
Teems and feeds all; whose selfsame mettle,   180
Whereof thy proud child, arrogant man, is puffed,
Engenders the black toad and adder blue,
The gilded newt and eyeless venomed worm,
With all th'abhorrèd births below crisp heaven

Whereon Hyperion's quickening fire doth shine –
Yield him, who all thy human sons doth hate,
From forth thy plenteous bosom, one poor root.
Ensear thy fertile and conceptious womb,
Let it no more bring out ingrateful man.
190 Go great with tigers, dragons, wolves, and bears,
Teem with new monsters, whom thy upward face
Hath to the marbled mansion all above
Never presented. – O, a root! Dear thanks! –
Dry up thy marrows, vines and plough-torn leas,
Whereof ingrateful man with liquorish draughts
And morsels unctuous greases his pure mind,
That from it all consideration slips –
    Enter Apemantus
More man? Plague, plague!

APEMANTUS
I was directed hither. Men report
200 Thou dost affect my manners, and dost use them.

TIMON
'Tis, then, because thou dost not keep a dog,
Whom I would imitate. Consumption catch thee!

APEMANTUS
This is in thee a nature but infected,
A poor unmanly melancholy sprung
From change of fortune. Why this spade? This place?
This slave-like habit and these looks of care?
Thy flatterers yet wear silk, drink wine, lie soft,
Hug their diseased perfumes, and have forgot
That ever Timon was. Shame not these woods
210 By putting on the cunning of a carper.
Be thou a flatterer now, and seek to thrive
By that which has undone thee. Hinge thy knee,
And let his very breath whom thou'lt observe

Blow off thy cap. Praise his most vicious strain
And call it excellent. Thou wast told thus.
Thou gavest thine ears, like tapsters that bade welcome,
To knaves and all approachers. 'Tis most just
That thou turn rascal; hadst thou wealth again,
Rascals should have't. Do not assume my likeness.

TIMON

Were I like thee, I'd throw away myself.   220

APEMANTUS

Thou hast cast away thyself, being like thyself
A madman so long, now a fool. What, thinkest
That the bleak air, thy boisterous chamberlain,
Will put thy shirt on warm? Will these moist trees,
That have outlived the eagle, page thy heels
And skip when thou pointest out? Will the cold brook,
Candied with ice, caudle thy morning taste,
To cure thy o'ernight's surfeit? Call the creatures
Whose naked natures live in all the spite
Of wreakful heaven, whose bare unhousèd trunks,   230
To the conflicting elements exposed,
Answer mere nature – bid them flatter thee.
O, thou shalt find –

TIMON   A fool of thee. Depart.

APEMANTUS

I love thee better now than e'er I did.

TIMON

I hate thee worse.

APEMANTUS   Why?

TIMON   Thou flatterest misery.

APEMANTUS

I flatter not, but say thou art a caitiff.

TIMON

Why dost thou seek me out?

APEMANTUS   To vex thee.

TIMON

 Always a villain's office or a fool's.
 Dost please thyself in't?

APEMANTUS   Ay.

TIMON   What, a knave too?

APEMANTUS

240 If thou didst put this sour cold habit on
 To castigate thy pride, 'twere well; but thou
 Dost it enforcedly. Thou'dst courtier be again
 Wert thou not beggar. Willing misery
 Outlives incertain pomp, is crowned before.
 The one is filling still, never complete,
 The other at high wish. Best state, contentless,
 Hath a distracted and most wretched being,
 Worse than the worst, content.
 Thou shouldst desire to die, being miserable.

TIMON

250 Not by his breath that is more miserable.
 Thou art a slave whom Fortune's tender arm
 With favour never clasped. But, bred a dog,
 Hadst thou, like us from our first swath, proceeded
 The sweet degrees that this brief world affords
 To such as may the passive drudges of it
 Freely command, thou wouldst have plunged thyself
 In general riot, melted down thy youth
 In different beds of lust, and never learned
 The icy precepts of respect, but followed
260 The sugared game before thee. But myself –
 Who had the world as my confectionary,
 The mouths, the tongues, the eyes, and hearts of men
 At duty, more than I could frame emplovment;
 That numberless upon me stuck, as leaves

Do on the oak, have with one winter's brush
Fell from their boughs, and left me open, bare,
For every storm that blows – I to bear this,
That never knew but better, is some burden.
Thy nature did commence in sufferance, time
Hath made thee hard in't. Why shouldst thou hate men? 270
They never flattered thee. What hast thou given?
If thou wilt curse, thy father, that poor rag,
Must be thy subject; who in spite put stuff
To some she-beggar and compounded thee
Poor rogue hereditary. Hence, be gone.
If thou hadst not been born the worst of men,
Thou hadst been a knave and flatterer.

APEMANTUS
Art thou proud yet?

TIMON   Ay, that I am not thee.

APEMANTUS
I, that I was no prodigal.

TIMON
I, that I am one now.   280
Were all the wealth I have shut up in thee,
I'd give thee leave to hang it. Get thee gone.
That the whole life of Athens were in this!
Thus would I eat it.
      He eats a root

APEMANTUS   Here, I will mend thy feast.
      He offers Timon food

TIMON
First mend my company, take away thyself.

APEMANTUS
So I shall mend mine own by th'lack of thine.

TIMON
'Tis not well mended so, it is but botched.

If not, I would it were.

APEMANTUS
What wouldst thou have to Athens?

TIMON
290 Thee thither in a whirlwind. If thou wilt,
Tell them there I have gold. Look, so I have.

APEMANTUS
Here is no use for gold.

TIMON   The best and truest;
For here it sleeps, and does no hired harm.

APEMANTUS
Where liest a-nights, Timon?

TIMON
Under that's above me.
Where feedest thou a-days, Apemantus?

APEMANTUS Where my stomach finds meat; or, rather,
where I eat it.

TIMON Would poison were obedient, and knew my mind!
300 APEMANTUS Where wouldst thou send it?

TIMON To sauce thy dishes.

APEMANTUS The middle of humanity thou never knewest, but the extremity of both ends. When thou wast in
thy gilt and thy perfume, they mocked thee for too
much curiosity. In thy rags thou knowest none, but art
despised for the contrary. There's a medlar for thee.
Eat it.

TIMON On what I hate I feed not.

APEMANTUS Dost hate a medlar?

310 TIMON Ay, though it look like thee.

APEMANTUS An th' hadst hated meddlers sooner, thou
shouldst have loved thyself better now. What man didst
thou ever know unthrift that was beloved after his
means?

TIMON Who, without those means thou talkest of, didst thou ever know beloved?

APEMANTUS Myself.

TIMON I understand thee: thou hadst some means to keep a dog.

APEMANTUS What things in the world canst thou nearest 320 compare to thy flatterers?

TIMON Women nearest. But men – men are the things themselves. What wouldst thou do with the world, Apemantus, if it lay in thy power?

APEMANTUS Give it the beasts, to be rid of the men.

TIMON Wouldst thou have thyself fall in the confusion of men, and remain a beast with the beasts?

APEMANTUS Ay, Timon.

TIMON A beastly ambition, which the gods grant thee t'attain to! If thou wert the lion, the fox would beguile 330 thee. If thou wert the lamb, the fox would eat thee. If thou wert the fox, the lion would suspect thee when peradventure thou wert accused by the ass. If thou wert the ass, thy dullness would torment thee, and still thou livedst but as a breakfast to the wolf. If thou wert the wolf, thy greediness would afflict thee, and oft thou shouldst hazard thy life for thy dinner. Wert thou the unicorn, pride and wrath would confound thee and make thine own self the conquest of thy fury. Wert thou a bear, thou wouldst be killed by the horse. Wert thou 340 a horse, thou wouldst be seized by the leopard. Wert thou a leopard, thou wert german to the lion, and the spots of thy kindred were jurors on thy life. All thy safety were remotion, and thy defence absence. What beast couldst thou be that were not subject to a beast? And what a beast art thou already, that seest not thy loss in transformation!

APEMANTUS If thou couldst please me with speaking to
me, thou mightst have hit upon it here. The common-
350 wealth of Athens is become a forest of beasts.

TIMON How has the ass broke the wall, that thou art out
of the city?

APEMANTUS Yonder comes a poet and a painter. The
plague of company light upon thee! I will fear to catch
it, and give way. When I know not what else to do, I'll
see thee again.

TIMON When there is nothing living but thee, thou shalt
be welcome. I had rather be a beggar's dog than
Apemantus.

APEMANTUS

360 Thou art the cap of all the fools alive.

TIMON

Would thou wert clean enough to spit upon!

APEMANTUS

A plague on thee! Thou art too bad to curse.

TIMON

All villains that do stand by thee are pure.

APEMANTUS

There is no leprosy but what thou speakest.

TIMON

If I name thee.

I'll beat thee – but I should infect my hands.

APEMANTUS

I would my tongue could rot them off.

TIMON

Away, thou issue of a mangy dog!

Choler does kill me that thou art alive.

370 I swoon to see thee.

APEMANTUS

Would thou wouldst burst!

TIMON   Away, thou tedious rogue!

I am sorry I shall lose a stone by thee.

He throws a stone at Apemantus

APEMANTUS

Beast!

TIMON

Slave!

APEMANTUS

Toad!

TIMON

Rogue, rogue, rogue!
I am sick of this false world, and will love naught
But even the mere necessities upon't.
Then, Timon, presently prepare thy grave.
Lie where the light foam of the sea may beat   380
Thy grave-stone daily. Make thine epitaph,
That death in me at others' lives may laugh.

He addresses the gold

O thou sweet king-killer, and dear divorce
'Twixt natural son and sire, thou bright defiler
Of Hymen's purest bed, thou valiant Mars,
Thou ever young, fresh, loved, and delicate wooer,
Whose blush doth thaw the consecrated snow
That lies on Dian's lap! Thou visible god,
That sold'rest close impossibilities,
And makest them kiss; that speakest with every tongue,   390
To every purpose! O thou touch of hearts!
Think thy slave man rebels, and by thy virtue
Set them into confounding odds, that beasts
May have the world in empire.

APEMANTUS   Would 'twere so!
But not till I am dead. I'll say th' hast gold.
Thou wilt be thronged to shortly.

TIMON   Thronged to?

APEMANTUS   Ay.

TIMON
  Thy back, I prithee.
APEMANTUS   Live, and love thy misery.
TIMON
  Long live so, and so die! I am quit.
      Enter the Bandits
APEMANTUS
  More things like men! Eat, Timon, and abhor them. *Exit*
400 FIRST BANDIT Where should he have this gold? It is
  some poor fragment, some slender ort of his remainder.
  The mere want of gold, and the falling-from of his
  friends, drove him into this melancholy.
SECOND BANDIT It is noised he hath a mass of treasure.
THIRD BANDIT Let us make the assay upon him. If he
  care not for't, he will supply us easily. If he covetously
  reserve it, how shall's get it?
SECOND BANDIT True; for he bears it not about him.
  'Tis hid.
410 FIRST BANDIT Is not this he?
THIRD BANDIT Where?
SECOND BANDIT 'Tis his description.
THIRD BANDIT He. I know him.
ALL THE BANDITS Save thee, Timon.
TIMON Now, thieves?
ALL THE BANDITS
  Soldiers, not thieves.
TIMON   Both two – and women's sons.
ALL THE BANDITS
  We are not thieves, but men that much do want.
TIMON
  Your greatest want is, you want much of meat.
  Why should you want? Behold, the earth hath roots;
420 Within this mile break forth a hundred springs;
  The oaks bear mast, the briars scarlet hips;

126

The bounteous housewife Nature on each bush
Lays her full mess before you. Want? Why want?

FIRST BANDIT

We cannot live on grass, on berries, water,
As beasts, and birds, and fishes.

TIMON

Nor on the beasts themselves, the birds, and fishes;
You must eat men. Yet thanks I must you con
That you are thieves professed, that you work not
In holier shapes. For there is boundless theft
In limited professions. Rascal thieves,   430
Here's gold. Go, suck the subtle blood o'th'grape
Till the high fever seethe your blood to froth,
And so 'scape hanging. Trust not the physician;
His antidotes are poison, and he slays
More than you rob. Take wealth and lives together.
Do villainy, do, since you protest to do't,
Like workmen. I'll example you with thievery.
The sun's a thief, and with his great attraction
Robs the vast sea. The moon's an arrant thief,
And her pale fire she snatches from the sun.   440
The sea's a thief, whose liquid surge resolves
The moon into salt tears. The earth's a thief,
That feeds and breeds by a composture stolen
From general excrement. Each thing's a thief.
The laws, your curb and whip, in their rough power
Has unchecked theft. Love not yourselves. Away.
Rob one another. There's more gold. Cut throats.
All that you meet are thieves. To Athens go,
Break open shops – nothing can you steal
But thieves do lose it. Steal less for this I give you,   450
And gold confound you howsoe'er. Amen.

THIRD BANDIT 'Has almost charmed me from my profession by persuading me to it.

FIRST BANDIT 'Tis in the malice of mankind that he
thus advises us, not to have us thrive in our mystery.

SECOND BANDIT I'll believe him as an enemy, and give
over my trade.

FIRST BANDIT Let us first see peace in Athens. There is
no time so miserable but a man may be true.

Exeunt Bandits

Enter Flavius

FLAVIUS

460 O you gods!
Is yond despised and ruinous man my lord?
Full of decay and failing? O monument
And wonder of good deeds evilly bestowed!
What an alteration of honour
Has desperate want made!
What viler thing upon the earth than friends,
Who can bring noblest minds to basest ends!
How rarely does it meet with this time's guise,
When man was wished to love his enemies!

470 Grant I may ever love, and rather woo
Those that would mischief me than those that do!
'Has caught me in his eye. I will present
My honest grief unto him, and as my lord
Still serve him with my life. My dearest master!

TIMON

Away! What art thou?

FLAVIUS   Have you forgot me, sir?

TIMON

Why dost ask that? I have forgot all men.
Then, if thou grantest th' art a man, I have forgot thee.

FLAVIUS

An honest poor servant of yours.

TIMON

Then I know thee not.

I never had honest man about me, I. 480
All I kept were knaves, to serve in meat to villains.

FLAVIUS

The gods are witness,
Ne'er did poor steward wear a truer grief
For his undone lord than mine eyes for you.

TIMON

What, dost thou weep? Come nearer. Then I love thee,
Because thou art a woman and disclaimest
Flinty mankind, whose eyes do never give
But thorough lust and laughter. Pity's sleeping.
Strange times, that weep with laughing, not with
          weeping!

FLAVIUS

I beg of you to know me, good my lord, 490
T'accept my grief, and whilst this poor wealth lasts
To entertain me as your steward still.

TIMON

Had I a steward
So true, so just, and now so comfortable?
It almost turns my dangerous nature mild.
Let me behold thy face. Surely this man
Was born of woman.
Forgive my general and exceptless rashness,
You perpetual-sober gods! I do proclaim
One honest man. Mistake me not, but one – 500
No more, I pray – and he's a steward.
How fain would I have hated all mankind,
And thou redeemest thyself. But all, save thee,
I fell with curses.
Methinks thou art more honest now than wise.
For by oppressing and betraying me
Thou mightst have sooner got another service;
For many so arrive at second masters

Upon their first lord's neck. But tell me true –
510 For I must ever doubt, though ne'er so sure –
Is not thy kindness subtle-covetous,
A usuring kindness, and as rich men deal gifts,
Expecting in return twenty for one?

FLAVIUS

No, my most worthy master, in whose breast
Doubt and suspect, alas, are placed too late.
You should have feared false times when you did feast.
Suspect still comes where an estate is least.
That which I show, heaven knows, is merely love,
Duty, and zeal to your unmatchèd mind,
520 Care of your food and living. And believe it,
My most honoured lord,
For any benefit that points to me,
Either in hope or present, I'd exchange
For this one wish, that you had power and wealth
To requite me by making rich yourself.

TIMON

Look thee, 'tis so. Thou singly honest man,
Here, take. The gods, out of my misery,
Ha' sent thee treasure. Go, live rich and happy,
But thus conditioned: thou shalt build from men,
530 Hate all, curse all, show charity to none,
But let the famished flesh slide from the bone
Ere thou relieve the beggar. Give to dogs
What thou deniest to men. Let prisons swallow 'em,
Debts wither 'em to nothing. Be men like blasted woods,
And may diseases lick up their false bloods!
And so farewell, and thrive.

FLAVIUS

O, let me stay and comfort you, my master.

TIMON

If thou hatest curses,

Stay not. Fly, whilst thou art blest and free.
Ne'er see thou man, and let me ne'er see thee.   540
Exit Flavius; Timon retires to his cave
at the rear of the stage

  Enter Poet and Painter   V.1

PAINTER As I took note of the place, it cannot be far
where he abides.

POET What's to be thought of him? Does the rumour
hold for true that he's so full of gold?

PAINTER Certain. Alcibiades reports it. Phrynia and
Timandra had gold of him. He likewise enriched poor
straggling soldiers with great quantity. 'Tis said he gave
unto his steward a mighty sum.

POET Then this breaking of his has been but a try for his
friends?   10

PAINTER Nothing else. You shall see him a palm in
Athens again, and flourish with the highest. Therefore
'tis not amiss we tender our loves to him in this supposed distress of his. It will show honestly in us, and is
very likely to load our purposes with what they travail
for, if it be a just and true report that goes of his having.

POET What have you now to present unto him?

PAINTER Nothing at this time but my visitation; only I
will promise him an excellent piece.

POET I must serve him so too, tell him of an intent that's   20
coming toward him.

PAINTER Good as the best. Promising is the very air
o'th'time; it opens the eyes of expectation. Performance
is ever the duller for his act, and but in the plainer
and simpler kind of people the deed of saying is quite
out of use. To promise is most courtly and fashionable.
Performance is a kind of will or testament which argues
a great sickness in his judgement that makes it.

  Enter Timon from his cave

TIMON (*aside*) Excellent workman! Thou canst not paint
30   a man so bad as is thyself.

POET I am thinking what I shall say I have provided for
   him. It must be a personating of himself; a satire against
   the softness of prosperity, with a discovery of the infinite
   flatteries that follow youth and opulency.

TIMON (*aside*) Must thou needs stand for a villain in
   thine own work? Wilt thou whip thine own faults in
   other men? Do so, I have gold for thee.

POET
Nay, let's seek him.
Then do we sin against our own estate,
40   When we may profit meet and come too late.

PAINTER
True.
When the day serves, before black-cornered night,
Find what thou wantest by free and offered light.
Come.

TIMON (*aside*)
I'll meet you at the turn. What a god's gold,
That he is worshipped in a baser temple
Than where swine feed!
'Tis thou that riggest the bark and ploughest the foam,
Settlest admirèd reverence in a slave.
50   To thee be worship; and thy saints for aye
Be crowned with plagues, that thee alone obey.
Fit I meet them.

     He comes forward

POET
Hail, worthy Timon!

PAINTER   Our late noble master!

TIMON
Have I once lived to see two honest men?

POET

Sir,
Having often of your open bounty tasted,
Hearing you were retired, your friends fall'n off,
Whose thankless natures – O abhorrèd spirits! –
Not all the whips of heaven are large enough –
What, to you,   60
Whose star-like nobleness gave life and influence
To their whole being! I am rapt, and cannot cover
The monstrous bulk of this ingratitude
With any size of words.

TIMON

Let it go naked, men may see't the better.
You that are honest, by being what you are,
Make them best seen and known.

PAINTER   He and myself
Have travelled in the great shower of your gifts,
And sweetly felt it.

TIMON   Ay, you are honest men.

PAINTER

We are hither come to offer you our service.   70

TIMON

Most honest men! Why, how shall I requite you?
Can you eat roots, and drink cold water? No?

POET *and* **PAINTER**

What we can do, we'll do, to do you service.

TIMON

Y'are honest men. Y'have heard that I have gold.
I am sure you have. Speak truth; y'are honest men.

PAINTER

So it is said, my noble lord, but therefore
Came not my friend nor I.

TIMON

    Good honest men! Thou drawest a counterfeit
    Best in all Athens. Th' art indeed the best;
80   Thou counterfeitest most lively.

PAINTER   So, so, my lord.

TIMON

    E'en so, sir, as I say. (*To the Poet*) And for thy fiction,
    Why, thy verse swells with stuff so fine and smooth
    That thou art even natural in thine art.
    But, for all this, my honest-natured friends,
    I must needs say you have a little fault.
    Marry, 'tis not monstrous in you, neither wish I
    You take much pains to mend.

POET *and* PAINTER   Beseech your honour
    To make it known to us.

TIMON   You'll take it ill.

POET *and* PAINTER

    Most thankfully, my lord.

TIMON   Will you indeed?

POET *and* PAINTER

90   Doubt it not, worthy lord.

TIMON

    There's never a one of you but trusts a knave
    That mightily deceives you.

POET *and* PAINTER   Do we, my lord?

TIMON

    Ay, and you hear him cog, see him dissemble,
    Know his gross patchery, love him, feed him,
    Keep in your bosom. Yet remain assured
    That he's a made-up villain.

PAINTER

    I know none such, my lord.

POET   Nor I.

TIMON

Look you, I love you well; I'll give you gold,
Rid me these villains from your companies.
Hang them or stab them, drown them in a draught,   100
Confound them by some course, and come to me,
I'll give you gold enough.

POET *and* **PAINTER**

Name them, my lord, let's know them.

TIMON

You that way, and you this – but two in company –
Each man apart, all single and alone,
Yet an arch-villain keeps him company.
(*To the Painter*) If, where thou art, two villains shall
        not be,
Come not near him. (*To the Poet*) If thou wouldst not
    reside
But where one villain is, then him abandon.
Hence, pack! There's gold. You came for gold, ye slaves.   110
(*To the Painter*) You have work for me. There's pay-
    ment. Hence!
(*To the Poet*) You are an alchemist, make gold of that.
Out, rascal dogs!
        He beats them off the stage, and retires to his cave
        Enter Flavius and two Senators

FLAVIUS

It is in vain that you would speak with Timon;
For he is set so only to himself
That nothing but himself which looks like man
Is friendly with him.

FIRST SENATOR   Bring us to his cave.
It is our part and promise to th'Athenians
To speak with Timon.

SECOND SENATOR   At all times alike

120 Men are not still the same. 'Twas time and griefs
That framed him thus. Time, with his fairer hand,
Offering the fortunes of his former days,
The former man may make him. Bring us to him,
And chance it as it may.

FLAVIUS   Here is his cave.
Peace and content be here! Lord Timon, Timon,
Look out, and speak to friends. Th'Athenians
By two of their most reverend Senate greet thee.
Speak to them, noble Timon.

Enter Timon out of his cave

TIMON
Thou sun, that comforts, burn! Speak and be hanged.
130 For each true word a blister, and each false
Be as a cantherizing to the root o'th'tongue,
Consuming it with speaking!

FIRST SENATOR   Worthy Timon –

TIMON
Of none but such as you, and you of Timon.

FIRST SENATOR
The senators of Athens greet thee, Timon.

TIMON
I thank them, and would send them back the plague,
Could I but catch it for them.

FIRST SENATOR   O, forget
What we are sorry for ourselves in thee.
The senators with one consent of love
Entreat thee back to Athens, who have thought
140 On special dignities, which vacant lie
For thy best use and wearing.

SECOND SENATOR   They confess
Toward thee forgetfulness too general-gross;
Which now the public body, which doth seldom
Play the recanter, feeling in itself

A lack of Timon's aid, hath sense withal
Of it own fault, restraining aid to Timon,
And send forth us to make their sorrowed render,
Together with a recompense more fruitful
Than their offence can weigh down by the dram –
Ay, even such heaps and sums of love and wealth   150
As shall to thee blot out what wrongs were theirs,
And write in thee the figures of their love,
Ever to read them thine.

TIMON   You witch me in it,
Surprise me to the very brink of tears.
Lend me a fool's heart and a woman's eyes,
And I'll beweep these comforts, worthy senators.

FIRST SENATOR
Therefore so please thee to return with us,
And of our Athens, thine and ours, to take
The captainship, thou shalt be met with thanks,
Allowed with absolute power, and thy good name   160
Live with authority. So soon we shall drive back
Of Alcibiades th'approaches wild,
Who like a boar too savage doth root up
His country's peace.

SECOND SENATOR   And shakes his threat'ning sword
Against the walls of Athens.

FIRST SENATOR   Therefore, Timon –

TIMON
Well, sir, I will – therefore I will, sir, thus:
If Alcibiades kill my countrymen,
Let Alcibiades know this of Timon,
That Timon cares not. But if he sack fair Athens,
And take our goodly agèd men by th'beards,   170
Giving our holy virgins to the stain
Of contumelious, beastly, mad-brained war,
Then let him know – and tell him Timon speaks it

In pity of our agèd and our youth –
I cannot choose but tell him that I care not,
And let him take't at worst. For their knives care not,
While you have throats to answer. For myself,
There's not a whittle in th'unruly camp
But I do prize it at my love before
180   The reverend'st throat in Athens. So I leave you
To the protection of the prosperous gods
As thieves to keepers.

FLAVIUS   Stay not, all's in vain.

TIMON
Why, I was writing of my epitaph;
It will be seen tomorrow. My long sickness
Of health and living now begins to mend,
And nothing brings me all things. Go, live still;
Be Alcibiades your plague, you his,
And last so long enough.

FIRST SENATOR   We speak in vain.

TIMON
But yet I love my country, and am not
190   One that rejoices in the common wrack,
As common bruit doth put it.

FIRST SENATOR   That's well spoke.

TIMON
Commend me to my loving countrymen –

FIRST SENATOR
These words become your lips as they pass through
        them.

SECOND SENATOR
And enter in our ears like great triumphers
In their applauding gates.

TIMON   Commend me to them,
And tell them that to ease them of their griefs,
Their fears of hostile strokes, their aches, losses,

Their pangs of love, with other incident throes
That nature's fragile vessel doth sustain
In life's uncertain voyage, I will some kindness do   200
  them –
I'll teach them to prevent wild Alcibiades' wrath.

FIRST SENATOR

I like this well. He will return again.

TIMON

I have a tree, which grows here in my close,
That mine own use invites me to cut down,
And shortly must I fell it. Tell my friends,
Tell Athens, in the sequence of degree
From high to low throughout, that whoso please
To stop affliction, let him take his haste,
Come hither ere my tree hath felt the axe,
And hang himself. I pray you do my greeting.   210

FLAVIUS

Trouble him no further; thus you still shall find him.

TIMON

Come not to me again, but say to Athens,
Timon hath made his everlasting mansion
Upon the beachèd verge of the salt flood,
Who once a day with his embossèd froth
The turbulent surge shall cover. Thither come,
And let my grave-stone be your oracle.
Lips, let four words go by, and language end:
What is amiss, plague and infection mend!
Graves only be men's works, and death their gain!   220
Sun, hide thy beams. Timon hath done his reign. *Exit*

FIRST SENATOR

His discontents are unremovably
Coupled to nature.

SECOND SENATOR

Our hope in him is dead. Let us return,

And strain what other means is left unto us
In our dear peril.

FIRST SENATOR   It requires swift foot.   *Exeunt*

V.2   *Enter two other Senators, with a Messenger*

THIRD SENATOR
Thou hast painfully discovered. Are his files
As full as thy report?

MESSENGER   I have spoke the least.
Besides, his expedition promises
Present approach.

FOURTH SENATOR
We stand much hazard if they bring not Timon.

MESSENGER
I met a courier, one mine ancient friend,
Whom, though in general part we were opposed,
Yet our old love made a particular force,
And made us speak like friends. This man was riding
From Alcibiades to Timon's cave
With letters of entreaty, which imported
His fellowship i'th'cause against your city,
In part for his sake moved.

Enter the two other Senators, from Timon

THIRD SENATOR   Here come our brothers.

FIRST SENATOR
No talk of Timon, nothing of him expect.
The enemy's drum is heard, and fearful scouring
Doth choke the air with dust. In, and prepare.
Ours is the fall, I fear; our foe's the snare.   *Exeunt*

Enter a Soldier in the woods, seeking Timon

SOLDIER

By all description this should be the place.
Who's here? Speak, ho! No answer? What is this?
(*He reads*)
Timon is dead, who hath outstretched his span.
Some beast read this; there does not live a man.
Dead, sure, and this his grave. What's on this tomb
I cannot read. The character I'll take with wax.
Our captain hath in every figure skill,
An aged interpreter, though young in days.
Before proud Athens he's set down by this,
Whose fall the mark of his ambition is.   *Exit* 10

Trumpets sound. Enter Alcibiades with his Powers V.4
before Athens

ALCIBIADES

Sound to this coward and lascivious town
Our terrible approach.
      The Trumpeter sounds a parley
      The Senators appear upon the walls
Till now you have gone on and filled the time
With all licentious measure, making your wills
The scope of justice. Till now, myself, and such
As stepped within the shadow of your power,
Have wandered with our traversed arms, and breathed
Our sufferance vainly. Now the time is flush,
When crouching marrow in the bearer strong
Cries of itself 'No more'. Now breathless wrong   10
Shall sit and pant in your great chairs of ease,
And pursy insolence shall break his wind
With fear and horrid flight.
FIRST SENATOR   Noble and young,

When thy first griefs were but a mere conceit,
Ere thou hadst power or we had cause of fear,
We sent to thee, to give thy rages balm,
To wipe out our ingratitude with loves
Above their quantity.

SECOND SENATOR   So did we woo
Transformèd Timon to our city's love
20   By humble message and by promised means.
We were not all unkind, nor all deserve
The common stroke of war.

FIRST SENATOR   These walls of ours
Were not erected by their hands from whom
You have received your grief; nor are they such
That these great towers, trophies, and schools should
        fall
For private faults in them.

SECOND SENATOR   Nor are they living
Who were the motives that you first went out;
Shame, that they wanted cunning, in excess
Hath broke their hearts. March, noble lord,
30   Into our city with thy banners spread.
By decimation and a tithèd death –
If thy revenges hunger for that food
Which nature loathes – take thou the destined tenth,
And by the hazard of the spotted die
Let die the spotted.

FIRST SENATOR   All have not offended.
For those that were, it is not square to take,
On those that are, revenges. Crimes like lands
Are not inherited. Then, dear countryman,
Bring in thy ranks, but leave without thy rage.
40   Spare thy Athenian cradle and those kin
Which, in the bluster of thy wrath, must fall
With those that have offended. Like a shepherd

Approach the fold and cull th'infected forth,
But kill not all together.

SECOND SENATOR   What thou wilt,
Thou rather shalt enforce it with thy smile
Than hew to't with thy sword.

FIRST SENATOR   Set but thy foot
Against our rampired gates and they shall ope,
So thou wilt send thy gentle heart before,
To say thou'lt enter friendly.

SECOND SENATOR   Throw thy glove,   50
Or any token of thine honour else,
That thou wilt use the wars as thy redress
And not as our confusion, all thy powers
Shall make their harbour in our town till we
Have sealed thy full desire.

ALCIBIADES   Then there's my glove.
Descend, and open your unchargèd ports.
Those enemies of Timon's, and mine own,
Whom you yourselves shall set out for reproof,
Fall, and no more. And, to atone your fears
With my more noble meaning, not a man
Shall pass his quarter, or offend the stream   60
Of regular justice in your city's bounds,
But shall be remanded to your public laws
At heaviest answer.

BOTH SENATORS   'Tis most nobly spoken.

ALCIBIADES
Descend, and keep your words.
    The Senators descend
    Enter Soldier

SOLDIER
My noble general, Timon is dead,
Entombed upon the very hem o'th'sea;
And on his grave-stone this insculpture which

With wax I brought away, whose soft impression
Interprets for my poor ignorance.

ALCIBIADES (*reading the epitaph*)

70   *Here lies a wretched corse, of wretched soul bereft.*
   Seek not my name. A plague consume you wicked caitiffs
       left!
   Here lie I Timon, who alive all living men did hate.
   Pass by and curse thy fill, but pass, and stay not here thy
       gait.

These well express in thee thy latter spirits.
Though thou abhorredst in us our human griefs,
Scornedst our brains' flow and those our droplets which
From niggard nature fall, yet rich conceit
Taught thee to make vast Neptune weep for aye
On thy low grave, on faults forgiven. Dead
80 Is noble Timon, of whose memory
Hereafter more. Bring me into your city,
And I will use the olive with my sword,
Make war breed peace, make peace stint war, make each
Prescribe to other, as each other's leech.
Let our drums strike.   *Exeunt*

COMMENTARY

THE Act and scene divisions are those of Peter Alexander's edition of the *Complete Works* (1951). Biblical quotations are from the Bishops' Bible.

I.1   Act and scene divisions in this play were first provided by editors in the eighteenth century. The Folio text opens with the conventional heading '*Actus Primus. Scæna Prima.*', but after that there are no divisions whatever in it. The first 288 lines can, however, be justifiably regarded as a distinct dramatic unit, fulfilling several necessary functions. They offer a vivid picture of the society in which Timon lives; they bring out his generosity and his addiction to conspicuous consumption; they give a preview of the play's main action in the Poet's description of the allegory he has written; and they introduce three of the leading figures: Timon himself, Apemantus, and Alcibiades. But, while the scene has been skilfully planned, there is a striking contrast, at the level of execution, between the first part of it, up to the entrance of Apemantus at line 177, and what follows. In the first part, the medium is consistently blank verse; the manner confident and assured; the imagery rich and impressive. In the second, blank verse and prose mingle with each other in a disconcerting fashion, making it hard to decide where irregular blank verse ends and prose begins; the texture of the writing becomes noticeably thinner; and the action loses much of its forward impetus. The unevenness, so characteristic of this play, is already evident.

(stage direction) *Merchant, at several doors.* After '*Merchant*' the Folio adds '*and Mercer*'; but there is no part for this character, who looks like a false start on Shakespeare's part, and he has therefore been omitted from this edition. The *several doors* are separate doors, one on either side of the stage, which were the principal means of access to it for Shakespeare's actors. Having made their entry, the Poet and the Painter converse on one side of the stage, and the Jeweller and the Merchant on the other.

1   *y'are* (colloquial) ye are

2   *long* for a long time
    How goes the world? how do you do? how are things with you? (But the Painter, to show off his wit, takes the phrase in its more literal sense.)

3   *wears* wears away, deteriorates

4   *strange* out of the ordinary, unusual event

5   *record* (pronounced with the stress on the second syllable) records of the past

6   *Magic of bounty* (an apostrophe to Timon)

7   *conjured* enforced by magical spells

9   *'tis.* Literally 'it is', this is a normal Shakespearian usage for 'he is' or 'she is', like '*c'est*' in French.
    fixed certain, indisputable

10 *breathed* accustomed, inured (like a horse made 'long-winded' by training)

11 *continuate* lasting, continual
    goodness generosity, bounty

12 *passes* excels, surpasses

13 *see't* (colloquial) see it

14 *touch the estimate* pay as much as the price it is valued at, rise to my figure

15 *the vile* worthless men, men who do not deserve praise

16 *stains the glory* dims the splendour, diminishes the worth
    happy (1) felicitous; (2) fortunate in having such a fitting subject

17   *good form* well-cut shape

18   *water* lustre

19   *rapt* absorbed, engrossed

19–20   *some dedication | To the great lord*. In Shakespeare's day
        it was customary for the professional writer to dedicate
        his work to an aristocratic patron – as Shakespeare
        himself dedicated both *Venus and Adonis* and *The Rape
        of Lucrece* to the Earl of Southampton – in the hope of
        a reward.

20   *idly* effortlessly, casually

21–5   *Our poesy . . . it chafes*. The main idea in this passage is
        that poetry is something that flows naturally and spon-
        taneously from the mind of the poet, and that true
        poetry cannot therefore be produced at will or under
        compulsion.

21   *gum which oozes*. The Folio reads 'Gowne, which vses'.
        This makes no sense, and can be best explained as the
        compositor's misreading of 'Gomme, which ouses' in
        the manuscript he was working from.

22   *i'th'* (colloquial) in the

23–4   *Our gentle flame | Provokes itself* the flame (of poetic
        inspiration) kindles of its own accord

24–5   *like the current flies | Each bound it chafes* like the stream
        slides away from each bank it chafes against. This
        image again endorses the notion that poetry is recalci-
        trant to any form of external stimulus, unlike the fire
        in the flint which can only be brought out by chafing the
        flint against steel or some other hard matter.

25   *chafes*. The Folio reading is 'chases'; but the confusion
        of the 'long s' (ſ) with 'f' is a common one; and the
        emendation gains support from 'The troubled Tiber
        chafing with her shores' (*Julius Caesar*, I.2.101).

27   *Upon the heels of my presentment* immediately after my
        presentation of it (to Timon)

28   *piece* picture, work of art

30   *This comes off well and excellent* this (pointing to some
        detail in the picture) is most admirably managed

31   *Indifferent* not bad, pretty good. The Painter affects
        modesty in order to fish for praise. The lavishness of
        the Poet's answer betrays its insincerity.

31-2   *How this grace | Speaks his own standing!* how elo-
        quently the gracefulness of this figure expresses the
        dignity and importance of the subject! It is never made
        clear that the portrait is of Timon himself, though this
        seems likely.

33-4   *How big imagination | Moves in this lip!* how pregnantly
        the imagination of the man portrayed is suggested by
        this lip!

34-5   *To th'dumbness of the gesture | One might interpret* it
        would be easy to supply the right words to fit this dumb
        gesture. Compare 'There was speech in their dumb-
        ness, language in their very gesture' (*The Winter's
        Tale*, V.2.13-14). At the back of what the Poet says
        there lies the Renaissance commonplace that a poem is
        a speaking picture, and a painting a dumb poem.

36   *a pretty mocking of the life* a pretty fair counterfeit of
        the living man

37   *a touch* a bit of technique

38   *It tutors nature* it instructs nature (by being better than
        the real thing, and so offering an ideal towards which
        nature can strive). The attitude to art expressed by the
        Poet has much in common with that set out by Sir
        Philip Sidney in *An Apology for Poetry* – see *Eliza-
        bethan Critical Essays*, edited by G. Gregory Smith
        (1904), Volume 1, pages 156-7.

38-9   *Artificial strife | Lives in these touches livelier than life*
        the strife of art (to surpass nature) is vindicated in this
        painting, which has more essential life in it than the
        living man who is the subject of it. The notion of art
        vying with nature was a familiar one at the time when
        the play was written. Shakespeare refers to it fre-
        quently – see *Venus and Adonis*, lines 289-94; *The Rape
        of Lucrece*, lines 1373-7; and *The Winter's Tale*,
        V.2.92-100.

39   *touches livelier*. The Folio reading is 'touches, liue-
        lier'; but it is hard to see how the strife of art with
        nature can be 'livelier' than life itself, since it is part of
        life. The omission of the comma removes this diffi-
        culty and makes the entire sentence a logical extension
        of the previous one.

40   *followed* sought after, courted

41   *happy man*. The Folio gives 'happy men', which has
        been defended on the grounds that the Poet envies the
        senators because they enjoy the privilege of being
        admitted to Timon's presence. In fact, however,
        Timon receives all and sundry. What the Poet really
        envies is Timon's good fortune in having even the
        senators as his clients.

43   *You see this confluence, this great flood of visitors*. The
        Poet indicates the *confluence* of clients because it pro-
        vides a convenient excuse for introducing his poem
        and also a living illustration of its main contention.

44   *rough work* unpolished poem

45   *this beneath world* this lower world, the world we live in
        (as distinct from the superior world of the heavenly
        bodies)

46   *entertainment* welcome

46-7   *My free drift | Halts not particularly* the frank unham-
        pered tenor of my work does not stop to single out any
        individual (for attack)

47   *moves itself* (1) moves; (2) busies itself, is active

48   *tax* criticism, censure. The Folio reads 'wax', which is
        retained by most editors, on the grounds that it is a
        reference by Shakespeare to the use of wax writing-
        tablets, and possibly also to the myth of Icarus, the son
        of Daedalus, who flew too near the sun after his father
        had equipped him with a pair of wings attached to his
        back by wax. The wax melted; and Icarus plunged into
        the sea and was drowned. No convincing explanation
        has yet been produced, however, of precisely what is
        meant by 'a wide sea of wax'. In this edition *tax*, which

was first suggested in the nineteenth century, has been preferred for two reasons. First, it appears in *All's Well That Ends Well*, where Helena speaks of being exposed to 'Tax of impudence' (II.1.170), that is, censure for being shameless and immodest. It is, therefore, a good Shakespearian word. Secondly, and more important, the whole context seems to demand it. The Poet's words, 'My free drift ... tract behind' (lines 46–51), are, in effect, a condensed version of Jaques's defence of the satirist in *As You Like It* (II.7.70–87). Like the Poet, Jaques claims the right to speak freely (lines 47–9), and says that his target is general vices, not individuals. Moreover, there are two striking verbal parallels. Jaques, too, connects the sin he is taxing with the sea:

> Why, who cries out on pride
> That can therein tax any private party?
> Doth it not flow as hugely as the sea ...?
>
> > (lines 70–72)

He also compares his taxing to the flight of a bird. Referring to the man who is untouched by it, he says:

> if he be free,
> Why then my taxing like a wild-goose flies,
> Unclaimed of any man.   (lines 85–7)

This statement is close to the Poet's in line 50, where he speaks of flying *an eagle flight*. *Tax*, then, commends itself as the better reading, by virtue both of its greater intelligibility and of the associations with the sea and with bird-flight that it seems to have had for Shakespeare.

48   *No levelled malice* no malice aimed at any specific individual

49   *one comma* the least detail (a comma being the least emphatic of stops)

50   *flies.* The subject, to be understood, is *the course I hold.*
    forth on straight on

51   *tract* trace, mark of its passage

52   *How shall I understand you?* what do you mean?

53   *unbolt* explain

54   *conditions* temperaments

55   *glib* smooth

56   *quality* character, nature
        tender down offer

58   *hanging* (like clothes upon the wearer). The point is
        that it is Timon's fortune, his outside, that makes him
        attractive to others, not *his good and gracious nature* in
        itself.

59   *properties* appropriates
        to his love and tendance to offering him loving attention

60   *glass-faced* mirror-faced (because the flatterer reflects
        the moods and opinions of the man he flatters)

64   *in Timon's nod* in having received the recognition of a
        nod from Timon

68   *ranked with all deserts* surrounded by rows of men of all
        degrees of worth

69   *this sphere* this globe, this earth

70   *To propagate their states* to increase their worldly
        prosperity

72   *personate* represent
        frame nature, mould

73   *ivory* white

74-5   *Whose present grace to present slaves and servants |
        Translates his rivals* and her sudden favour to him in-
        stantly transforms his rivals (for that favour) into his
        slaves and servants. In both cases where it is used
        present means: (1) existing now; (2) immediate.

75   *conceived to scope* devised to the purpose

78-9   *Bowing his head against the steepy mount | To climb his
        happiness* bending forward in his effort to climb the
        steep slope and attain his good fortune

79-80   *would be well expressed | In our condition* would well
        express the condition of mankind

80   *hear me on* hear what else I have to say, listen further

81   *fellows but of late* comrades and equals only a short time before

82   *better than his value* (1) of more worth than he; (2) worth more than he
    on the moment immediately

83   *Follow his strides* become his obsequious followers
    his lobbies fill with tendance fill his ante-rooms, dancing attendance on him

84   *sacrificial whisperings*. According to Onions (*A Shakespeare Glossary*, 1911, etc.), this means whispers 'having the character of sacrifice or worship offered to a god'. It seems far more likely, however, that the clients are offering to make large sacrifices to curry favour with the great man, and that they whisper them to him in order to keep them secret from the other clients.

85   *Make sacred even his stirrup* treat his stirrup as if it were holy. The allusion is to the custom of some menial holding a great man's stirrup while he mounted.

85–6   *through him | Drink the free air* make out that they are indebted to him for the air they breathe

86   *marry* indeed, to be sure (originally the name of the Virgin Mary used as an oath)

88   *Spurns down* kicks down

90   *hands*. The Folio reads 'hand'; but the plural seems necessary here.
    fall. This is C. J. Sisson's emendation for the 'sit' of the Folio, which is too weak a word for this context. In Elizabethan handwriting 'fall' could be confused with 'sitt'. Most editors read 'slip'.

91   *declining* falling, sinking

93   *moral paintings* paintings pointing a moral

94   *demonstrate* (stressed on the second syllable)
    quick sudden. But the other meaning – 'pregnant' – appears to have suggested *pregnantly* in the next line.

96   *mean eyes* the eyes of humble men

97   *The foot above the head* the foot of Fortune poised over the head of the prosperous man. There is probably a

reference also to the proverb 'Do not make the foot the head', that is, 'Don't upset or invert the proper order of things'. Such a reversal may well be imminent for Timon.

(stage direction) *Trumpets sound . . . every suitor*. These are the words given in the Folio – the rest of the direction is the work of the editor – carefully designed to ensure that the first impression the hero makes on the audience is the right one.

99   *Five talents*. Exactly what a talent meant to Shakespeare is one of the problems of the play (see An Account of the Text, pages 257–8). Writers contemporary with him made it equivalent to anything from £100 to £180.

100   *strait* strict, exacting

101   *Your honourable letter* a letter from your honour

102   *those have* those who have

102–3   *which failing | Periods his comfort* but if the letter is not forthcoming, that puts an end to all his hopes of happiness

104   *of that feather* to of such a kind as to. Compare 'Birds of a feather flock together.'

     shake off cast off, discard. The conviction Timon states here is rich in irony, for he thinks men in general share it.

105   *know him* know him to be

106   *a help* some assistance

108   *ever binds him* binds him eternally to you by ties of gratitude. There is a quibble here on *free* in the previous line.

109   *Commend me to him* give him my kind regards

     ransom the money needed to free him from the debtors' gaol

110   *being enfranchised, bid him* bid him, when he is set free

111   *the feeble* the feeble man

112   *But to* but it is also necessary to

114   *Freely* gladly, readily

     father (term of respect used in addressing an old man)

116   *so* indeed
120   *fellow* (term of contempt)
        creature puppet, hanger-on
122   *first* beginnings
123   *more raised* of higher rank, more important
124   *one which holds a trencher* a waiter (a *trencher* was a
        wooden plate)
126   *confer* bestow
        got acquired, earned
127   *fair* beautiful
        o'th'youngest for a bride only just of marriageable age
128-9 *And I have bred her at my dearest cost | In qualities of the
        best* and I have spared no expense to have her educated
        in the best possible way
130   *Attempts* tries to win
131   *her resort* visiting her, access to her
132   *spoke* spoken
133   *Therefore he will be, Timon* therefore he is going to be
        honest, Timon. This cryptic statement comes close to
        being a demand that Timon, having given his word
        that Lucilius is an honest man, should see to it that
        Lucilius abandon his pursuit of the girl.
134   *His honesty rewards him in itself* (a version of the pro-
        verb 'Virtue is its own reward')
135   *It must not bear my daughter* it is not going to carry off
        my daughter as well
136   *apt* impressionable, susceptible to a love suit
137   *precedent passions* former feelings, amorous desires
        when we were young. The stress falls on the second
        syllable in *precedent*.
139   *accepts of* accepts (a fairly common usage in Shake-
        speare)
140   *If in her marriage my consent be missing* if she marries
        without my consent. In Shakespeare's day young
        people were not supposed to marry without the ap-
        proval of their parents, who, indeed, were usually re-
        sponsible for arranging the match.

142   *from forth the beggars of the world* from among the poorest beggars I can find anywhere

143   *all* entirely, utterly

        How shall she be endowed what dowry will you give her

144   *mated with an equal husband* married to a husband who is her equal in rank and fortune

145   *on the present* immediately, forthwith

147   *strain* strain my fortunes

148   *a bond in men* an obligation that one man owes to another. This idea, that society is held together by men's readiness to be generous to one another, is basic to Timon's behaviour at this stage in the play.

149   *counterpoise* balance exactly, give an equivalent for

150   *weigh with* equal in fortune to

151   *Pawn me to this your honour* if you will pledge your honour to me that you will do this

153–5   *Never may ... owed to you* may I never regard any possession or fortune that falls to my lot as anything but yours to be held in trust for you

154   *keeping* temporary possession of something that truly belongs to another

155   *owed to you* acknowledged to be yours

156   *Vouchsafe my labour* deign to accept my work

157   *anon* shortly

161   *the natural man* man as he really is, 'the thing itself' (*King Lear*, III.4.106)

162   *traffics with* has mercenary dealings with, perverts

163   *but outside* merely deceptive appearance, nothing but a hypocrite. It is ironical that Timon is incapable of applying this generalization to those about him.

        pencilled painted (a *pencil* was an artist's paint-brush)

164   *Even such as they give out* exactly what they profess to be

165   *Wait attendance* remain in attendance, don't go away

168   *needs* of necessity, of course

169   *suffered under praise* had to put up with a lot of praise.

Timon is joking, but the Jeweller misunderstands him
and takes *under praise* as 'underpraise'; hence comes
his question.

170   *mere* absolute, downright

171   *for't* (colloquial) for it
     as 'tis extolled according to the rate at which it is praised

172   *unclew* undo, ruin (literally, to unwind a ball of wool)
     rated priced

173   *As those which sell would give* at cost price, at the same
     price as the seller would give for it

174-5 *Things of like value, differing in the owners, | Are prizèd
     by their masters* things of the same value, when owned
     by different men, are valued according to the status of
     their owners

176   *mend* increase the value of

177   *Well mocked* a neat bit of flattery
     (stage direction) *Enter Apemantus.* Many editors move
     this entry, which occurs here in the Folio, to line 179;
     but the Elizabethan stage was of considerable depth,
     and a character would therefore need time in which to
     make his way to the front of it.

178   *the common tongue* the general opinion

180   *Will you be chid?* are you prepared for a scolding?

181   *We'll bear, with your lordship* we'll suffer, together with
     your lordship

183-4 *Till I be gentle, stay thou for thy good morrow, | When
     thou art Timon's dog, and these knaves honest* you will
     get no greeting from me until I really am gentle, and
     that will be when you become Timon's dog and these
     knaves turn honest (that is, never)

186-99 *Are they not Athenians ... Wrought he not well that
     painted it?* These lines are printed as verse in this
     edition because some of them are regular blank verse
     lines, and the rest seem to preserve some kind of
     rhythm, though it is very irregular.

190   *I called thee by thy name* (when he described them all as
     knaves)

196   *if doing nothing be death by th'law* if the legal penalty for doing nothing be death

198   *The best, for the innocence* very well, because, being a mere picture, it can do no harm

199   *Wrought he not well* did he not show great creative ability

201   *filthy* contemptible, nasty

202   *a dog.* The point of the Painter's remark is that Apemantus belongs to the school of philosophers known as the Cynics, who snarled at all notions of human goodness and derived their name from '*kunos*', the Greek for a dog.

203   *of my generation* of the same breed as I am

206   *I eat not lords.* These words are important because they introduce the theme of cannibalism which is so pronounced in the play. Apemantus is saying that Timon's 'friends' eat their host, since they consume all he has; they are parasites preying on him.

207   *An thou shouldst* if you were to do that
           thou'dst thou wouldst

208   *eat lords* (1) consume all that lords have by eating it and spending it; (2) swallow lords up by having sexual intercourse with them
           come by acquire

210   *apprehension* interpretation, way of taking it. There is a bawdy quibble here on the idea of grasping mentally and that of grasping physically.

211-12   *So thou apprehendest it. Take it for thy labour* that's the interpretation you put on it. Take it for your pains

214   *plain-dealing* (alluding to the proverb 'Plain dealing is a jewel')

215   *doit* (Dutch coin, worth half a farthing)

219   *Thou liest.* Apemantus is repeating the charge, which goes back to Plato, that all poets are by definition liars, since they deal with the imaginary and fictional. Compare Touchstone's remark 'the truest poetry is the most feigning' (*As You Like It*, III.3.17-18).

226   *him* (Timon)

237   *That I had no angry wit to be a lord.* This has never been satisfactorily explained, and no convincing emendation has been put forward. The meaning required is something like 'that I had no more sense than to be a lord'.

240   *Traffic confound thee* trade ruin you

245   *horse* horsemen

246   *All of companionship* all belonging to the same party

247   *entertain them* receive them hospitably
    give them guide show them in

250   *piece* picture
    of your sights to see you, at the sight of you

251   *So, so, there!* just look at that!

252   *Aches* (pronounced as two syllables – 'aitches')
    contract and starve cripple and destroy

253   *sweet* smooth, hypocritical

254   *courtesy* show of politeness
    The strain of man's bred out the race of man has become exhausted and degenerated

256   *saved* anticipated and so prevented

257   *hungerly on your sight* hungrily on the sight of you

258   *depart* part, take leave of one another

259   *different* various
    let us in let us go in

262   *That time serves still* there is always time for that

263   *The more.* The Folio reads 'The most'; but normal English usage seems to demand the emendation.
    thou that still omittest it you who constantly neglect it, you who never profit by the opportunity to be honest

274   *unpeaceable dog* dog that will not stop barking
    spurn kick

277   *opposite to humanity* (1) antagonistic to mankind; (2) utterly inhuman

278   *shall we in* shall we go in

279   *outgoes* surpasses, goes beyond

280   *heart* essence

281   *pours it out* pours things out (*it* is indefinite)

282   *meed* gift, service

285   *All use of quittance* all customary rates of repayment
with interest

    use (1) normal practice; (2) interest on a loan

    carries has

I.2   This scene, one of the most powerful in the play, is
built on a telling contrast. Its primary function is to
dramatize the generosity of Timon, which it does by a
lavish use of all the capacity for staging pageantry and
revels that the Elizabethan theatre had at its disposal,
and to enable him to declare the faith by which he lives
(lines 86–105). But over against the feasting and the
public display are set the quiet asides of Flavius, revealing the true state of Timon's fortunes and the utter
folly of what he is doing.

    (stage direction) *States* senators, members of the
governing body

    Ventidius which Timon redeemed from prison. It looks as
though Shakespeare was reminding himself of who
Ventidius was.

    dropping coming casually

    like himself in his ordinary dress, not in his best

5   *free* liberal

6   *service* promise of service

8   *mistake* misunderstand the nature of

9   *freely* unreservedly

9–10   *there's none | Can truly say he gives, if he receives.* Com-
pare Luke 6.34–5: 'And if ye lend to them of whom ye
hope to receive, what thank have ye? ... But love ye
your enemies, and do good, and lend, looking for
nothing again'.

11   *If our betters play at that game* if men of high rank
expect to be paid for their gifts

11–12   *dare | To imitate* run the risk of imitating, defy heaven
by imitating

12   *faults that are rich are fair* the faults of rich men
      receive no criticism, rich men can get away with any-
      thing

14   *Ceremony* formal display of respect. It is evident from
      Timon's request to the company that they should sit
      down (line 18) that at this point they are all standing,
      and probably bowing as well.

15   *To set a gloss on faint deeds* to give a fair appearance to
      half-hearted actions

16   *Recanting goodness, sorry ere 'tis shown* generosity that
      takes back its offers, regretting them before they have
      even been made

17   *there needs none* there is no need for *Ceremony*

20   *confessed it* acknowledged the truth of what you say,
      made that our creed

21   *confessed it? Hanged it, have you not?* made the idea of
      mutuality your creed? Have you not rather murdered
      it? (Apemantus is alluding to the proverb 'Confess and
      be hanged'.)

24   *to have thee thrust* to provoke you into thrusting

25   *th' art* (colloquial) thou art
      humour disposition, warped attitude of mind

26   *Does not become* that is unfitting for
      much too blame far too blameworthy, quite disgraceful

27   *Ira furor brevis est* anger is a madness that does not last
      long (Horace, *Epistles*, I.2.62)

28   *yond man* that man there
      ever always. The Folio reading is 'verie'; but *ever* is
      required in antithesis to *brevis*.

30   *affect* (1) like; (2) wish for

32   *apperil* peril, risk

33   *on't* (colloquial) of it

35   *I myself would have no power* I have no wish for the
      power to silence you

36   *meat* food in general, hospitality

37-8 *'Twould choke me, for I should ne'er flatter thee*. Ape-
      mantus appears to be saying that the food, which has

been prepared for flatterers and is to be paid for with
flattery, would choke him, since he will not flatter.
There may well be a reference to the proverb 'A
flatterer's throat is an open sepulchre'.

40–41   *all the madness is he cheers them up to't* the maddest
thing of all is that he actually eggs them on to it

41   *to't.* The Folio reads 'too'. This makes quite good
sense, but *to't* is far more pointed.

43   *without knives.* It was customary at the time when the
play was written for guests to bring their own knives
with them.

44   *Good for their meat, and safer for their lives* it would
mean that less of the hosts' food would be consumed,
and their lives would be in less danger

45   *There's much example for't* there are plenty of instances
to illustrate the truth of what I say

45–8   *The fellow . . . to kill him.* The obvious 'example' here
is that of Judas Iscariot (see Matthew 26.23: 'He that
dipped his hand with me in the dish, the same shall
betray me'). The allusion has been prepared for by the
use of *dip* at line 40.

46   *parts* shares

46–7   *pledges the breath of him in a divided draught* drinks a
health to his life from a cup that is passed round

48   *huge* great, important

50   *my windpipe's dangerous notes* the most vulnerable
places, and so the most dangerous to me, in my windpipe. There seems to be a quibble on *windpipe* and
'bagpipe', and another on *notes*, meaning (1) marks or
signs, and (2) musical notes. The general sense is that a
man tilting back his head to drink exposes his throat to
the knife of an enemy.

51   *harness* armour

52   *in heart* in all sincerity. Timon is proposing a toast.
  health toast – and so the cup from which the toast was
drunk

53   *flow* circulate

54   *Flow* come in a flood. Apemantus is quibbling to reveal the Second Lord's greed.

            brave rare, fine (ironical)

55   *tides* (1) tides of the sea; (2) times, turns. Apemantus means that the Second Lord will take care not to miss his turn; and that, when it comes, he will drink inordinately.

55–6   *Those healths will make thee and thy state look ill* (a version of the proverb 'To drink health is to drink sickness')

56   *state* fortune

57   *a sinner* a cause of sin, a provoker of sin

58   *i'th'mire* in the mud, in trouble

59   *there's no odds* there's nothing to choose between them

61   *pelf* property, possessions

63   *fond* foolish, misguided

64   *To* as to

65   *Or a harlot for her weeping* (compare the proverb 'Trust not a woman when she weeps')

67   *keeper* gaoler

69   *fall to't* begin your dinner

71   *dich* may it do to. This word is thought to be a corruption of 'do it'. Its rustic flavour fits in with Apemantus's pose as the rugged incorruptible man who prefers the simple life.

72   *field* battle-field, wars

73   *service* (quibbling on (1) service; (2) military service)

74   *of enemies* upon enemies

75   *of friends* with friends

76   *So* provided that, so long as

            bleeding new freshly bleeding

79   *Would* I would that, I wish that

80–81   *and bid me to 'em* and invite me to eat them

83   *use our hearts* make trial of our love

85   *for ever perfect* eternally happy, at the height of bliss. These words, like the entire speech to which they be-

long, are extremely affected, betraying the utter in-
sincerity of the speaker.

89   *charitable* kindly, loving

   from thousands from among thousands

90   *told more* spoken better

92   *confirm you* confirm your professions of friendship

93   *what* why, for what purpose

96   *instruments* musical instruments

97   *keeps.* In Shakespeare's English the relative often takes
   a singular verb when the antecedent is plural.

100   *properer* more fittingly, more appropriately

101   *comfort* joy, happiness

102   *commanding* having at their disposal

103   *joy's e'en made away ere't can be born* joy dies in the very
   moment of its birth before it is fully alive

104   *cannot hold out water* are not watertight

104-5   *To forget their faults* to hide their weakness in filling
   with tears

106   *Thou weepest to make them drink* (a sneer at the ab-
   surdity of Timon's tears being made a reason for his
   'friends' to drink)

108   *sprung up* sprang up. There seems to be a three-
   fold quibble here: (1) leapt up like a child in the
   womb; (2) exulted; (3) flowed forth as from a
   fountain.

109   *a bastard* (Apemantus's way of saying that the statement just made is not genuine, not true)

110   *promise* assure

111   (stage direction) *Sound tucket* blow the trumpet. The
   direction is in the imperative because it is addressed to
   those who were in charge of 'effects' in Shakespeare's
   theatre.

112   *trump* blast on the trumpet

114   *Please you* if it please you, please

116   *What are their wills?* what do they want?

118   *which bears that office to signify their pleasures* whose job
   it is to say what they propose

120–23   *Hail to thee . . . plenteous bosom.* These lines are printed
         as prose in the Folio.

123   *gratulate* greet and gratify
         plenteous bosom generous heart

123–4   *Th'ear, | Taste, touch, smell, all.* The Folio, shifting into
         verse at this point, reads 'There tast, touch all'. How-
         ever, since *The five best senses* have already been men-
         tioned, and since the masquers come only to please the
         sight, it seems essential that the other four senses
         should be referred to here. 'There' for *Th'ear*,
         probably written as 'Th'ere' by Shakespeare, is an easy
         mistake to make. The omission of *smell* can be ac-
         counted for on the assumption that the similarity be-
         tween the last three letters in this word and *all* led the
         compositor to overlook it.

125   *They only now come but* their sole purpose in coming is.
         Shakespeare often joins 'only' with 'but' in cases
         where modern English would require nothing more
         than 'only'. Compare 'He only lived but till he was
         a man' (*Macbeth*, V.6.79).

127   *Music make* let music make

128   FIRST LORD. The Folio speech heading is '*Luc.*'
         which could mean either Lucullus or Lucius; but as
         neither of them is named in the stage direction at the
         opening of the scene it seems better to adopt the
         neutral form.
         ample amply
         (stage direction) *Music. Enter Cupid . . . and playing.*
         The Folio provides no direction whatever at this point.
         The reading given here is a conflation of two previous
         directions which anticipate this entry: '*Enter Cupid
         with the Maske of Ladies*' at line 119, and '*Sound
         Tucket. Enter the Maskers of Amazons, with Lutes in
         their hands, dauncing and playing*' at line 111.

129   *Hoy-day* (exclamation of contemptuous surprise)
         sweep of vanity sweeping movement of vain people,
         parade of vanity

131-2 *Like madness is the glory of this life | As this pomp
shows to a little oil and root* the vainglory of this life
is just as much madness in the eye of reason as the
pomp of the feast is when compared with my simple
meal

133 *disport ourselves* amuse ourselves

134-6 *And spend our flatteries . . . and envy* and lavish flattery
in drinking the healths of those men upon whom, when
they are old, we vomit that flattery back in the form of
poisonous spite and envy

134 *drink* (1) drink the health of; (2) consume

137 *depravèd or depraves* slandered or a slanderer

138 *spurn* hurt, insult, contemptuous thrust

139 *Of their friends' gift* of their friends' giving, given by
their friends

142 *Men shut their doors against a setting sun* (an adaptation
of the proverb 'The rising, not the setting, sun is worshipped by most men')
(stage direction) *adoring of* obeisance to, scraping and
bowing to

143 *done our pleasures much grace* greatly embellished our
enjoyments

144 *Set a fair fashion on* given real elegance to
entertainment feast

145 *kind* gracious

147 *entertained me with mine own device* delighted me with
your performance of my own dramatic spectacle. The
words suggest that Timon had arranged for the masque
himself, in order to please his guests, but had then
found unexpected personal pleasure in it.

148 *I am to thank* I must thank

149 FIRST LADY. The Folio prefix is '*1 Lord*'; but Timon
has addressed his speech to the Ladies, and Apemantus's reply makes it plain that this speech must be
spoken by a woman. If the prefix were merely written
as '*La*' in the copy, the compositor might well have
misread it as '*Lo*'.

149   *you take us even at the best* you give us our due and more than our due, you are most flattering to us

150–51   *Faith, for the worst is filthy, and would not hold taking, I doubt me* indeed, for the worst part of you is obscene, and would not bear *taking*, I fear

151   *taking* (1) regarding; (2) handling; (3) taking sexually. Apemantus implies that the Ladies are rotten with venereal disease.

152   *an idle banquet attends you* a trifling dessert that awaits you. Compare 'We have a trifling foolish banquet towards' (*Romeo and Juliet*, I.5.122).

153   *Please you to dispose yourselves* if you would please take your places

154   *Flavius*. It is only in this scene, where he makes his first appearance, that this character is given a name in the Folio. Later in the play he is always '*Steward*'.

157   *There is no crossing him in's humour* he will not be thwarted in his inclination

158   *tell him well* tell him plainly

159   *he'd be crossed then, an he could* he'd be only too glad to have his debts cancelled then, if he could. Flavius is quibbling on the two senses of *crossed*: (1) thwarted; (2) having the list of one's debts crossed through as a sign of payment.

160   *had not eyes behind* cannot be prudent. 'He has an eye behind' was a proverbial way of describing a cautious man.

161   *for his mind* because of his good intentions

162   *be* are

167   *you honour* you to honour

168   *advance* promote, raise the standing of

169   *Kind my lord* my kind lord

170   *so far already in your gifts* so deeply indebted to you already for your gifts

173   *alighted* (from their horses)

174   *fairly* kindly, very

176   *near* closely, deeply, intimately

178   *let's be provided to show them entertainment* let everything be laid on to welcome them properly

181   *Out of his free love* moved by unrestrained love

182   *trapped in silver* with silver harness

183   *fairly* courteously, in the spirit in which they are offered

184   *worthily entertained* given the reception they deserve

190   *fair* fitting, generous

193   *know his purse* recognize the state of his finances
        yield me this allow me even

195   *Being* since it is
        good valid, effective

196   *state* means, fortune

199   *for't* for it, for being so kind
        put to their books entered in their account books. Flavius means that Timon no longer owns his land, because it has been mortgaged.

203   *Than such that do e'en enemies exceed* than he that feeds such 'friends' as are worse than open enemies

206   *bate* deduct, reduce, undervalue

207   *trifle* trifling token

210–11   *gave good words . . . of* spoke well of, commended

213–14   *pardon me . . . in that* please don't ask me to, excuse me for declining the offer

215   *You may take my word* you can be sure I mean what I say

216   *praise but what he does affect* praise anything except that which he is fond of

216–17   *weigh my friend's affection with mine own* think my friend's desires as important as my own

217   *I'll tell you true* I assure you

218   *call to* call on, visit

220   *all and your several visitations* your visits collectively and individually

221   *kind* kindly
        'tis not enough to give there is not enough for me to give you

222   *deal* give away, distribute

225   *It comes in charity to thee* anything given to you is an act of true charity

        living source of income, livelihood

227   *pitched field* battle-field

228   *defiled*. Alcibiades is quibbling on the proverb 'Whoso toucheth pitch shall be defiled' (Ecclesiasticus 13.1).

229   *virtuously* strongly, powerfully

231   *endeared* bound by obligation, indebted

232   *All to you* entirely to you, all the obligation is on my side

234   *Keep* continue, dwell

235   *Ready for* ready to help

        coil fuss, bother

236   *Serving of becks and jutting-out of bums* offering of bows and thrusting-out of backsides. Apemantus's sarcastic words give a vivid picture of the ridiculous postures adopted by Timon's 'friends' in their efforts to flatter him.

237   *legs* (1) bows; (2) legs, in the normal sense

238   *dregs* impurities, corrupt matter

239   *false hearts* false-hearted men

        sound legs legs strong enough to enable them to make deceptive bows

240   *curtsies* (1) bows; (2) acts of courtesy

242   *good* kind, generous

243   *I'll nothing* I wish for nothing, I refuse to take anything

246   *I fear me* I fear

        in paper in the form of promissory notes

247   *What needs* what necessity is there for

248   *an you begin to rail on society once* if ever you begin to rail against companionship, the minute you begin to rail against companionship

249   *give regard to* take notice of, heed

250   *with better music* making a better noise, saying nicer things

251   *So* very well

252   *then* later (when you have given yourself away and
       have nothing left)
       lock thy heaven withhold thy heaven. By *thy heaven*
       Apemantus appears to mean his good advice which
       might have saved Timon. There is probably a half-
       veiled allusion to the proverb 'He that refuses to buy
       counsel cheap shall buy repentance dear'.

II.1   Here, for the first time in the play, the scene moves
       away from Timon's house. After the feverish and
       riotous prodigality of what has gone before, so indica-
       tive of instability, there is a positive menace in the
       purposeful activity of this quiet interlude in which
       Timon's whole way of life is submitted to the cold
       scrutiny of a keen business-man. Hitherto, we have
       seen that way of life from the inside, as it were; now,
       we are shown it from the outside. The shift of per-
       spective is in itself sufficient to show that there has
       been a change of location; but it is quite likely, though
       by no means certain, that this change was also em-
       phasized in Shakespeare's theatre by the use of the
       inner stage, with a 'discovery' of the Senator busy
       with his accounts. If this device were resorted to,
       however, it would be appropriate for the Senator to
       advance, while speaking his first lines, to the front of
       the stage, so that every word he uttered would make
       the maximum impact on the audience.

1   *late* lately. The Senator is reckoning up his loans to
       Timon.
       five thousand. The unit is not specified, but 'five
       thousand crowns' (see III.4.30–31) is probably what is
       meant.

3   *it* (the sum he owes me)

3–4   *Still in motion | Of raging waste* always active in mad
       dissipation

4   *hold* last, continue

5	*steal but* let me but steal, I have only to steal
9	*it foals me straight* it bears foals for me immediately
10	*And able horses* and strong full-grown horses at that
	porter. The porter here is thought of as the guardian of the gate whose main function is to keep people out – the Senator's own attitude to hospitality is all too evident.
11	*still* constantly
12–13	*No reason | Can sound his state in safety* no rational man can examine Timon's financial position and call it safe
13	*sound.* Shakespeare seems to have conflated two different meanings of this word into one complex meaning: (1) to sound the depth of water with a fathom-line; (2) to proclaim, to declare openly.
14	*pleasure* will, command
15	*haste you* make haste (reflexive use)
16	*moneys* sums of money, money. It is, perhaps, significant that Shylock habitually uses the plural form (see *The Merchant of Venice*, I.3.105, 113, 126, etc.), suggesting that Shakespeare connected it with the practice of usury.
	ceased stopped, put off
17	*With slight denial* by a negligent off-hand refusal
17–19	*when ... right hand, thus* when he speaks words of compliment and makes polite gestures. The behaviour described here is very similar to that which Volumnia recommends Coriolanus should use in order to win over the citizens of Rome (see *Coriolanus*, III.2.72–80).
18	*Commend me* give my kind regards
20	*uses cry* need clamours
20–21	*I must serve my turn | Out of mine own* I must meet my needs out of my own money
21	*His days and times* the days and precise times fixed for repayment by him of the loans I have made
22	*reliances.* Shakespeare uses the plural to show that more than one loan and more than one date of repayment are involved.

fracted dates broken promises to repay on certain dates

23   *smit* done grave damage to (past participle of 'smite')

24   *must not break my back to heal his finger* am under no
compulsion to ruin myself in order to help him out of a
slight embarrassment. 'To break one's back' was a
proverbial expression, signifying financial ruin.

25   *Immediate* pressing, requiring immediate satisfaction

25–6   *my relief | Must not be tossed and turned to me in words*
the help I need must not be bandied back to me in the
form of empty words. The metaphor is from tennis.

27   *find supply immediate* be supplied at once in hard cash
Get you gone go, take yourself off

29   *visage of demand* demanding visage

30–32   *When every feather . . . a phoenix.* The allusion here is
to the fable of the crow which decked itself out in
feathers stolen from other birds. Robert Greene made
use of it when, in his *Groatsworth of Wit* (1592), he
described Shakespeare as 'an upstart Crow, beautified
with our feathers'.

30   *sticks in his own wing* is restored to the bird it came
from. The saying 'If every bird had his own feathers
you would be naked' was proverbial.
his (normal Shakespearian equivalent of modern 'its')

31   *gull* (1) unfledged nestling; (2) dupe, credulous ass

32   *Which flashes now a phoenix* who now displays himself
as a phoenix. The phoenix was a mythical bird, of
gorgeous plumage, fabled to be the only one of its
kind, and to live five or six hundred years in the
Arabian desert, after which it burnt itself to ashes on a
funeral pile, and emerged from its ashes with renewed
youth, to live through another cycle of years. Shakespeare was fascinated by this myth, and dealt with it at
length in his subtle metaphysical poem *The Phoenix
and the Turtle*.

34   *I go, sir?* The Folio reads 'I go sir?', which many
editors omit, on the grounds that the compositor has
unconsciously repeated the previous line. Other editors

emend to 'Ay, go sir!', which is quite possible. The reading of the Folio has been retained in this edition because it produces a nice bit of comedy. Urged on by the Senator's repeated commands to him to hasten away, Caphis is about to set off without the precious documents, and has to be recalled as he is making for the door.

35 *And have the dates in. Come.* This is the reading of the Folio. It is retained in this edition, contrary to the practice of most editors, because it makes quite good sense, meaning 'And see that the dates are entered on the bonds. Get on with it'. Timon is exactly the kind of man who would sign to a bond without noticing whether it was dated or not, thus leaving himself wide open to being cheated. Many editors, unwilling to envisage this possibility, emend to 'And have the dates in compt', meaning 'And have the dates reckoned up and noted down'.

II.2 In this scene the consequences of II.1 – which has a representative quality about it, since it now becomes plain that similar scenes must have been taking place at Varro's and Isidore's – now begin to come home to Timon, leading to a clarification of the situation that exists between him and Flavius, and to a partial realization of his own position by the hero. But, while the function of the scene is clear enough and the main outlines of it are firm and distinct, there is also some undigested matter in it. In particular, the appearance of the Fool at line 49 raises unresolved problems. He is not properly built into the structure of the play, for after this scene he never comes on again; beyond the fact that his mistress is a bawd, there is no indication of the household he belongs to; and the only purpose he serves is to enable Shakespeare to make some connexions, as he had done in *Measure for Measure* through the comments of Pompey, between usury and prostitution. Thematically these connexions are important, being developed later in the exchanges between Timon and Phrynia and Timandra in IV.3; but the Fool himself seems to be a loose end, the temporary embodiment of an idea that Shakespeare chose not to follow out.

The setting is unlocalized. It must be near Timon's house, since he is about to dine (line 17), but it cannot be in the house, because Apemantus tells the Fool *I will go with you to Lord Timon's* (lines 91–2).

1 *senseless* regardless

2 *know* learn, trouble to find out

3 *cease* discontinue

   flow of riot flood-tide of extravagant living

4 *How things go from him* of how things vanish from his possession

   nor resumes no care nor takes any care (double negatives are quite normal in Shakespeare)

5 *to continue* to come as a sequel

5–6 *Never mind | Was to be so unwise, to be so kind* never was there such a determination to be so stupid, such a determination to be so generous

7 *shall* is to, ought to

   hear till feel hear what the consequence of his folly must be until he feels it

   feel (subjunctive)

8 *round* blunt, plain-spoken

9 *Fie* (exclamation of impatience, occasioned by the fact that Timon has been spending the day in hunting instead of looking after his affairs)

10 *Good even* (form of greeting used at any time after noon)

14 *Would we were all discharged!* I wish we had all been paid the money we have come for!

15 *I fear it* I fear that's not going to happen, I fear the worst

17 *dinner* (the main meal of the day, usually served between 11 a.m. and noon in Shakespeare's England)
     we'll forth again we'll go out again (probably back to their hunting)

18 *With me?* have you business with me, do you wish to speak to me?
     What is your will? what do you want?

19 *note* account, list
     dues debts

22 *Please it* may it please

23 *To the succession of new days this month* from one day to the next this past month

24 *awaked by great occasion* forced by urgent need

25 *To call upon his own* to ask for repayment of the money he lent you

26 *with your other noble parts you'll suit* you'll act in conformity with your other noble qualities

27 *his right* that which is due to him

28 *repair* return
     next morning tomorrow morning

29 *Contain thyself* don't get excited, be content

31 *prays* requests, asks for

33 *wants* needs, hardships

34 *'Twas due on forfeiture* the money was due under penalty of your forfeiting the security for it

35 *and past* and more ago

37 *expressly to your lordship* to your lordship and to no one else

38 *breath* time to breathe

39 *keep on* proceed, carry on, go ahead without me

40 *wait upon you instantly* join you without delay

41 *How goes the world* what is happening, to what state have things come

41–2 *encountered | With* met with, assailed by

42 *of broken bonds* for broken bonds. The Folio reads 'of debt, broken Bonds'; but this ruins the metre, and also the word 'debt' seems unnecessary, since 'debts'

occurs in the next line. It has, therefore, been omitted
from this edition. An emendation preferred by many
editors is 'of date-broke bonds'.

43	*the detention* the charge of withholding payment
44	*Against my honour* contrary to my reputation as an honourable man
45	*unagreeable to* unsuitable for
46	*Your importunacy cease* abandon your importunities
47	*That* so that
49	*entertained* treated
	draw near come this way, come in
51	*ha'* (colloquial) have
52	*abuse* malign, revile
54	*How dost* how are you
55	*dialogue* hold a conversation
	shadow reflection, mirror image (implying that Varro's Servant is the fool)
56	*I speak not to thee* (a way of saying that Apemantus is not a real man but a mere shadow of one)
58-9	*There's the fool hangs on your back already* you have already got the title of fool hanging on your back (as a result of Apemantus's remark at line 57)
60-61	*No, thou standest single, th' art not on him yet* no, you stand fool all to yourself, for you are not yet on his back; if you were, it would be fool upon fool
63	*He* he who
63-4	*Poor rogues . . . and want.* This sentence would fit in far better if it came after *yourselves* at line 69.
64	*bawds between gold and want* go-betweens bringing together those who have money and those who want it
71	*Gramercies* many thanks (from French *grand merci* – God reward you greatly)
73	*e'en setting on water* just putting a pan of water on the fire to heat it
73-4	*to scald such chickens as you are.* Shakespeare is quibbling here. Scalding is a method of removing feathers from poultry; so, when the Fool calls the three servants

chickens, he implies that they are simpletons who deserve to be 'plucked', as they will be in the house of the bawd he serves. But 'sweating' or 'scalding' in a tub was also the treatment for venereal disease, which the servants will contract by visiting his mistress.

74 *Corinth* (probably the part of the city inhabited by courtesans; ancient Corinth was notorious for its licentiousness)

75 *Good* good chap, my good fellow

76 *mistress'*. The Folio has 'Masters'; but in view of the reference to the Fool's mistress at line 72 the emendation seems necessary.

77 *captain* (used as familiar term of address)

79 *rod* stick or cane used for chastisement

80 *profitably* in a manner that would do you good, that is, by beating you

81 *superscription* address

89–90 *famish a dog's death* die a dog's death by starvation

91 *E'en so* precisely, just so (twisting the Page's *gone* to mean 'spiritually ruined', 'damned')

  Thou outrunnest grace God's grace will never overtake you

94 *If Timon stay at home* so long as Timon's at home, there will always be a fool there

101 *I think no usurer but has* I think there is no usurer who has not

101–2 *My mistress is one*. Shakespeare associates usury with lechery in *Measure for Measure* (III.2.5–6), where Pompey calls lechery 'of two usuries, the merriest'. 'Lechery and covetousness go together' was proverbial.

104 *mistress'*. The Folio reads 'Masters', as at line 76.

106 *render one* give one (that they have lost money and caught disease)

108 *whoremaster* whoremonger, fornicator

108–9 *which notwithstanding, thou shalt be no less esteemed* in spite of which you will be no worse thought of than you are now (because practising lechery is only the same thing as practising usury)

112   *'Tis a spirit* (because it can take on any appearance it likes)

112–13   *Sometime ... sometime ... sometime* at one time ... at another ... at yet another

112   *'t* it

113   *philosopher* learned man, alchemist

113–14 *with two stones more than's artificial one* with two stones (his testicles) more than his artificial stone (the philosopher's stone which was supposed to have the power of transmuting base metals into gold)

115–17 *in all shapes ... walks in.* Shakespeare often repeats a preposition for the sake of clarity when it is at some distance from the verb with which it is connected.

116   *fourscore to thirteen* (years of age)

121   *become* been fitting for, done credit to

123   *Aside* stand aside

126–7   *lover, elder brother, and woman.* All three were proverbially associated with folly. Compare 'It is impossible to love and be wise', 'The younger brother has the more wit', and 'Women have no souls'.

127   *sometime* from time to time, at times

128   *walk near* withdraw but don't go away
      anon shortly

129–32 *You make me marvel ... leave of means* I simply can't understand why you did not make my financial position fully clear to me before now, so that I might have regulated my expenditure according to what my means would allow

130   *Had you.* Shakespeare is using the word order of a direct question in an indirect context.

133   *leisures* times when you were free, convenient times
      Go to rubbish! (exclamation of protest)

134–7 *Perchance some single ... excuse yourself* perhaps on some rare occasions you may have brought the matter up, but it was when you knew my disinclination for the

177

subject would cause me to reject your efforts, and you
have made my reluctance then serviceable to yourself
now as a convenient excuse

139 *throw them off* have nothing to do with them, brush
them aside

140 *found them* found their accuracy

142 *Return so much* give such and such a sum in recompense

143 *'gainst th'authority of manners* contrary to what good
manners would dictate

144 *To hold your hand more close* to be tighter-fisted, less
generous

145 *Not seldom, nor no slight checks* reproofs that were
neither rare nor slight. *Seldom* is an adjective.

146 *Prompted you in* warned you about, reminded you
about (language drawn from the theatre)
ebb flowing-out

147 *flow* flowing-in, flood-tide

148 *Though you hear now too late, yet now's a time* though
you hear the truth too late, yet now I can at least tell it
to you

149–50 *The greatest of your having lacks a half | To pay your
present debts* the utmost that you have is only half
enough to pay your immediate debts

151 *engaged* mortgaged

152–3 *stop the mouth | Of* satisfy, silence demands for

153 *present dues* debts due for payment now

154 *What shall defend the interim?* what shall we do to
defend the immediate future against the attacks of
creditors?
at length in the end

155 *How goes our reck'ning?* what will the final account
look like?

156 *Lacedaemon* (another name for Sparta)

160 *my husbandry of falsehood* falsehood in my management
of your affairs
of. The Folio reading is 'or', giving a very awkward
and unconvincing construction.

162 *set me on the proof* put me to the test

   So the gods bless me as I hope for the gods' blessing

163 *offices* kitchen and servants' quarters

   oppressed crowded

164 *feeders* (1) servants; (2) parasites, locusts

   vaults wine-cellars

165 *drunken spilth of wine* drunkards' spilling of wine, wine spilled by drunkards

166 *brayed with minstrelsy* echoed with rowdy song

167 *retired me* retired (reflexive use)

   wasteful cock tap of a wine-cask that has been left running

168 *set mine eyes at flow* begun to weep (in sympathy with the 'weeping' cask)

170 *prodigal bits* morsels lavishly supplied and prepared

171 *englutted* swallowed down

   Who is not Timon's? who is there that does not claim to be utterly devoted to Timon?

172 *means* financial resources

173 *Great Timon . . . royal Timon!* Flavius is giving an ironical rendering of what Timon's 'friends' say.

176 *Feast-won, fast-lost* what is gained by giving feasts is quickly lost. There may well be the secondary meaning to *fast-lost* – 'lost by having only fasting to offer'. The words are an ironical inversion of Shylock's proverb 'Fast bind, fast find' (*The Merchant of Venice*, II.5.52); his whole way of life being the exact opposite of Timon's.

176–7 *One cloud of winter showers,* | *These flies are couched* a single cloud bringing winter showers is enough to drive these flies to shelter

177 *flies* flesh-flies, parasites (like Mosca in Ben Jonson's *Volpone*)

   sermon preach to, lecture

178 *No villainous bounty yet hath passed my heart* no act of generosity that I need feel ashamed of has yet received the sanction of my heart

180–81 *Canst thou the conscience lack | To think* are you so lacking in sound judgement as to think

181 *Secure thy heart* set your mind at rest

182 *would broach the vessels of my love* wanted to tap the vessels filled with love for me (meaning his friends)

183 *try the argument* test the contents. The *argument* of a book or a play is the summary of its contents.

184 *frankly* as freely, as unrestrainedly

185 *Assurance bless your thoughts!* may your ideas be blessed by being proved right!

186 *in some sort* in a way
are crowned are glorified, have acquired a royal dignity

187 *That* so that

188 *try* test, try the quality of

189 *mistake* misjudge, are mistaken about

191 *Within there!* you within there! (command for attention)
Flaminius. The Folio reads '*Flauius*', but he is on stage already, and one of the servants who appear must be called Flaminius, since the speech heading at line 199 is '*Flam.*' in the Folio.

193 *severally* separately

195 *Commend me* remember me kindly

196 *occasions* needs
time opportunity

197 *toward* for

202–3 *Of whom, even to the state's best health, I have | Deserved this hearing* by whom I have deserved to be listened to; indeed, the health and prosperity of the body politic demand that I should be. The exact meaning of *even to the state's best health* has been much disputed. There are those who think it implies that Timon by his generosity had ministered to the well-being of the state; others hold he is saying that the state ought to support his claims to the limit, so long as the prosperity of the state is not imperilled. The present editor's view is that Timon is putting forward the first idea.

203   *o'th'instant* at once

204   *I have been bold* I have gone so far as

205   *For that* because

        most general way most compendious way, best way of trying many at a time

206   *signet* seal usually affixed to a ring (taken as a proof of authenticity)

208   *in return* for my pains

209   *corporate* belonging to one body of people

210   *at fall* at a low ebb

        want treasure are short of money

211   *would* would like to do

214   *May catch a wrench* may be wrenched away from its natural bent

215   *intending* pretending to be occupied with

        other serious matters other matters of a really serious kind

216   *distasteful looks* looks indicating a dislike of the whole business

        hard fractions harsh and disjointed remarks

217   *half-caps* half-courteous salutes (disdainful semi-politeness)

        cold-moving frigid, chilling

219   *cheerly* cheerily

220   *hereditary* as a natural legacy of their age

221   *caked* clotted, set solid. Compare the modern metaphorical use of the phrase 'hardening of the arteries'.

222   *'Tis lack of kindly warmth they* lack of kindly warmth is the reason why they

        kindly (1) innate; (2) generous

        kind (1) kind – in the modern sense; (2) natural

223   *nature* the life of man

        as it grows again toward earth as it approaches the grave, as it moves again towards the dust from which it came. There may also be a reference to the tendency for old people to become bent.

226   *Ingeniously* ingenuously, with absolute sincerity

230   *in scarcity of* hard up for

231   *cleared him* freed him from prison and from debt

232   *good* valid, genuine

233   *Touches* affects

233-4   *which craves to be remembered | With those five talents*
and this necessity calls for practical remembrance on
his part in the form of those five talents

234   *That had* when you have it

235   *instant* immediately, urgently

236   *'mong his friends can sink* can sink while he is surrounded by friends

237   *it* (that Timon's fortunes can sink)

238-9   *That thought is bounty's foe – | Being free itself, it thinks
all others so* the thought that is the real enemy to the
generous man is his notion that because he is generous
everyone else must be. The passage is a difficult one,
though the general sense is clear enough. What seems
to happen is that Flavius begins with *That thought* –
Timon's statement that his fortunes cannot sink – and
then defines it in his own way, seeing it as the cause of
his master's troubles.

III.1   The first three scenes of this Act are of especial interest
from the technical point of view, for in them Shakespeare resorts to a dramatic method which he does not
use elsewhere in his tragedies in the same concentrated
fashion – that of deliberately repeating a scene, with
variations, in order to drive a point home. It looks very
much as though he had been influenced here by the
example of Ben Jonson, who was particularly fond of
this device and employs it to devastating effect in
Volpone, where this pattern of action is established in
I.3–5, and then developed consistently throughout the
play. Taken together, these three scenes add up to a
most telling indictment of a whole society. They also
make it plain that in this tragedy the antagonist to the
hero will not be a specific individual but a way of life.

6	*hits right* fits perfectly, coincides beautifully
7	*ewer* pitcher with a wide spout (used to bring water for washing the hands before and after a meal, which was, of course, eaten with the fingers in Shakespeare's day)
8	*respectively* respectfully
10	*complete* highly accomplished
15	*pretty* excellent, good. This vague and affected epithet is in keeping with the dandified manner characteristic of Lucullus.
19	*supply* fill
	instant occasion urgent need
	use make use of
20	*furnish him* provide him with what he requires
21	*nothing doubting* having no doubts about, being sure of
	present immediately available
22	*La, la, la, la!* well, well, well, well! (affected exclamation of derision)
23	*'tis* he is (compare I.1.9)
24	*keep so good a house* be so hospitable. Complaints about the 'decay of housekeeping' were frequent at the time when the play was written. There is a good account of what aristocratic 'housekeeping' involved in the way of expenditure in Lawrence Stone's *The Crisis of the Aristocracy* (1965), pages 555–62.
25	*on't* of it
25-6	*come again to supper to him* returned to have supper at his house
26	*of purpose to have him* on purpose to persuade him to
27	*embrace* receive, take
	by from
28	*Every man has his fault* (a proverbial expression, but Lucullus gives it an unexpected twist)
	honesty generosity
29	*from't* away from it
31	*noted thee always wise* observed that you are always discreet, that you always know what is to your own advantage

32   *Here's to thee.* This is a very neat dramatic reversal;
      the wine, intended at line 9 for Flaminius, is now
      drunk to his health.

33   *speaks your pleasure* is pleased to say so

34-5 *I have observed thee always for a towardly prompt spirit*
      I have always marked you as a well-disposed man
      ready to meet another's thoughts half-way

35   *give thee thy due* not to flatter you

36   *what belongs to reason* what is reasonable

36-7 *use the time well, if the time use thee well* make good
      use of an opportunity, if the opportunity comes your
      way

37   *parts* qualities

40   *wise* skilled in the ways of the world

42   *bare* mere

43   *solidares.* No such coins ever existed. Shakespeare
      seems to have made the word up out of the Latin
      solidus, regarded as the Roman equivalent of the
      English shilling. It is quite possible that Shakespeare
      deliberately invented this impressive word to denote a
      paltry sum. Compare the fun that he had with 'guer-
      don' and 'remuneration' in *Love's Labour's Lost*,
      III.1.128–41, 158–63.

44   *wink at* connive with

46   *differ* change, be other than it was

47   *And we alive that lived?* and that we, to whom life
      meant something so different, should still be alive
      today?

51-2 *May these add to the number that may scald thee! | Let
      molten coin be thy damnation.* The idea at the back of
      these words, a commonplace among moralists and
      poets at the time when the play was written, is that the
      wicked are punished in hell by being forced to commit,
      without intermission, the sin they were most given to
      on earth. So, the punishment visited on the avaricious
      man is that he has to swallow molten gold.

53   *Thou disease of a friend and not himself!* Flaminius

means that Lucullus bears the same relationship to true friendship that a malignant disease does to a healthy body.

54 *milky* weak, timorous

55 *It turns* (1) that it changes; (2) that it turns sour (developing the associations of *milky* in the previous line)

56 *passion* anger

57 *Unto this hour*. The Folio reads 'vnto his Honor'. This has been defended on the grounds that Flaminius is ironically describing Lucullus as a man who is 'a slave to his sense of honour'; but the emphasis in these lines is on time, on the rapidity with which the attitude of Lucullus has changed. The emendation therefore seems essential.

60 *work upon't* occupy themselves with it, thrive on it

61 *that part of nature* that part of his physical being

63 *his hour*. This could mean either 'its [sickness's] duration' or 'his [Lucullus's] last hour'. In any case the basic meaning remains the same: Flaminius prays that Lucullus may die a lingering death.

III.2 (stage direction) *three Strangers*. These three characters are 'strangers' in the sense that they are unknown to Timon (see lines 3–4) and that they have no part whatever in the action. Once this scene is over, they disappear from the play, never to return. Yet, brief though their appearance is, the impact they make is a telling one. There is something mysterious, almost numinous, about them. Their standards of judgement are religious; and the verdict they pass at the end of the scene carries great weight, since they are disinterested detached observers, utterly without bias. They speak for, and also direct, the reactions of an audience or a reader.

3 *know him for no less* know he is all you say he is

5 *and which* and it is one that

185

6-7   *his estate shrinks from him* his fortune falls away from him

8   *want for* want, be short of

12   *so many talents* an unspecified number of talents. This expression makes no sense whatever at a point where a specific number is obviously required, and where, in order to be consistent with what Timon says at II.2.197-8 and with Flaminius's request at III.1.20, the figure should be fifty. The explanation must be that by the time he wrote this scene Shakespeare had come to realize that he did not know what a talent was worth, and therefore left the amount vague, intending to put in a precise and appropriate figure when he came to revise the play for production. See An Account of the Text, pages 257-8.

    urged extremely put in a very strong plea

13   *what necessity belonged to't* how indispensable it was

22   *his* (those received by Lucullus)

22-3   *had he mistook him* had Timon made a mistake, made a slip. This reflexive use of 'mistake' is not found elsewhere in Shakespeare.

23-4   *denied his occasion* refused him in his hour of need

25   *by good hap* by good luck

26   *sweat* made great efforts, been sweating

27   *You are kindly met* I'm delighted to meet you

28   *Commend me* give my best wishes

29   *exquisite* excellent, special

32-3   *endeared to* bound by obligation to, in the debt of

35   *'Has* he has

    present occasion urgent need

36   *supply his instant use* make good his immediate need

38   *but merry with me* only pulling my leg, only having a game with me

39   *fifty five hundred talents.* This is the reading of the Folio. It has been preserved in this edition, because it seems to indicate more uncertainty on Shakespeare's part about the value of the talent. It is likely that he

wrote both 'fifty' and 'five hundred' in the manuscript, probably in figures, intending to cross out the figure that proved to be inappropriate.

41   *virtuous* deserving, a consequence of his goodness

42   *urge it half so faithfully* plead for it half so confidently, with half as much conviction

45–6   *disfurnish myself against* leave myself unprovided for meeting

46   *good time* fortunate opportunity

47–9   *that I should purchase the day before for a little part and undo a great deal of honour* that I laid out money the day before for the purchase of a small share of honour and so ruined my chances of acquiring a large share (by helping Timon). The passage is difficult and much disputed. It can, however, be made to yield tolerable sense as it stands, if 'of honour' is understood after *a little part*, thus preserving the antithesis with *a great deal*.

48   *should* (used to indicate the past tense in a dependent clause)

       purchase. Both the *Oxford English Dictionary* and Onions in his *A Shakespeare Glossary* (1911, etc.) give the meaning 'to exert oneself, strive' in this context. But it seems essential that the paying out of money should be involved. Schmidt's definition in his *Shakespeare-Lexicon* (1874, etc.), 'to make a bargain', is therefore preferred.

       a little part. In the opinion of the present editor these words are a reference to 'the sale of honours', particularly knighthoods, by King James I, at the time when the play was written. 'Purchase' was the word commonly used for the acquiring of a title for cash; and the excuse would be a plausible one, since it was moneyed men like Lucius who were eager to obtain what Bacon, when he applied for it, called 'the almost prostituted title of knighthood'.

       undo destroy, ruin

50   *do* take action, be of service

51   *use* make use of, borrow from

52–3   *but I would not, for the wealth of Athens, I had done't
        now* but I could not bring myself, for the wealth of
        Athens, to wish that I had actually done so now

53   *Commend me bountifully* be generous in your com-
        mendations of me

54–5   *conceive the fairest of me* put the best possible con-
        struction on my behaviour

55   *kind* benevolent

57   *pleasure* gratify, do the kindness of a loan to

61   *look you out a good turn* seek for a good turn I can do you

62   *shrunk* diminished in fortune, brought low

63   *speed* prosper, flourish

65   *the world's soul* the principle that animates human life,
        the way of the world. Ben Jonson's Volpone addresses
        his gold with the words 'Hail, the world's soul and
        mine' (*Volpone*, I.1.3); and Shakespeare may well have
        had them in mind.

66   *just of the same piece* exactly of the same kind (literally,
        'cut out of the same piece of cloth')

67   *spirit*. The Folio reading is 'sport', which has been
        interpreted as 'the mockery that every flatterer exer-
        cises on his victim'; but the context requires a parallel
        to *soul*, and the compositor may easily have misread
        spirit as 'sport'.

68   *That dips in the same dish*. The allusion is to Judas at
        the Last Supper (Matthew 26.23).
        in my knowing to my knowledge

70   *kept his credit with his purse* kept up his (Lucius's)
        credit with his (Timon's) money

72   *his men* (Lucius's men)

73   *treads upon* presses on, leaves an imprint on. There
        may also be a quibble on 'trades upon', meaning 'has
        commerce with'.

74   *monstrousness*. The monstrous nature of ingratitude is
        referred to repeatedly in *King Lear*; compare 'In-

gratitude . . . More hideous . . . Than the sea-monster!' (I.4.259–61) and 'Monster ingratitude!' (I.5.37).

75   *When he looks out in an ungrateful shape* when human nature shows itself in the shape of ingratitude

76–7   *He does deny him, in respect of his, | What charitable men afford to beggars* what Lucius refuses to give Timon is, in comparison with what Lucius possesses, no more than the alms charitable men usually give to beggars

79   *tasted* sampled, tried the qualities of (but the literal sense also applies)

80   *Nor came any of his bounties over me* nor did any of his generous acts light upon me

81   *protest* solemnly declare, affirm in public

82   *For* because of

85–6   *I would have put my wealth into donation, | And the best half should have returned to him* I would have made a free gift of my wealth, and the better half of it should have gone to him

86   *returned* gone back to its proper place

89   *policy* self-interest that will resort to any means to attain its end

       sits above has a higher place than, overrules

       conscience (pronounced as three syllables)

III.3   This brief scene offers the final and most devastating variation on the theme of ingratitude, for Sempronius's excuse is even more outrageous than those of Lucullus and Lucius. The grudging aggressiveness of Sempronius is established in the first line he speaks, and consolidated by everything he says thereafter.

1   *'Bove* above

5   *Owes.* This form of the third-person plural is quite common in Shakespeare's work.

6   *touched* tested, tried for genuineness (referring to the practice of rubbing metals upon a touchstone in order to determine whether they were precious or base)

9   *Has.* Shakespeare often uses the singular form of the verb when that verb precedes the subject in the plural.

13   *Thrice.* The Folio reading is 'Thriue', which could be forced to yield the sense 'thrive on his money'; but, in view of Sempronius's emphasis on *Three* (line 10), the emendation seems fully justified.

      give him over give him up, pronounce him incurable

14   *'Has* he has

      much disgraced badly insulted

15   *That might have known my place* since he ought to have known my place among his friends (not after the other three)

15–16 *I see no sense for't | But his occasions might have wooed me first* I see no good reason why he should not have applied to me first in his troubles

17   *in my conscience* to my knowledge

19–20 *And does he think so backwardly of me now | That I'll requite it last?* and does he think of me as being so backward now that I must be the last man to repay him?

19   *backwardly of me* (1) of me as being backward; (2) of me in the reverse order to what he should

21   *an argument of laughter* a subject for laughter, a reason for my being derided

22   *and I 'mongst lords.* The Folio reading is 'and 'mong'st Lords', which is defective both in sense and in metre, as those responsible for the second Folio (1632) recognized when they altered it to ''mong'st Lords I'. The justification for the reading adopted in this edition is that it is better both syntactically and metrically.

24   *'Had* he had

      but for my mind's sake if only in recognition of my kindly feelings towards him

25   *courage* disposition, inclination

26   *faint* feeble, half-hearted

27   *Who bates* he who depreciates

      know see, make the acquaintance of

28   *goodly* fine, proper (ironical)

28–31   *The devil knew not ... set him clear.* The idea at the back of this passage, later developed in considerable detail by Ben Jonson in his play *The Devil is an Ass* (1616), is that the devil thwarted himself when he made man clever in evil, since man now excels the devil himself in this respect, causing him to look relatively innocent, and so to forfeit his supremacy in wickedness, which he does not want to do.

29   *politic* cunning in self-interest, clever at being wicked

30   *crossed* thwarted, tricked
   I cannot think but I can't help thinking that, I am driven to the conclusion that

31   *set him clear* make him appear innocent by comparison
   How fairly with what a plausible appearance of goodness

32   *foul* wicked
   Takes virtuous copies to patterns his behaviour on that of the virtuous in order to

33–4   *like those that ... would set whole realms on fire.* Shakespeare was probably thinking here of the Gunpowder Plot of 1605 and of those who took part in it.

33   *under* under the pretext of

35   *politic love* self-interest masquerading as love

37   *dead* (used figuratively, not literally)

38   *were ne'er acquainted with their wards* never knew what their locks were, were always left unlocked

39   *Many* for many, during many

40   *sure* safe (from arrest for debt)

41   *a liberal course allows* a generous way of life yields

42   *keep his house* stay indoors, stay at home (where the officers of the law could not arrest him for debt)

III.4   The last five lines of the previous scene lead directly into this, for the action now returns to Timon's house, where the doors are locked (see line 80), and which has become his *gaol* (line 82), besieged by a horde of

creditors. There is a careful building-up of dramatic tension which culminates in the appearance of Timon himself, who has not been seen since the end of Act II.
(stage direction) The direction in the Folio is vividly descriptive but, at the same time, quite unsuitable for use in a production, since it lacks explicitness. It runs as follows: '*Enter Varro's man, meeting others. All Timons Creditors to wait for his comming out. Then enter Lucius and Hortensius.*'

6   *Sir* (intended, no doubt, as a mock address)
       at once to one and all
8   *Labouring for* about to strike, about to give birth to
9   *seen* visible
10   *wonder on't* wonder at it
11   *are waxed* have grown
12   *prodigal course* prodigal's course
13   *Is like the sun's* is like the sun's annual course (because after his long days of extravagance come the short days of penury)
       recoverable (1) capable of being redeemed; (2) capable of being retraced
17   *I am of your fear for that* I share your fear about that
18   *t'observe a strange event* to make a scientific analysis of a curious phenomenon (metaphor taken from astronomical observation)
20   *gift* giving
22   *against my heart* contrary to my wish, repugnant to my feelings
23–4   *how strange it shows | Timon* what an extraordinary thing it is that Timon
26   *for 'em* to pay for them
27   *charge* task, employment
28   *spent of* done his spending out of, spent some of
29   *stealth* stealing, theft
30   crowns. Shakespeare is now dealing in units that he understands, not in unintelligible talents; and the sums involved begin to make sense. Three thousand crowns

is £750, the sort of amount that an Elizabethan gentleman might well borrow.

32   *'Tis much deep* it's very heavy

33-4   *Your master's confidence was above mine, | Else surely his had equalled* your master's confidence in Timon was greater than my master's, otherwise my master's loan to him would have equalled your master's

39   *attend* are waiting for
        signify so much let him know as much, tell him

40-41   *I need not tell him that; he knows. You are too diligent.* The Folio reads: 'I need not tell him that, he knowes you are too diligent', which editors render as 'I need not tell him that; he knows you are too diligent'. The reading offered in this edition is more pointed, and has the further advantage of making the last four words a direct reproof of one servant by another.

41   *diligent* officious

43   *in a cloud* (1) in a disguise; (2) under a cloud, in a state of gloom and disgrace

47   *certain money* some money, certain sums of money

50   *preferred* presented, proffered

53   *take down th'interest* swallow the interest (in the form of food and drink)
        maws bellies

54   *You do yourselves but wrong to stir me up* you only injure your own cause by provoking me

56   *Believe't* believe me when I say

57   *reckon* add up, keep account of

58   *serve* do, suffice

59   *serve* be a servant (quibbling on the previous use)

61-2   *cashiered* dismissed, sacked

64   *broader* more bluntly, with less restraint

64-5   *than he that has no house to put his head in* (because the homeless man has nothing to lose)

65-6   *rail against great buildings.* From about 1570 until the end of the reign of James I there was a positive craze in England for the building of what have been described as 'prodigy houses'. Many of them were in fact very handsome, but they did provide a target for the satirists of the time. The opening lines of Ben Jonson's poem 'To Penshurst' are a fine example of the more judicious criticism levelled at them.

69   *repair* return

70   *I should derive much from't* it would be of great assistance to me

71   *take't of my soul* I assure you from the bottom of my heart

71–2   *leans wondrously to discontent* is becoming deeply perturbed in spirit

72   *comfortable temper* cheerful disposition

73   *keeps his chamber* keeps to, stays in, his private apartment

74   *are* who are (omission of the nominative relative pronoun is very common in Shakespeare)

75   *And if it be so far beyond his health.* This passage has been much debated, because it is far from clear what *it* refers to. The simplest solution is to take *it* as meaning 'to come out', since this is what all the creditors are waiting for and have uppermost in mind. The line would then mean 'and if he is so ill that it is quite beyond his capacity to come out'.

77   *And make a clear way to the gods* and smooth his path to heaven

78   *for an answer.* The Folio reading is 'for answer', which gives an unmetrical line. It is easy to see how the compositor might have overlooked the shorter of two words that begin in exactly the same way.

80   *opposed against my passage* closed to prevent my going through them

81   *free* (1) free from restraint; (2) generous

82   *retentive* confining, restraining

83   *The place which I have feasted.* Timon in his rage sees his house as though it were one of his false friends, generalizing his own experience much as Lear does when, on first seeing Edgar as 'poor Tom', he says

'What, has his daughters brought him to this pass?'
(*King Lear*, III.4.63).

85   *Put in* make your claim

91   *Knock me down with 'em; cleave me to the girdle.* The
concealed pun is used to devastating effect here. Timon
takes *bills* in the sense, not of 'bills owed', but of 'hal-
berds', long-handled weapons with a curved blade that
could indeed cleave a man to the girdle.

93   *in sums* into sums of money

95   *Tell out my blood* count my blood drop by drop

100   *the gods fall upon you!* may the gods set upon you! (like
an avenging army)

101–2   *throw their caps at their money* give their money up as
irrecoverably lost, whistle for their money. 'To throw
one's cap' at a person was a proverbial expression for
abandoning all hope of overtaking him.

103   *desperate* (1) irrecoverable, past hoping for; (2) mad

104   *e'en put my breath from me* quite put me out of breath,
left me panting

107   *What if it should be so?* how about doing that? The idea
of the banquet is just beginning to take shape in
Timon's mind.

111   *So fitly!* that's the way! Timon is still thinking about
his plan, which is now fully formed.

112   *Sempronius – all.* The Folio reads '*Sempronius Vllorxa*:
All'; but the very odd name 'Ullorxa' occurs nowhere
else in the text, and it is hypermetrical. It may represent
the compositor's attempt to make something of a bit of
doodling by Shakespeare.

115   *so much left to furnish out* enough left to supply

116   *Be it not in thy care* let it not be your responsibility,
don't worry about that

III.5   No other scene in the play is more puzzling than this.
Its main function is clear enough: to show how deeply
engrained ingratitude, hypocrisy, and self-interest are

in the life of Athens. But there is also much that is obscure about it. It begins abruptly, without any preparation, and never so much as explains who the man referred to in line 2 as *he* actually is. Moreover, while Alcibiades has appeared before, there has been nothing up to this point to indicate that he is now going to assume the major role in an action that will run parallel to that involving Timon.

(stage direction) The direction here is that of the Folio. What it suggests is that the Senators come forward and confer for a moment, while Alcibiades waits by the door at which he has come in.

1   *my voice to't* my vote for it ('it' being the death sentence)

    the fault's bloody the offence involves bloodshed

3   *emboldens* encourages

4   *bruise him* crush him, destroy him. The Folio reading is 'bruise 'em'; but it is difficult to see what ''em' can refer to in a dialogue that is concerned with one specific man.

7   *your virtues* your virtuous selves. Instead of addressing the Senators as 'your honours', Alcibiades endows them with the quality he intends to appeal to.

8–9   *pity is the virtue of the law, | And none but tyrants use it cruelly.* The sentiment expressed in these lines is one that appears frequently in Shakespeare's work, the best known example of it being Portia's speech beginning 'The quality of mercy is not strained' and ending 'When mercy seasons justice' (*The Merchant of Venice*, IV.1.181–94).

8   *virtue* essence

10–11   *lie heavy | Upon* oppress

12   *stepped into the law* put himself within the power of the law

    past depth bottomless, unfathomable

14   *setting his fate aside* leaving aside his unfortunate destiny (which led him into this action). Many editors

find this interpretation of *fate* forced and emend it to 'fault'.

16   *soil the fact* sully the deed

17   *An.* The Folio reads 'And'; but as the entire line is in brackets in the Folio the emendation is a certain one. *buys out* redeems, cancels out

18   *fair* honourable

19   *Seeing his reputation touched to death* seeing his reputation injured in a way that would have been death to it (had he let the injury pass). For the importance that a gentleman attached to his reputation see *Othello*, II.3.255–8, where Cassio describes it as 'the immortal part of myself'.

21–3   *And with such sober . . . an argument.* This passage is a difficult one; but the main idea it expresses is that the man succeeded in bringing his initial burst of anger under control to such an extent as to make his action appear as the result of a calm reasonable resolution, not of a mad fury.

21   *sober and unnoted passion* passion so cool as to pass unnoticed

22   *behove* moderate, manage (a most unusual extension of the normal meaning 'to have use for or need of') *spent* exhausted

23   *but proved an argument* only been proving a logical proposition

24   *undergo too strict a paradox* undertake to maintain too strained a paradox

25   *fair* beautiful

26   *took* taken

27   *bring manslaughter into form* make manslaughter a form of legal procedure

27–8   *set quarrelling | Upon the head of valour* place quarrelling under the category of valour (or, possibly, 'make quarrelling the height of valour')

28   *which* (quarrelling)

29   *misbegot* unlawfully begotten, bastard

30 *When sects and factions were newly born.* This looks like an anachronistic reference to the proliferation of religious sects in sixteenth-century England.

32 *breathe* speak

33 *make his wrongs his outsides* treat injuries done to him as mere external things

34 *wear.* In addition to its normal sense this also means 'bear, put up with'.
    carelessly in a care-free way, without brooding over them

35-6 *And ne'er prefer his injuries to his heart, | To bring it into danger* and never do his injuries the honour of promoting them to the dignity of being taken to heart, because that endangers the heart itself. In the familiar analogy of the human body to the state the heart was thought of as the court or place of counsel. Compare 'The counsellor heart' and 'the court, the heart' (*Coriolanus*, I.1.114 and 134).

37 *us kill* us to kill, to revenge them

38 *for ill* for the sake of doing evil, for an evil cause

39 *gross* palpable, blatant
    clear innocent

40 *To revenge is no valour, but to bear* true valour lies not in revenging wrongs but in putting up with them

41 *under favour* by your leave

42 *like a captain* as a soldier (not as a parson or a moralist)

43 *fond* foolish (ironical)

44 *not endure all threats* not submit to all they are threatened with
    Sleep upon't disregard it

46 *Without repugnancy* without fighting back, without offering any resistance

47 *the bearing* the patient suffering of injuries

47-8 *what make we | Abroad?* what are we doing away from home? why do we spend our lives on the battle-field?

49 *if bearing carry it* if bearing wins the day
    bearing (1) putting up with wrongs; (2) bearing

198

children; (3) bearing the weight of men, in the sense of having sexual intercourse with them

50　*more captain* a better soldier

51　*fellow loaden with irons* the man weighed down with shackles, the prisoner. The description is so specific that there is no need, as some editors do, to emend the 'fellow' of the Folio to 'felon'.

53　*be pitifully good* be good by showing pity

54　*Who cannot condemn rashness in cold blood?* Alcibiades is pointing out that it is all too easy to condemn a rash act when one is not involved in it, and asking the Senators to do better than this by using their imaginations.

55　*sin's extremest gust* the most violent outburst of sin (taking *gust* in the sense of a gust of wind. Alternatively *gust* can be interpreted to mean 'relish, taste', giving the sense 'the utmost degree of appetite for sin'.)

56　*in defence, by mercy* done as an act of self-defence, and viewed with the mercy that such an action deserves

57　*To be in anger is impiety* to continue in anger is a sin against God. Compare 'Be ye angry, and sin not: let not the sun go down upon your wrath' (Ephesians 4.26).

58　*who is man* what man is there
　　angry (pronounced as three syllables)

60　*breathe* speak

62　*sufficient* (1) adequate; (2) capable of paying
　　briber giver of bribes. Alcibiades is personifying the *service* his friend has done, and, at the same time, suggesting that bribes are, apparently, the only thing the Senators are interested in.

64　*Why, I say.* The reading of the Folio is 'Why say'. The missing word was inserted in the second Folio and is accepted by editors.
　　'has he has
　　fair excellent

66   *bear himself* conduct himself, behave

68   *He has made too much plenty with 'em.* This line is obscure. The Second Senator must mean either that Alcibiades's friend 'has been altogether too liberal in giving wounds, dealing them out to friend and foe alike', or, twisting *made plenteous wounds* to 'made plenty o' 's wounds', that he 'has made an excessive profit out of his wounds by using them to cadge drinks and so forth'. The reading adopted is that of the second Folio; the first Folio has 'him' for *'em*, which yields no sense, unless *too much* be taken as 'too-much', in which case it might mean 'he has made excess his plenty, he has confused abundance with excess'.

69   *sworn rioter* inveterate rioter, one who seems to have taken an oath to continue in riotous living

        a sin (drunkenness)

74   *cherish factions* encourage conspiracies, foster plots

        inferred alleged (probably by the professional informers, or 'intelligencers' as they were called, employed by the state in Shakespeare's day)

75   *His days are foul and his drink dangerous* his days are spent in wickedness, and his drinking is a danger to the state

77   *parts* good qualities

78–9   *might purchase his own time | And be in debt to none* might be thought to have earned him the right of dying in his own good time without being indebted to anyone else for that part of his natural life that is still left to him

79   *more to move you* to move you more

80   *to* in addition to

81   *for* because

        your reverend ages you in your reverend old age

82   *Security* (1) safety; (2) security for debts owed you (charging them obliquely with being usurers)

        pawn pledge (carrying on the second meaning of *Security*)

83	*his good returns* his making a good return to you for your clemency, his repaying you with interest for sparing his life
86	*For law is strict, and war is nothing more.* The sense of this line would be improved if *law* and *war* were transposed.
88	*On height of our displeasure* on pain of incurring our utmost displeasure
89	*another* the blood of another
91	*know me* recognize who I am and what I have done
92	*Call me to your remembrances* recall what I have done for you
93	*I cannot think but* I can only think, I am driven to think *your age has forgot* you, as a consequence of being old, have forgotten
94	*It could not else be* otherwise it could not happen that
94–5	*I should prove so base	To sue and be denied such common grace* I should be regarded as of so little account as to plead for and be refused such a common favour
97	*spacious in effect* (1) having large consequences; (2) having the effect of putting a large space between you and us
102	*Attend our weightier judgement* expect a more severe sentence from us
103	*not to swell our spirit* in order to prevent our anger increasing further. This gloss is far from certain. The abrupt switch from Alcibiades to the condemned man is suspicious; and the passage may well be corrupt.
104	*presently* at once, immediately
105	*the gods keep you old enough* may the gods preserve you to such an old age, so prolong your lives
105–6	*that you may live	Only in bone* that you may be mere living skeletons
108	*told* counted
	let out lent, loaned
110	*hurts* wounds, injuries
111	*balsam* balm, medicinal ointment

113   *It comes not ill* it does not fall out badly, it's not such a bad thing after all

114   *worthy* worthy of, deserving

115   *cheer up* put new life into by my words

116   *lay for hearts* seek to win men's hearts

117   *worst lands.* The Folio reading is 'most Lands'; but it is difficult to see what particular honour there is in being at war with 'most lands'. To attack a wicked state, on the other hand, might well be considered an honourable thing to do; and it is the ingratitude of Athens that is uppermost in Alcibiades's mind throughout this speech.

118   *Soldiers should brook as little wrongs as gods* soldiers should be no more ready to put up with injuries than the gods are

III.6   It is here that the play reaches its climax in the most powerful dramatic scene that it presents. Beginning with a concise ironical repetition and summing-up of the initial situation, the scene then moves on to a startling reversal of it, which comes as a complete surprise to Timon's false friends and as a partial surprise to the audience, who, while knowing that something important is about to happen, have not been let into the secret of precisely what it is to be. This reversal of the action coincides with, and is indeed an extension of, the reversal that has taken place in Timon himself. He emerges here as the antithesis of his former self.

(stage direction) The Folio direction, quite inadequate for any production, is simply '*Enter diuers Friends at seuerall doores*'; and these '*Friends*', when they speak, are not identified by name but merely marked in the speech headings as 1, 2, 3, and 4. This edition follows C. J. Sisson in naming them Lucullus, Lucius, Sempronius, and Ventidius. That these are, in fact, the

characters intended is evident not only from what they
say but also from Timon's previous order to Flavius:
*Go, bid all my friends again, | Lucius, Lucullus, and
Sempronius – all* (III.4.111–12).

2   *this honourable lord* (Timon)

3   *did but try us* was only testing us

4   *tiring* exercising themselves, active (literally, a term
from falconry, meaning 'feeding ravenously')

5   *encountered* met

    it is not so low with him his financial position is not so bad

7   *persuasion* evidence

9–10   *earnest inviting* pressing invitation

10   *many my near occasions* my numerous personal engage-
ments

11   *put off* refuse

    conjured me beyond them made an appeal to me that is
more pressing than my own affairs

13   *in debt to* badly needed by

15–16   *my provision was out* my resources were exhausted (or
'were out on loan')

17–18   *I am sick of that grief too, as I understand how all things
go* I share your grief, especially as I now understand
the state of affairs

21   *pieces* gold coins (exact value not clear)

26   *With all my heart* hearty greetings

28–9   *Ever at the best, hearing well of your lordship* very well
indeed, as we always are when we know things are well
with your lordship

30   *willing* willingly

32–3   *Nor more willingly leaves winter. Such summer birds are
men.* Behind Timon's aside there lies the proverb
'Swallows, like false friends, fly away upon the
approach of winter'.

34   *stay* wait

35–6   *if they will fare so harshly o'th'trumpet's sound* if they
will be content with such harsh fare as the sound of
the trumpet

36   *to't presently* sit down to eat shortly. This is one of the very few instances where Shakespeare uses 'presently' in something like the modern sense.

37-8   *it remains not unkindly with your lordship that* your lordship harbours no hard feelings against me because

38   *returned you* sent back to you
        empty empty-handed

41   *what cheer?* how are things with you?

42   *e'en* quite

44   *so unfortunate a beggar* so unfortunate as to have no money

47   *cumber your better remembrance* trouble your kind memory
        (stage direction) *The banquet is brought in.* The Folio direction is placed after line 41; but, as there is no indication of the banquet in the speeches until this point, this edition follows the normal practice of editors.

50   *Royal cheer* dishes fit for a king

58   *upon what?* upon what cause?

61   *toward* about to take place, forthcoming

62   *the old man still* still the same old Timon as he always was

63   *Will't hold?* will it last? can it continue?

64   *time will –.* Lucius is clearly referring to a proverb or well known saying, such as 'Time will show'.

65   *conceive* understand your meaning

66   *with that spur* with the same eagerness

67   *diet* food and drink, fare

67-8   *in all places alike* the same no matter where you sit

68   *a City feast* a formal banquet of the kind given by the City of London (where there was much ado about precedence)

69   *upon the first place* about who is to sit above whom

70   *require* demand

73   *reserve still to give* always keep something in reserve for future giving

75   *forsake* (1) refuse; (2) renounce

79   *as they are* no better than they should be, wantons
      fees creatures holding their lives from you (as the
      medieval tenant held land from his lord)

80   *the common leg of people* the common people who are
      the leg of the state. This passage, given here in the
      form in which it occurs in the Folio, has been the sub-
      ject of much discussion; but the simplest way to take it
      is to see it as a reference to the familiar analogy be-
      tween the state – the body politic – and the human
      body. In *Coriolanus*, where Shakespeare handles this
      analogy at length, the First Citizen speaks of 'Our
      steed the leg' (I.1.115), implying that the leg, though
      an inferior part of the body, nevertheless supports and
      carries the rest of it. Timon means that there is nothing
      to choose between the heads of the state – the Senators
      – and the common people, since they are all equally
      bad. Many editors emend the 'legge' of the Folio to
      'lag', meaning 'that which comes last, the tail'; but
      there is no example of 'lag' as a noun elsewhere in
      Shakespeare's work.

81–2   *what is amiss in them, you gods, make suitable for destruc-*
      tion because of what is wrong in them, you gods, make
      them fit for destruction

82   *For* as for
      present friends (1) friends present here; (2) friends
      whose friendship depends on presents

82–3   *are to me nothing* mean nothing to me, are not friends
      at all to me

85   (stage direction) *The dishes are uncovered and seen to be*
      full of warm water and stones. There is no direction in
      the Folio at this point, but the water is demanded by
      Timon's reference to *lukewarm water* at line 89, and
      the stones by what Ventidius says at line 118. In the
      anonymous *Timon* the hero offers his guests stones
      painted to resemble artichokes (*Narrative and Dramatic*
      Sources of Shakespeare, edited by Geoffrey Bullough,

Volume 6 (1966), page 328). There is a good account of the anonymous *Timon* in the essay by M. C. Bradbrook listed under Further Reading on page 46.

89 *knot* company, conspiracy. Compare 'A knot you are of damnèd bloodsuckers' (*Richard III*, III.3.5).

 mouth-friends friends in words only. Compare 'mouth-honour' (*Macbeth*, V.3.27). Timon may also be implying that they are *friends* only for what they can stuff into their mouths.

89–90 *Smoke and lukewarm water | Is your perfection* smoke and lukewarm water is the perfect image of you. The conjunction of these words with *mouth-friends* suggests that Shakespeare was thinking of Christ's message to the Laodiceans: 'because thou art lukewarm, and neither cold nor hot, I will spew thee out of my mouth' (Revelation 3.16).

90 *last* final action

91 *stuck* adorned, decked out

 with your. The Folio reading is 'you with', which is patently wrong in this context.

92 *it* (the flattery)

96 *fools of fortune*. This phrase normally means 'sports or dupes of fortune', which is not satisfactory in this vituperative context. Perhaps Timon is calling them 'fortune's licensed jesters' with reference to the way in which they have made sport of him and gained by it.

 trencher-friends spongers, friends for the sake of free meals

 time's flies fair-weather flies, parasites

97 *Cap-and-knee slaves* slaves that are always bowing and scraping, sycophants

 vapours unsubstantial things

 minute-jacks fickle fellows, men who change their minds at every minute. There is probably an allusion here to the 'Jack of the clock', the automatically operated figure that strikes the bell. Compare *Richard III*, IV.2.108–15.

98–9   *Of man and beast the infinite malady | Crust you quite o'er!* may every foul disease that man and beast are subject to, infinite as the number is, cover you entirely with scabs. Compare *Hamlet*, I.5.71–3:

> And a most instant tetter barked about,
> Most lazar-like, with vile and loathsome crust,
> All my smooth body.

100   *Soft* stay, stop
       physic medicine

101   (stage direction) *He throws the stones at them, and drives them out.* This direction, though not in the Folio, seems to be called for by what is happening.

105   *Of Timon* by Timon

107   *quality* cause (literally, 'original nature')

108   *Push!* (exclamation of impatience)

110   *humours* caprices, wild fancies

111   *sways* rules

116   *make no stay* not delay

IV.1   The new direction that the action of the play has now taken is confirmed by this scene, where, for the first time, as the opening line indicates, the action moves from Athens to the open country beyond it. This shift from the world of men to the natural world is endorsed by the fact that, again for the first time, we see the hero alone and find him resorting to soliloquy. The verse too makes a fresh kind of music, not heard in the play before. Troubled, bitter, and violent in the feelings it gives utterance to, it is, at the same time, beautifully articulated, moving to its conclusion in a series of great waves, as the hero defines that hatred of society which has now taken possession of his soul.

2   *girdles* girdlest. Shakespeare frequently drops the final 't' in the second person singular of a verb in order to produce something that an actor can speak without difficulty.

4   *Obedience fail* let obedience fail

4–5   *Slaves and fools | Pluck* let slaves and fools pluck

6   *minister* officiate, govern
           general filths common harlots, common drabs

7   *Convert* change
           green virginity young virgins

8   *hold fast* keep a firm grasp on the money you have

9   *render back* repay what you owe

10   *trusters* creditors
           Bound servants indentured servants, servants bound by
           a contract

11–12   *Large-handed robbers your grave masters are, | And pill
           by law.* Compare *King Lear*, IV.6.163–7:

> The usurer hangs the cozener.
> Through tattered clothes small vices do appear;
> Robes and furred gowns hide all. Plate sin with gold,
> And the strong lance of justice hurtless breaks;
> Arm it in rags, a pigmy's straw does pierce it.

11   *Large-handed* grasping, unrestrained (ironical use of a
           word that ought to mean 'generous')

12   *pill by law* rob in a legal manner
           to go to, hasten to

13   *o'th'brothel* belongs to the brothel
           Son. The Folio reading is 'Some', an obvious mistake
           for 'Sonne'.

14   *lined* stuffed, padded

16   *Religion to* religious veneration for

17   *Domestic awe* the respect owed by children to parents
           and by servants to the head of the household
           neighbourhood neighbourliness, the sense of mutual
           concern and solidarity that ought to exist between
           neighbours

18   *mysteries* professions, occupations

19   *Degrees* ordered ranks of society, established positions
           in the social hierarchy. For the Elizabethans this word

had a rich and universal sense that is fully explained by Ulysses in *Troilus and Cressida*, I.3.75-137.

20   *Decline to* sink into, degenerate into
    confounding contraries contraries which bring all to confusion

21   *And yet confusion live.* The condensed paradox of these words is best brought out by Dr Johnson, who paraphrases them thus: 'though by such confusion all things seem to hasten to dissolution, yet let not dissolution come, but the miseries of confusion continue'.
    incident to natural to

23   *for stroke* for being stricken
    cold chilling

25   *liberty* licence, licentiousness

28   *riot* dissoluteness
    blains blisters (the same word as in 'chilblains')

29   *Sow all th' Athenian bosoms* fall like seed in the vitals of all Athenians

31   *That their society* so that their association with one another
    as like

32   *merely* nothing but, unadulterated
    bear carry away

33   *detestable* (with stress on the first syllable)

34   *Take thou that too, with multiplying bans* may nakedness be yours too, with ever increasing curses

35   *will to* will go to
    shall find is certain to find

36   *more kinder* (double comparative for emphasis)

38   *within and out* within and without

IV.2   The loyalty and affection that Timon's servants feel for his ruined master stand in vivid contrast to his undiscriminating hatred for Athens and all who live in it, so powerfully voiced in the previous scene. The situation portrayed here was a familiar one at the time when the play was written, since the break-up of a great household frequently meant unemployment and beggary for many of those who had been employed in it and who knew no other home.

(stage direction) *two or three Servants*. The imprecision of this direction points to Shakespeare's manuscript as the copy for the play. He had probably not made up his mind when he began this scene exactly how many servants would be needed.

2	*undone* ruined
4	*Let me be recorded* let it be recorded of me, I vow
5	*broke* bankrupt
7	*his fortune* (Timon in his misfortune)
10	*his familiars to his buried fortunes* his intimate friends who were really attached to his fortunes that are now buried
13	*A dedicated beggar to the air* a beggar vowed to the open air, a beggar dedicated to a homeless life
14	*all-shunned* shunned by all
15	*like contempt* as though he were contemptibility itself
16	*implements* utensils, instruments
17	*Yet do our hearts wear Timon's livery* we are still Timon's servants in our hearts
18	*fellows* fellow-servants, colleagues
19	*Leaked* leaky, full of leaks
20	*mates* (1) associates; (2) subordinate officers of a ship *the dying deck* the deck that is sinking to its grave
21	*threat* threaten *part* depart
22	*this sea of air* (the open air which will be as dangerous and inhospitable to us as the sea is to men on a sinking boat)
23	*latest* last
25	*shake our heads* (in sorrow)
26–7	*As 'twere a knell unto our master's fortunes,*	*'We have seen better days'*. The same association of 'knell' and 'seen better days' is found in *As You Like It*, II.7.114–

15, where Orlando, seeking help for Adam, says to the Duke:

> If ever you have looked on better days;
> If ever been where bells have knolled to church. . . .

28   *put out all* all put out

29   *part* separate

30   *fierce* excessive, violent

31   *exempt* kept far, excluded

32   *point to* tend to, lead to

33   *Who would be* who would wish to be

      to live. Shakespeare often omits 'to' from the former of two clauses and inserts it in the latter of them, particularly when the finite verb is an auxiliary.

34   *But* merely

35   *all what state compounds* all that constitutes worldly grandeur

36   *But only painted* merely a pretended thing, a façade. For Shakespeare 'painted' frequently has a pejorative sense, denoting unreality and deception. Compare Claudius's reference to 'my most painted word' in his speech beginning 'O, 'tis too true!' (*Hamlet*, III.1.49–54) – a passage that is most illuminating on this matter.

      varnished friends pretended friends, those whose friendship is only a superficial gloss

37   *heart* goodness of heart, generosity

38   *blood.* This word is usually explained as 'temper' or 'disposition', a gloss that does not seem nearly paradoxical enough in this context. I suggest that *blood* here means 'prompting of passion', as it often does in Shakespeare, and thus, with reference to the sin of Adam in allowing passion to overmaster reason, 'form of original sin'.

39   *is he does* is that he does

40   *dares* can possibly dare

      half so kind again even half as kind on any future occasion

41   *does*. This reading is taken from the fourth Folio; the first Folio has 'do', which is just possible on the assumption that the verb has been attracted into the plural by *gods* earlier in the line, but which reads very awkwardly.

42   *to be* only to be

45   *He's flung* he has rushed off
      seat residence, abode

47   *to supply his life* the provisions necessary to keep him alive, the bare necessities of life

48   *that which can command it* that which can obtain the necessities of life (money)

49   *inquire him out* find him by making inquiries about him

50   *serve his mind* be obedient to his wishes

IV.3   Even as it stands this scene is much the longest in the entire play. In fact, however, it is still longer than it appears, because the division between it and V.1, first introduced by editors in the eighteenth century, is quite arbitrary and makes no sense whatever. In terms of both location and action IV.3 and V.1 are one continuous whole in which Timon confronts Athenian society and his own past. Generalizing from his personal experience, he now sees ingratitude and self-interest as universal principles, voicing his new insights in speeches of great force and intensity. Yet, at the same time, a kind of counter-movement is going on, for in the very process of giving expression to his bitterness and disillusion Timon also begins to come to terms with them, so that, by the end of V.1, where he disappears from the play and is seen no more, he is a very different man from the one who steps on to the stage at the opening of this scene.

(stage direction) *in the woods*. These words are Shakespeare's own, and they are important. The setting, contrasting vividly with that of the first three Acts, is part of the play's meaning, and its presence and reality are impressed on the mind of an audience by one evocative descriptive touch after another.

2   *Rotten humidity* foul unwholesome vapours

2–3   *Below thy sister's orb | Infect the air.* Shakespeare is referring here to the Ptolemaic idea of the universe, according to which everything below the sphere of the moon was imperfect and corruptible. Timon invokes the sun, normally the source of life in the sublunary part of the universe, to become instead a source of infection and disease.

2   *thy sister's orb* (the moon). In classical mythology Diana, the moon-goddess, was the sister of the sun-god Apollo.

3   *Twinned brothers* brothers brought forth as twins

5   *dividant* capable of being divided, different

    touch try, test

    several separate, different

6–8   *Not nature ... contempt of nature.* The manifold significances that the word 'nature' had for Shakespeare and his age make this an extremely difficult passage to paraphrase. The simplest meaning, and the one that fits the context best, is 'human nature, beleaguered as it is by every kind of affliction, cannot bear great prosperity, except by despising its own kind'. It is possible, however, that Timon is saying: 'human beings, because they are troubled by all sorts of physical ills, are incapable of resisting the temptations that wealth brings with it unless they are ascetics or saints'.

9   *me* for me. This use of the dative is primarily for emphasis, amounting substantially to 'I tell you' or 'believe me'.

    deject. The Folio has 'deny't', which is unsatisfactory, since the sense demands that the lord be treated in exactly the reverse way to the beggar, who is to be elevated. The misreading of 'deiect' as 'deniet' would be very easy. Moreover, the idea at the back of the line is that of the wheel of Fortune, carrying one man up to prosperity and casting another down into misery. Edgar describes himself as 'The lowest and most dejected thing of fortune' (*King Lear*, IV.1.3).

10–11   *The senator shall bear contempt hereditary, | The beggar native honour* the senator will be treated with the contempt bestowed on a beggar, as though he had inherited it; and the beggar with honour, as though he had been born to it

10   *senator.* The sense demands the singular, though the Folio reads 'Senators'.

12–13   *It is the pasture lards the wether's sides, | The want that makes him lean.* The reading of the Folio – a celebrated crux – is 'It is the Pastour Lards, the Brothers sides, | The want that makes him leaue'. The emendations of 'Pastour' to *pasture* and of 'leaue' to *lean* are generally accepted by editors. The justification for changing 'Brothers' to *wether's* is partly graphical, since the two words look very much alike in an Elizabethan hand, but more a matter of sense and consistency, which make an animal that grows fat on good pasture necessary at this point. Corin, the shepherd in *As You Like It*, states that 'good pasture makes fat sheep' (III.2.25–6).

12   *lards* makes fat

13   *want* lack (of good pasture)

16   *grise* step, stair on a flight of stairs

17   *smoothed* (1) made smooth, made easier; (2) flattered
    learnèd pate learned head (man of learning)

18   *Ducks* bows obsequiously
    golden wealthy, rich in gold
    obliquy obliquity, deviation from a right course of conduct. Shakespeare seems to have coined *obliquy*, which is not known apart from its occurrence here, as a portmanteau word containing the senses of both 'obliquity' and 'obloquy'.

19   *level* straightforward

20   *direct* downright

22   *His semblable* his like, his fellow-man, his own species

23   *fang* seize, take

24   *of* from

      sauce tickle, stimulate

25   *operant* potent, operative

27   *no idle votarist* not one who has taken a vow with no intention of keeping it (alluding to his preference for roots)

28   *clear* pure

      this (the gold)

33   *Pluck stout men's pillows from below their heads.* This is an allusion to the practice of drawing away the pillow from under the head of a dying man in order to let him expire more easily. As the men here are *stout* (strong), however, it is clearly murder that Timon is thinking of. In Ben Jonson's *Volpone* (II.6.87–8) Mosca proposes to Corvino that they get rid of Volpone by this means, saying:

> 'Tis but to pull the pillow from his head,
> And he is throttled.

35   *knit and break religions* knit men together in religious unity and break that unity to pieces

36   *hoar* white (because leprosy covers the skin with whitish scales)

      place thieves put thieves into high positions

37   *knee* the right to be bowed to

39   *makes* enables

      wappened stale, worn-out (probably in the sense of 'sexually exhausted')

40   *She* her, the very woman. Shakespeare sometimes treats the word 'she' as though it were an uninflected noun synonymous with 'woman'.

      the spital-house and ulcerous sores the inmates of a hospital with their ulcerous sores. The *spital-house*, used here as a collective noun, was thought of with contempt because of its associations with venereal disease. Compare Pistol's remarks to Nym in *Henry V*, II.1.70–74:

> O hound of Crete, think'st thou my spouse to get?
> No, to the spital go,
> And from the powdering tub of infamy
> Fetch forth the lazar kite of Cressid's kind,
> Doll Tearsheet she by name, and her espouse.

41   *cast the gorge at* vomit at the sight of

41–2   *embalms and spices | To th'April day again* preserves from corruption and perfumes so that she again looks as she did in her first youth

43   *puts* puttest

43–4   *puts odds | Among the rout of nations* set the disorderly mob of nations at variance with each other

44–5   *make thee | Do thy right nature* make you do the work you are properly fitted for (to set men at odds with each other)

45   *quick* (1) speedy; (2) alive, active

46   *go* be able to walk
    strong (1) powerful; (2) resolute, confirmed. Gold is thought of as a thief because it steals away from its owner.

48   *for earnest* as an instalment, as a pledge
    (stage direction) *Timandra*. Shakespeare took this name from North's translation of Plutarch's *Lives*, where Timandra is described as 'a concubine' of Alcibiades and as a courtesan.

50   *canker* spreading sore or ulcer

54   *Misanthropos* the man-hater (from the Greek). Shakespeare took this name from North's Plutarch, where Timon is referred to as 'Timon, surnamed Misanthropus (as who would say, Loup-garou, or the manhater)'.

55   *For thy part* as for you

56   *something* somewhat

57   *in thy fortunes am unlearned and strange* am uninformed about and unacquainted with your fortunes

59   *not desire* do not desire

60   *gules* red (heraldic term)

62   *fell* cruel, virulent

63   *destruction* capacity for destruction (suggesting that she is a source of venereal disease)

64   *cherubin* angelic
    Thy lips rot off! may your lips rot off!

65-6   *I will not kiss thee; then the rot returns | To thine own lips again* I will not kiss you; and as a result the rottenness you have wished on my lips will return to your own where it really belongs. Compare *Richard III*, I.3.239: 'Thus have you breathed your curse against yourself'. An alternative explanation is that Timon is alluding to the belief, prevalent in Shakespeare's day, that one could get rid of venereal disease by transmitting it to another.

68   *wanting* lacking

69   *renew* become new (with a quibble on the idea of re-newing a loan)

71   *friendship* friendly action, kind service

71-6   *None, but to . . . art a man.* These lines appear as prose in the Folio, which is odd in a verse context. In this edition, emendations introduced at lines 74 and 75 restore the blank-verse pattern.

72   *Maintain my opinion* support my view by your actions
    opinion (pronounced as four syllables)
    it (the thing I must do)

74-6   *If thou wilt promise, the gods plague thee, for | Thou art a man. If thou dost not perform, | Confound thee, for thou art a man.* The Folio reads 'If thou wilt not promise, the Gods plague thee, for thou art a man: if thou do'st performe, confound thee, for thou art a man'. The sense of this is not consistent with the order that Timon gives to Alcibiades in line 73, which expresses what he expects of all men and is, in fact, the *opinion* he asks Alcibiades to maintain. The transposition of *not* from its place before *promise* to the place before *perform* gives perfect sense, and, at the same time, turns prose into blank verse.

77   *in some sort* to some extent

80   *held with a brace of harlots* spent with a couple of harlots. There is probably also a quibble on *brace* in the sense of 'clamp', implying that Alcibiades is 'held down by the clamping influence of a couple of harlots'.

81–2   *Is this th'Athenian minion whom the world | Voiced so regardfully?* The sentiment and diction of these lines are very close to those of Lodovico's comment on Othello (*Othello*, IV.1.266–7):

> Is this the noble Moor, whom our full senate
> Call all-in-all sufficient?

81   *th'Athenian minion* the darling of Athens

82   *Voiced so regardfully* spoke of with such high esteem

84   *use* make use of (for sexual purposes)

85   *leaving* while they are leaving

86   *Make use of* profit from
       salt lecherous, lustful
       Season (1) make ready, prepare; (2) pickle, salt (alluding, with a quibble, to the 'powdering-tub' in which meat was pickled)

87   *tubs and baths* sweating-tubs and hot baths (used in the treatment of venereal disease)
       bring down reduce

88   *tub-fast* fasting that was part of the cure along with the sweating-tub. The Folio reads 'Fubfast'.
       diet strict diet prescribed by a physician

92   *want* lack, shortage
       make revolt cause mutiny

93   *penurious* poverty-stricken

93–6   *I have heard . . . trod upon them.* This unfinished sen-

tence is of importance because it is the first indication
we are given that Timon has been a great soldier, and
that Athens owes him much on this score.

96   *trod* would have trodden

97   *get thee gone* go, take yourself off

102   *on a heap* in ruins

104   *confound* destroy, ruin

      in thy conquest in the course of your victory over them

106-7   *That by killing . . . my country.* The conjunction of un-
satisfactory metre and inadequate sense suggests either
that there is corruption of the text here or that these
lines are merely a rough draft.

106   *That* seeing that, because

108   *Put up* pocket, put back in your purse

109-29 *Be as a . . . be gone.* This passage looks as though it has
been influenced by Thomas Nashe's description of the
Fall of Jerusalem and of the wickedness of London in
his *Christ's Tears over Jerusalem* (1593), a pamphlet
written during the very bad outbreak of the plague in
1592-3.

109   *a planetary plague* (a plague caused by the influence of
a malign planet or by some disorder among the planets)

109-11 *when Jove . . . sick air.* The view that the plague was
God's visitation on a country or a city as a punishment
for its wickedness was very common at the time when
the play was written. Nashe writes:

     'You usurers and engrossers of corn, by your hoard-
ing up of gold and grain till it is mould, rusty, moth-
eaten, and almost infects the air with the stench, you
have taught God to hoard up your iniquities and
transgressions, till mouldiness, putrefaction, and
mustiness enforceth him to open them: and being
opened, they so poison the air with their ill savour,
that from them proceedeth this perilsome contagion.
The land is full of adulterers, and for this cause the
land mourneth. The land is full of extortioners, full
of proud men, full of hypocrites, full of murderers.

> This is the cause why the sword devoureth abroad,
> and the pestilence at home.'
>
> (*The Works of Thomas Nashe*, edited by R. B.
> McKerrow (1904–10), Volume II, page 158)

110   *Will* determines to
      high-viced full of great vices

111   *sick* infected and infectious
      skip miss, omit

113   *Strike me* strike, I bid you
      the counterfeit matron the married woman whose
      modesty is a sham

114   *habit* dress
      honest modest, chaste

115–27 *Let not . . . a jot.* Compare the King's speech before
      Harfleur in *Henry V*, III.3.10–41.

116   *trenchant* sharp, cutting
      milk-paps teats

117   *window, bared.* The Folio reading is 'window Barne',
      which most editors emend to 'window-bars', meaning
      'lattice'. Graphically, however, *bared* is equally plaus-
      ible, and it has the advantage of fitting the context
      better, since complaints about women baring their
      breasts in order to tempt men are fairly frequent in
      Elizabethan satire. Thomas Nashe writes as follows in
      his *Christ's Tears over Jerusalem*: 'Their breasts they
      embusk [corset] up on high, and their round roseate
      buds immodestly lay forth, to show at their hands there
      is fruit to be hoped' (*The Works of Thomas Nashe*,
      Volume II, page 137). The paradox of *bared, bore* is
      also appropriate.

118   *the leaf of pity.* This looks like a reference to Deutero-
      nomy 20.14, where the Israelites are commanded to
      spare 'the women, and the children' when they
      capture an enemy city.
      writ written down

119   *set them down* write them down as
      traitors (because they betray men)

120   *exhaust* elicit, draw out

121–2   *whom the oracle | Hath doubtfully pronounced thy throat shall cut* who, according to one interpretation of the oracle's ambiguous declaration, is destined to cut your throat. The Folio reads 'the throat', which has been defended on the grounds that it means 'somebody's throat', but a more personal inducement seems to be required. Shakespeare is clearly trying – not very successfully – to find an English equivalent for the kind of ambiguity that the Latin use of the accusative with the infinitive in indirect speech can give. The most famous instance, which he actually quotes in *2 Henry VI*, I.4.62, is the answer that the Pythian Apollo gave to Pyrrhus when the latter inquired whether he would overcome the Romans: '*Aio te, Aeacida, Romanos vincere posse*'. This can mean either 'I declare that you, son of Aeacus, can conquer the Romans' or 'I declare that the Romans can conquer you, son of Aeacus'. What is needed here is a form of words that can mean both that the babe is destined to cut Alcibiades's throat and that Alcibiades is destined to cut the babe's throat; but English does not lend itself to this kind of statement.

123   *mince it* chop it to pieces
       sans remorse without pity
       Swear against objects take an oath not to be moved by objections to this course, abjure all pleas to the contrary

125   *Whose proof* the invulnerability of which armour

128   *large confusion* wide-spread havoc
       thy fury spent when your fury is exhausted

132   *Dost thou or dost thou not* whether you do or whether you don't

135   *And to make whores, a bawd* and enough to make a bawd forswear her trade of making women whores, and enough to enable a bawd to retire from business

136   *aprons mountant* rising aprons, aprons that are always

being lifted up for sexual purposes. Shakespeare has coined the word *mountant* by analogy with such heraldic terms as 'rampant' and 'couchant', thus making the lifted apron the device of the whore. Timon's intention is, of course, to throw money into the aprons held out to receive it.

136   *oathable* fit to be trusted on oath

137–8   *swear ... | Into* swear with such vehemence as to throw into

138   *strong* violent
      heavenly agues celestial shivering fits

139   *Spare* forbear

140   *conditions* characters, natural inclinations
      still constantly, always

142   *strong in whore* resolute in whoring
      burn him up (1) inflame him with passion; (2) infect him with venereal disease

143   *close fire* (1) ardent passion (because a *close* or 'enclosed' fire gives out most heat); (2) secret infection
      predominate prevail over
      his smoke (1) his empty phrases – the *pious breath* of line 141 (compare 'Sweet smoke of rhetoric' in *Love's Labour's Lost*, III.1.58); (2) the steam of the sweating-tub, his attempted cure

144   *be no turncoats* be no renegades (don't let him convert you). Another meaning of *turncoat* is implicit in what follows.

144–5   *Yet may your pains, six months, | Be quite contrary* yet may all your efforts, six months hence, be directed to the opposite end (that is, to being *turncoats*, but this time in the sense of 'people who alter their outward appearance'). This passage is obscure and has caused much discussion. The explanation proposed does at least lead on to the lines that follow, where the assumption of a different appearance is much emphasized. I take *six months* as being the maximum time that Timon thinks Phrynia and Timandra can retain their natural beauty.

146 *thin roofs* scalps with a very sparse covering of hair (loss of the hair being a consequence of syphilis)
burdens of the dead hair taken from dead bodies. Shakespeare refers to the use of hair acquired in this way in *The Merchant of Venice*, III.2.92–6:

> So are those crispèd snaky golden locks,
> Which make such wanton gambols with the wind
> Upon supposèd fairness, often known
> To be the dowry of a second head,
> The skull that bred them in the sepulchre.

149 *mire* sink into the mire, become bogged down in the mire
150 *A pox of wrinkles!* a pox on wrinkles! (Elizabethan equivalent of the modern 'to hell with wrinkles!')
152 *Consumptions* wasting diseases (reference here is to venereal diseases rather than tuberculosis)
153 *hollow* (used proleptically to indicate that the bones are 'made hollow' by the disease)
strike their sharp shins strike their shins with disease and make them sharp
154 *spurring* ability to use the spur (probably with a quibble on 'sexual potency')
Crack the lawyer's voice (a further reference to the effects of syphilis)
155 *title* claim to possession of land or goods
156 *sound his quillets shrilly* utter his subtle verbal distinctions in a loud voice
Hoar the flamen make the priest white with disease
157–8 *That scolds against the quality of flesh | And not believes himself* who inveighs against the natural desires of the flesh without believing a word of what he says, who fails to practise what he preaches
158 *Down with the nose* (referring to yet another effect of syphilis)

160   *his particular to foresee* in order to provide in advance for his private profit

161   *Smells from the general weal* goes hunting in a manner that is opposed to the welfare of society. The basic idea here is that of a hound that leaves the pack to follow a quarry of his own.

           curled-pate curly-headed

162   *the unscarred braggarts of the war* those who brag about their exploits in war yet have never been in danger of a wound

164   *defeat and quell* render impotent and destroy

165   *The source of all erection* the basic impulse from which the erection of the male sexual organ proceeds

166   *Do you* make it your business to

167   *grave* serve as graves for, entomb

169   *mischief* destruction, harm

           earnest the instalment of money necessary to engage your services, the money that makes the contract binding

170   *towards Athens* for our march towards Athens

172   *If I hope well* if my hopes are realized

175   *find it* find it true by experience

176   *Thy beagles* your small hounds. Timon means Phrynia and Timandra, of course, who are, in their way, just as much hunters of men as Alcibiades the soldier is in his.

177   *That nature* to think that my physical being

           sick of surfeited with

178   *Common mother* (the earth, mother of all things)

180   *Teems* brings forth, gives birth to

           mettle essential substances, life-giving principle

181   *Whereof* with which

           puffed inflated (with a sense of his own importance)

183   *eyeless venomed worm* blindworm or slow-worm. Like the toad and the newt, it was considered poisonous in Shakespeare's England, though, in fact, all three are quite harmless.

184   *crisp* shining, bright

185   *Hyperion* the sun. Hyperion was the sun-god in Greek mythology.

        quickening life-creating

186   *thy human sons doth hate*. The Folio reading is 'the humane Sonnes do hate', which does not fit the context of an address to the earth.

188   *Ensear* dry up. Compare *King Lear*, I.4.279: 'Dry up in her the organs of increase'.

        conceptious prolific

190   *Go great* become pregnant

191   *Teem with* be fruitful in, bring forth

        upward upturned

192   *marbled mansion all above* (sky)

        marbled shining like marble

194   *marrows*. The *marrows* referred to here are the secretions of marrow in the bones, used here in a figurative manner to denote the rich fertility of the earth as seen in her *vines and plough-torn leas*.

        leas fields

195   *Whereof* from which

        liquorish draughts pleasantly alcoholic drinks

196   *unctuous* rich in fat

        greases his pure mind makes his mind, that was originally pure, gross and lewd

197   *That* so that

        consideration capacity for moral reflection

200   *affect* deliberately imitate

202   *would* would prefer to

        Consumption catch thee ! may wasting disease lay hold on you!

203   *a nature but infected* merely an attitude of mind that you have caught by infection

204   *sprung* proceeding, resulting

205   *fortune*. The Folio reading is 'future', but *change of fortune* is what the play is about, and the emendation is accepted by most editors.

206   *habit* dress

208   *perfumes* perfumed mistresses

210   *putting on the cunning of a carper* assuming the role of a fault-finder

       cunning skill, professional expertise

212   *undone* ruined

       Hinge bend, make flexible

213   *let his very breath whom thou'lt observe* let the very breath of the man whose favours you are seeking to court

214   *strain* quality of character

215   *Thou wast told thus* you were told this kind of thing. There may also be a multiple quibble on 'tolled', meaning (1) allured, enticed into a trap; (2) taken toll of, fleeced.

216   *gavest thine ears* listened readily

220   *throw away myself* (as something utterly useless)

221   *like thyself* true to your own nature

222   *thinkest* do you think

223   *chamberlain* one who waits on a king or a lord in his bedchamber

224   *warm* warmed, carefully aired

       moist damp, dripping. Many editors emend to 'mossed' on the grounds that it is the great age of the trees that matters. This aspect of them is, however, sufficiently emphasized by the clause that follows; and, as the eighteenth-century critic Walter Whiter first pointed out, the words *warm* and *moist* were both associated with shirts. See Walter Whiter, *A Specimen of a Commentary on Shakespeare*, edited by Alan Over and Mary Bell (1967), pages 71–2.

225   *the eagle* (traditionally supposed to live to a great age)

       page thy heels follow at your heels like a page

226   *skip when thou pointest out* leap into action when you indicate

227   *Candied* congealed, encrusted

227–8   *caudle thy morning taste,* | *To cure thy o'ernight's surfeit* provide a warm medicinal drink for the filthy taste in

the mouth that you wake up with after the debauches
of the night before

228–32   *Call the creatures . . . mere nature.* Compare *King Lear*,
III.4.26–32:

> You houseless poverty –
> Nay, get thee in. I'll pray, and then I'll sleep.
> Poor naked wretches, wheresoe'er you are,
> That bide the pelting of this pitiless storm,
> How shall your houseless heads and unfed sides,
> Your looped and windowed raggedness, defend you
> From seasons such as these?

229   *Whose naked natures* who in their natural nakedness
    in exposed to

230   *wreakful* revengeful, vindictive
    unhousèd houseless, unsheltered
    trunks bodies (but Apemantus is probably thinking of
    the trees as well as of the animals)

232   *Answer mere nature* have to face nature as it really is

233   *of* in

236   *caitiff* contemptible wretch

239   *a knave too.* Timon has called Apemantus a fool at line
    233; now, by admitting that he takes pleasure in vexing
    others, Apemantus has proved himself to be a villain
    as well.

240   *habit* disposition, behaviour

241   *'twere well* it would be a good thing, it would do you
    credit

242   *enforcedly* by compulsion

243–4   *Willing misery | Outlives incertain pomp, is crowned
    before* the man who accepts a lowly condition of life is
    likely to outlive him who strives for a pomp that is
    bound to be uncertain of duration, and his desires are
    sooner completely satisfied. The advantages of a
    humble status in life were one of the great common-
    places of the age.

245   *The one* (incertain pomp)

245 *filling still* always needing more to fulfil its ambitions
  complete full

246 *at high wish* at the height of its wishes
  Best state, contentless a man in the most prosperous
  circumstances, if he is discontented

247 *distracted* harassed
  being existence

248 *Worse than the worst, content* far worse than the life of
  the poorest man who is contented with his lot

249 *being miserable* since you are utterly miserable yet not
  resigned to being so

250 *by his breath* by the persuasion of him

252–3 *clasped. But, bred a dog,* | *Hadst thou.* The Folio read-
  ing is 'claspt: but bred a Dogge. | Hadst thou', which
  editors render as 'clasped, but bred a dog. | Hadst
  thou'. The objection to this is that it gives the impression that Apemantus is entirely the victim of Fortune, which has not only denied him her favours but
  seen to it that he has been brought up like a dog.
  Timon's point, however, brought out by the reading
  adopted in this edition, is that while it is true that
  Fortune has never treated Apemantus kindly, his basic
  nature is such that had he been fortunate he would
  have been completely dissolute.

252 *bred a dog* being a dog by birth

253 *Hadst thou* even if you had
  first swath first swaddling-clothes (earliest infancy)
  proceeded (1) moved upward by, advanced by; (2) taken,
  gained (technical term used in universities for the
  taking of a degree)

254 *degrees* (1) steps, stages; (2) academic degrees
  brief world affords short life on earth offers

255 *drudges.* The reading of the Folio is 'drugges', an
  Elizabethan spelling of *drudges*; but there may be a
  quibble on 'drugs', meaning 'poisons' in the form of
  riches.
  it (the world)

257   *riot* debauchery

      melted down thy youth wasted your youthful vigour away

259   *icy precepts of respect* chilling commands of rational moral reflection

260   *sugared game* sweetly tempting quarry (mistresses)

261   *confectionary* (1) place where sweetmeats are kept; (2) maker of sweetmeats

263   *At duty* at my service

      frame employment find employment for

264   *That*. The construction of this long sentence changes at this point, so that it is necessary to understand some such word as 'these' to provide an antecedent. The sense is 'these men that'.

264–7   *That numberless . . . that blows*. A close parallel to this passage occurs in *Cymbeline*, III.3.60–64, where Belarius says:

> Then was I as a tree
> Whose boughs did bend with fruit; but in one night
> A storm, or robbery, call it what you will,
> Shook down my mellow hangings, nay, my leaves,
> And left me bare to weather.

265   *one winter's brush* a single wintry onset, one wintry storm

266   *Fell* fallen

      open exposed

      bare (1) naked; (2) unprotected, unarmed

267   *I to bear* that I should have to bear, for me to bear

268   *That never knew but better* who have only known better circumstances

269   *nature* physical existence

      sufferance suffering, enduring hardship

270   *hard in't* hardened in it, inured to it

272   *rag* worthless object

273   *in spite* out of spite (as distinct from love), against her will

273–4   *put stuff | To* copulated with
274   *compounded* composed, begot
275   *hereditary* by right of inheritance, because your father was one
276   *worst* basest, lowest in worldly position
278   *yet* still, even now
281   *shut up* enclosed, summed up
283   *That* would that, if only
284   *mend* improve
285   *my*. The Folio reads 'thy', but the sense demands *my*.
287   *mended* repaired
        botched cobbled, clumsily repaired (because Apemantus will still have to endure the company of himself)
288   *If not, I would it were*. This is a very puzzling line. Timon is not likely to admit the possibility that Apemantus might find his own company anything but intolerable. It therefore seems better to take *it* here as a reference to Timon's own state, giving the sense 'if my company is not to be mended by your absence, I can only wish that it were'.
289   *have to Athens* have done in Athens, wish to be carried out for you in Athens. Timon, quibbling, takes it in the sense 'like to be sent to Athens'.
294   *a-nights* at night
295   *that's above me* that which is above me (the sky)
296   *a-days* by day
297   *meat* food
301   *sauce* give a relish to
302   *humanity* human existence
305   *curiosity* fastidiousness, attention to fashion
306   *medlar* (fruit like a small apple, not ripe for eating till nearly rotten)
310   *though it look like thee*. Timon is being ironical; he means 'especially as it looks like you', and he is referring to (1) the rottenness of the fruit; (2) the use of 'meddler' to denote one given to sexual promiscuity.

311   *An* if
      meddlers intriguers, self-interested busybodies

312-14 *What man didst thou ever know unthrift that was beloved*
      after his means? what man did you ever know to be a
      prodigal who was loved in proportion to his means?
      The point Apemantus is making is that the rational
      man gives in proportion to his means; only the foolish
      spendthrift allows himself to be flattered into giving
      beyond them.

318-19 *thou hadst some means to keep a dog.* The best way to
      understand this is to take the *dog* as a reference to
      Apemantus himself, whom Timon has called a dog at
      line 252. Timon is saying that only Apemantus loves
      Apemantus.

326-7 *fall in the confusion of men* degenerate into a beast in
      the general ruin of mankind

334-5 *still thou livedst but* you would always be living merely

337-9 *Wert thou the unicorn ... conquest of thy fury.* Timon is
      alluding to the tradition that the hunter captured the
      unicorn by standing in front of a tree and annoying the
      legendary beast. It charged; the hunter skipped away
      at the last moment; and the unicorn, embedding its
      horn in the tree, was at the hunter's mercy.

339-40 *Wert thou a bear, thou wouldst be killed by the horse.*
      According to Elizabethan beast lore, there was mortal
      hatred between the horse and the bear.

342   *german to* closely akin to

342-3 *the spots of thy kindred were jurors on thy life* the crimes
      of your cousin the lion would condemn you to death.
      There is a quibble on the spots, meaning 'vices', of the
      lion and the physical spots on the leopard's skin.

344   *remotion* taking yourself off, keeping out of the way

346-7 *that seest not thy loss in transformation* since you don't
      see how much you would lose by being turned into a
      beast

353   *Yonder comes a poet and a painter.* As these two charac-
      ters do not appear until V.1.1, it looks as though

Shakespeare changed his mind about their entry but failed to delete these misleading words.

355   *give way* retire, leave the place to them

360   *cap* top, chief

363   *do stand by* are compared with

377–82   *I am sick . . . may laugh.* These six lines look forward to the end of the play. For the time being at least, Timon's rage has blown itself out.

378   *But even* except only

        mere necessities absolute requirements. Timon is apparently thinking of the need to prepare for his own death.

379   *presently* immediately, at once

382   *death in me* death through me

383   *divorce* cause of separation

384   *natural* truly begotten. Shakespeare does not use 'natural' in the sense of 'illegitimate'.

385   *Hymen* (Greek and Roman god of marriage)

        Mars. The allusion here is to the adultery of Mars, the Roman god of war, with Venus, the goddess of beauty. They were caught in bed together by Venus's husband Vulcan.

387   *blush* (referring to the ruddy shine of gold)

387–8   *the consecrated snow | That lies on Dian's lap.* Diana was a virgin goddess and the patron of chastity. Shakespeare also associates her with the purity of snow in *Coriolanus* (V.3.65–7), where the hero addresses Valeria as

> The moon of Rome, chaste as the icicle
> That's curdied by the frost from purest snow
> And hangs on Dian's temple. . . .

As well as Diana, however, Shakespeare seems to have had at the back of his mind the myth of Danaë whom Jupiter seduced by appearing to her in a shower of gold.

389   *close* closely, firmly together

        impossibilities things apparently incapable of union

391   *touch* touchstone, tester of the true quality

392-3   *by thy virtue | Set them into confounding odds* by your power set men at such variance with each other that they utterly destroy themselves

393   *that* so that

398   *quit* rid of him

399   *More things like men! Eat, Timon, and abhor them.* This line is given to Apemantus in the Folio, but many editors assign it to Timon, on the grounds that Apemantus has already gone, though the Folio marks his exit at the end of it. The alteration ignores the depth of Shakespeare's stage. What happens is that Apemantus, who has been playing at the front of the stage with Timon, turns to go at the end of line 397; but, as he makes his way to the exit door at one side of the back wall, he sees the Bandits coming in at the other door and speaks this line to Timon as he is going out. The Bandits, on entering, do not move to the front of the stage immediately, but talk among themselves until they notice the figure at the front of the stage, decide that it is Timon, and then come forward.

  them. The Folio reads 'then', which is possible if *abhor* is taken in the intransitive sense of 'shrink with horror', but an action demanding an object seems more appropriate.

400   *Where should he have* whence can he have obtained

401   *slender ort of his remainder* tiny scrap of the remnant of his fortune

402   *mere want* absolute need, total lack

  falling-from falling-off, desertion

404   *noised* rumoured

405   *make the assay* make the test (technical term for deciding, by use of the touchstone, the amount of pure metal in an ore or alloy)

406   *for't* for it (the gold)

407   *shall's* shall we

411   THIRD BANDIT. The Folio reads '*All*'; but this cannot be correct as the First Bandit has already seen Timon

233

and the Second is aware that the man they are looking
at answers to the description they have of him.

416   *Both two* both. This emphatic form was common in
Elizabethan English.

417   *much do want* (1) are in desperate need (what the
Bandits mean); (2) want a great deal (the sense in
which Timon takes it)

418   *Your greatest want is, you want much of meat* your main
need arises from the fact that you want so much food

419–23 *Behold, the earth . . . before you.* In contrast to the world
dominated by the love of gold, in which he is living,
Timon paints a vivid picture of the Golden Age, when
there was no use of gold.

421   *mast* acorns

423   *full mess* plenteous course of dishes

427   *thanks I must you con* I must express my thanks to
you

430   *limited professions* professions to which the entry is
limited and that pay lip service to a code of conduct
Rascal good for nothing

431   *subtle* (1) fine, delicate; (2) treacherous
blood o'th'grape (wine)

432   *high fever* violent fever (brought on by intoxication)
seethe your blood to froth dissipates the vitality of your
blood by overheating it and turning it into froth

433   *'scape hanging* escape hanging (by dying of the fever)

433–5 *Trust not the physician . . . you rob.* The idea that the
physician killed more patients than he cured was a
commonplace of the time when Shakespeare was
writing. The abrupt transition from the subject of intoxication to that of doctors may have been suggested
by the proverb 'There are more old drunkards than old
physicians'.

435   *Take wealth and lives together.* As Sir Thomas More
had pointed out in his *Utopia* (1516), the fact that the
punishment for theft was hanging made it logical that
the thief should kill the man he robbed, since it dis-

posed of the main evidence against him without increasing the penalty.

436   *protest* openly profess

437   *example you with* provide you with precedents for

439   *arrant* notorious, confirmed. The moon was regarded as the planet that ruled over thieves. Compare the exchanges between Falstaff and Hal in *1 Henry IV* (I.2.25–33), where Falstaff speaks of 'our noble and chaste mistress the moon, under whose countenance we steal'.

441–2   *The sea's a thief, whose liquid surge resolves | The moon into salt tears.* The theory current in Shakespeare's day to explain the phenomenon of the sea's tidal flow was that the sea attracted moisture from the watery planet, the moon. The correct explanation was first put forward by Kepler in 1609, soon after *Timon of Athens* was written.

441   *resolves* dissolves, melts

443   *composture* compost, manure

444   *general excrement* the excrement of the universe. The earth was thought of as a general dunghill. Shakespeare's contemporary, John Marston, in his play *The Malcontent* (1604), writes: 'this earth is the only grave and Golgotha, wherein all things that live must rot; 'tis but the draught [privy] wherein the heavenly bodies discharge their corruption, the very muckhill on which the sublunary orbs cast their excrement' (IV.5).

445   *your curb and whip* which restrain and whip you

445–6   *in their rough power | Has unchecked theft* provide opportunities for unlimited theft to those who administer them arbitrarily. The main idea stated here is the same as that put forward in *King Lear*, IV.6.163: 'The usurer hangs the cozener'.

446   *Has.* The third person plural in '–s' is common in Shakespeare; but in this case the preceding singular noun *power* has probably attracted the form of the verb to it.

235

450–51   *Steal less for this I give you,* | *And gold confound you howsoe'er* if you steal any the less on account of what I am giving you, may gold bring you to ruin no matter what you do

452   *'Has* he has

454   *in the malice of mankind* because of his hatred for mankind

455   *mystery* profession

456   *as an enemy* as I would an enemy (that is, not at all)

458–9   *There is no time so miserable but a man may be true* no matter how bad things may become there is always time to turn honest. The First Bandit means that there will be plenty of time for thinking about turning over a new leaf when the opportunities for theft and looting offered by civil war come to an end.

461   *yond despised and ruinous man* that despised ruin of a man over there. Flavius views Timon as though he were the ruins of a great house.

462–3   *monument* | *And wonder* shocking reminder, astonishing memorial

463   *evilly bestowed* badly misplaced, conferred on wicked men

464   *alteration of honour* decline from a state of honour

468–9   *How rarely does it meet with this time's guise,* | *When man was wished to love his enemies!* how perfectly does the commandment that a man should love his enemies fit in with the practice of the present time! (since it is a fatal mistake to love one's 'friends')

471   *Those that would mischief me than those that do* those who wish to do me harm than those who actually do me harm

472   *'Has* he has

477   *th' art* (colloquial) thou art

483   *wear* have, feel

484   *undone* ruined

487   *Flinty* hard-hearted, as hard as flint
       give exude moisture as a stone floor will

488   *But thorough* except through, except when moved by

492   *entertain me* keep me in your service

494   *comfortable* ready to afford help or comfort

495   *dangerous* savage, disposed to violence

       mild. The Folio reads 'wilde', giving the possible sense of 'distracted, mad'; but something completely opposed to *dangerous* seems to be required.

498   *exceptless* indiscriminate, making no allowance for exceptions

502   *fain* gladly, readily

504   *fell* cut down

505   *wise* wise in the ways of the world, prudent

506   *oppressing* tyrannizing over

507   *service* position, situation

508   *so arrive at* thus obtain, thus make their way to

509   *Upon their first lord's neck* by treading on the neck of their first lord

511   *subtle-covetous* the last refinement of insidious covetousness

512   *A usuring kindness* a kindness that expects to be rewarded with interest. The Folio reads 'If not a Vsuring kindnesse'; but the 'If not' ruins the metre and does not help the sense.

515   *suspect* suspicion

516   *feared false times* feared that the occasions were deceptive

517   *Suspect still comes where an estate is least* suspicion always comes when a man's fortune is at its lowest ebb

518   *merely* purely, nothing but

520   *Care of* concern for, solicitude for

       living maintenance

522   *For* as for

       points to is destined for, looks likely to come

523–4   *I'd exchange | For* I'd exchange it for

526   *singly* uniquely

528   *Ha'* (colloquial) have. The Folio reading is 'Ha's', which is clumsy, especially before *sent*.

529 *But thus conditioned* but on this condition
   build from men build your house remote from human
   society

533–4 *Let prisons swallow 'em, | Debts wither 'em to nothing.*
   The debtors' prison was one of the horrors of Elizabethan life. Mosca, in Ben Jonson's *Volpone* (I.1.44–7),
   describes extortioners who

> Tear forth the fathers of poor families
> Out of their beds, and coffin them, alive,
> In some kind, clasping prison, where their bones
> May be forth-coming, when the flesh is rotten.

534 *Be men* let men be

540 (stage direction) *Exit Flavius; Timon retires to his cave
   at the rear of the stage.* The Folio reads '*Exit*' here,
   giving Timon an entry '*from his Caue*' at V.1.28. But,
   since he overhears most, if not all, of the conversation
   with which V.1 begins, it is clear that he never leaves
   the stage at all but merely takes up a position where he
   is unnoticed by the Poet and the Painter as they come
   in.

V.1 The entry of the Poet and the Painter, anticipated at
   IV.3.353 but then postponed, follows immediately on
   the departure of Flavius. There is no break in the
   action and no change of location here, though the
   return of these two characters does serve to bring the
   play back to its beginning, thus suggesting that the final
   phase is near.

3–37 *What's to be thought ... I have gold for thee.* In the
   Folio this piece of dialogue is printed as irregular verse.

5–6 *Phrynia and Timandra.* The Folio has the very odd
   reading '*Phrinica* and *Timandylo*', which does not look
   like a compositor's error.

6 *of him* from him

6–7 *poor straggling soldiers* (the Bandits, who call themselves
   soldiers at IV.3.416)

7   *straggling* straying

9   *breaking* going bankrupt

        but a try for merely a test of

11–12   *a palm in Athens again, and flourish with the highest*
        (probably an allusion to Psalm 92.12: 'The righteous
        shall flourish like a palm tree')

13   *we tender* that we should offer

14   *show honestly in us* appear an honourable action on our
        part

15–16   *to load our purposes with what they travail for* to reward
        our designs amply with just the things those designs
        are labouring to obtain

16   *goes of his having* is current about his wealth

18   *only* but

19   *piece* painting

20   *intent* projected work

21   *coming toward* intended for

22   *Good as the best* that's fine, couldn't be better
        air style, fashion

24   *his act* its doing, its being carried out

25   *the deed of saying* the doing of what one says one will
        do, keeping one's promises

26   *out of use* no longer practised

28   (stage direction) *Enter Timon from his cave.* Since
        Timon has heard the Painter's remarks, '*Enter*' in this
        Folio direction must mean 'show himself'.

31   *provided* planned in imagination

32   *a personating of himself* a symbolic representation of his
        own situation

33   *the softness of prosperity* the weak and gullible outlook
        created by a life of ease
        discovery disclosure, revelation, exposure

35   *Must thou needs* can't you help, are you compelled to
        stand for serve as a model for. Timon is emphasizing
        that the work the Poet intends to write will be a super-
        lative example of the flattery the Poet means to attack
        in it.

39-40   *Then do we sin against our own estate, | When we may*
        profit meet and come too late we commit a crime against
        our own creed of self-interest when we have a chance
        to do good to ourselves and let it go by

42-3   *When the day serves, before black-cornered night, | Find*
        what thou wantest by free and offered light when you
        have the chance to get what you want by the open light
        of day don't wait for night to come to shroud what you
        are doing. In Shakespeare's work generally, and par-
        ticularly in *Macbeth*, day is seen as hostile to crime and
        night as friendly to it; but in this case, suggests the
        Painter, Timon is so gullible that there is no need to
        wait for the cover of night before taking advantage of
        him, since it can be done better by daylight.

42   *serves* is convenient
        black-cornered full of dark lurking-places

45   *I'll meet you at the turn* I'll take you on at your own
        game. Compare *Hamlet*, III.4.209-10: 'O, 'tis most
        sweet | When in one line two crafts directly meet'. The
        turn referred to here is (1) the corner implicit in line
        42; (2) a subtle device.

46   *a baser temple* (the human body)

48   *'Tis thou that riggest the bark and ploughest the foam.*
        This is an interesting comment on the motives that led
        the Elizabethan seamen to make their voyages of dis-
        covery. It is not surprising, in the light of *aperçus* such
        as this, that Karl Marx found *Timon of Athens* so
        congenial.

49   *admirèd reverence* reverence full of wonder
        a slave your slave (the servile man who worships
        money)

50-51   *thy saints for aye | Be crowned with plagues, that thee*
        alone obey may your saints, who obey you only, be
        crowned with plagues to all eternity

52   *Fit I* the right moment has come for me to

54   *once* actually, really

56   *open* generous, liberal

57   *were retired* had withdrawn from society
        fall'n off become estranged from you

58–60   *Whose thankless natures . . . What, to you.* The mingling
        of two constructions here is probably deliberate on
        Shakespeare's part, in order to convey the insincerity
        of the Poet's simulated indignation. What the Poet
        means is 'for whose thankless natures . . . what, thank-
        less to you'.

61   *star-like* (1) shining like a star; (2) working like a star
        influence. The technical astrological term for the effect
        that the stars were supposed to exercise on human be-
        ings is appropriate here, since Timon's nobleness has
        just been called *star-like*.

62   *rapt* beside myself (with indignation)

64   *size* (1) quantity; (2) glutinous wash applied by painters
        to paper or canvas

65   *Let it go naked* if you let it go naked. Timon is quibbling
        on *bulk* in the sense of 'body', and he is also referring
        to the proverb 'The Truth shows best being naked'.

67   *them* (the thankless 'friends' you speak of)

76–7   *therefore | Came not my friend nor I* that is not the
        reason why my friend and I came

78   *counterfeit* (1) likeness, portrait; (2) spurious imitation,
        forgery

80   *Thou counterfeitest most lively* (1) you paint the most
        life-like portraits; (2) you put on a most convincing act
        (in pretending to be honest)
        So, so indifferently well

81   *fiction* (1) imaginative invention; (2) deceit, lies

82   *stuff* matter, ideas
        fine (1) refined, elegantly stated; (2) subtle, deceptive
        smooth (1) smooth-flowing; (2) flattering

83   *thou art even natural in thine art* your art has become
        second nature to you
        art (1) art as a poet; (2) artifice, art of lying

86   *Marry* indeed, to be sure
        monstrous unnatural, shockingly unexpected

87	*mend* remedy what is amiss
90	*Doubt it not* have no fear on that score
93	*cog* tell cheating lies
94	*patchery* roguery
95	*Keep* keep him. The construction is awkward and does not harmonize with the rest of the sentence. The suggestion of the New Cambridge editor, that 'Let him keep', meaning 'let him dwell', would give a complete verse line and make better sense, is an attractive one.
96	*made-up* complete, out-and-out
99	*Rid me* if you will do me the service of getting rid of
100	*draught* privy, jakes
101	*Confound* destroy
	course means
104	*You that way, and you this – but two in company* if you go that way and you this, there will still be two together (because each of them takes his own villainous self with him)
107	*If, where thou art, two villains shall not be* if there are not to be two villains wherever you go
109	*But* except
110	*pack* clear out, be off
111	*work* (the *excellent piece* the Painter talked of at line 19)
112	*an alchemist.* Timon calls the Poet an alchemist because he uses words in order to convert one thing into another, just as the alchemist was supposed to be able to convert base metals into gold. Shakespeare seems to have associated alchemy with flattery – see Sonnets 33 and 114.
114	*It is in vain.* The Folio reading is 'It is vaine'; but *in vain* is the normal Shakespearian usage, and it makes the line metrically better.
115	*set so only to himself* so wholly wrapped up in himself
117	*friendly* on terms of friendship
118	*our part and promise to th'Athenians* the part we have promised the Athenians we will play

120   *still* always, constantly

121   *framed him thus* made him what he is, moulded him into this shape

        Time, with his fairer hand. Time in Renaissance art had a double face; it was both destroyer and creator – the cause of suffering and death, but also of joy and life. See *The Winter's Tale*, IV.1, and also Erwin Panofsky, *Studies in Iconology* (1939), Chapter 3.

124   *chance it* let it fall out, let things happen

129   *that comforts* that comfortest, that cheerest

131   *cantherizing* cauterizing, searing with a hot iron. Many editors emend to 'cauterizing', but the form 'cantherizing' appears to have existed in Shakespeare's day as a confusion of 'cauterizing' and 'cantharides'.

132   *Worthy* (1) excellent, noble (the sense in which the Senator uses it); (2) deserving (the sense in which Timon takes it)

133   *Of none but such as you, and you of Timon* I have deserved to be punished by having you inflicted on me, and you deserve me as your scourge

137   *What we are sorry for ourselves in thee* what we ourselves are sorry for in your case (that is, the wrongs we have done you)

138   *with one consent* with a unanimous voice

139   *thee back* you to come back

        who and they

139–40   *thought | On* remembered, called to mind

140   *dignities* high offices

141   *For thy best use and wearing* until you, who are best fitted for them, assume them

142   *forgetfulness* neglect, ingratitude

        general-gross universally blatant

143   *Which* as to which, so that. This loose and ungrammatical use of 'which' is fairly common in Shakespeare, who frequently writes as people speak.

        public body state

145   *withal* moreover, in addition

146   *it* its

      fault. The Folio reads 'fall', which is just possible in the sense of 'fall from grace', though this seems excessive in the context. But there appears to have been some confusion of the two words in Shakespeare's England; Evans in *The Merry Wives of Windsor* (I.1.230–31) uses 'fall' for 'fault' when he says: 'It is a fery discretion answer, save the fall is in the ord "dissolutely" . . .'.

      restraining in withholding

147   *sorrowed* sorrowful

      render rendering of the account, admission of their debt

148   *fruitful* plenteous

149   *can weigh down by the dram* can equal when scrupulously weighed out by the dram

150   *heaps and sums of love and wealth*. The characteristic Athenian confusion between love and wealth, and their notion that love can be measured and bought, still persist.

152–3   *And write in thee the figures of their love, | Ever to read them thine*. Shakespeare is bringing out still further the absurdity of the Athenian equation of love and money. The citizens are asking Timon to regard himself as a sort of walking account-book in which he will find the amount of the Athenians' love for him written down, with the assurance that they are his for ever.

153   *witch me in it* enchant me with the prospect

156   *beweep these comforts* weep over this joyful news

157   *so please thee to* if you will please

159   *captainship* leadership, command

160   *Allowed* invested

162   *Of Alcibiades th'approaches wild* the violent attack of Alcibiades

171   *stain* disgraceful pollution

172   *contumelious* insolent, insulting

176   *let him take't at worst* let him put the worst construction

on it, make the worst possible interpretation of my statement that I care not

their knives (the knives of Alcibiades's men)

177 *to answer* to take the consequences, for those knives to cut

178 *whittle* clasp-knife

179 *But I do prize it at my love before* that I do not value in terms of my love above

181 *prosperous* propitious, favourable

182 *As thieves to keepers* as I would leave thieves to the mercy of their gaolers (who would show them none)

183 *Why, I was writing of my epitaph.* The transition of ideas at this point is very abrupt indeed. It is as though Timon suddenly recollects the serious business that he must have been engaged on before Flavius and the Senators arrived. He is looking forward to death; and the meditative tone is sustained through the next three lines, until he turns to the Senators again.

184-6 *My long sickness ... all things.* The idea of life as a continued disease from which death was the only deliverance was a commonplace of the time. Shakespeare gives memorable expression to it in the Duke's speech 'Be absolute for death ... That makes these odds all even' (*Measure for Measure*, III.1.5–41).

185 *mend* improve, get better

186 *nothing* oblivion

188 *last so long enough* continue in that state for as long a time as possible. The idea here is the same as the wish that Alcibiades expresses about the Senators at III.5.105–6.

190 *the common wrack* the destruction of the commonwealth

191 *common bruit* popular rumour

193 *become* do credit to

194 *triumphers* generals granted a Roman triumph

195 *applauding gates* gates crowded with applauding citizens

196 *ease them of* give them relief from

197 *aches* (pronounced 'aitches')

199 *nature's fragile vessel* (the human body)
  sustain suffer, undergo

201 *prevent* (1) anticipate (which is what Timon means);
  (2) avoid, frustrate (which is what the Senators think
  he means)

203–10 *I have a tree . . . And hang himself.* This passage is very
  close to one in Plutarch's *Life of Marcus Antonius*,
  which runs as follows in North's translation:

> 'It is reported of him also that this Timon on a time,
> the people being assembled in the market-place
> about dispatch of some affairs, got up into the pulpit
> for orations, where the orators commonly use to
> speak unto the people; and silence being made, every
> man listening to hear what he would say, because it
> was a wonder to see him in that place, at length he
> began to speak in this manner:
>
> ' "My Lords of Athens, I have a little yard in my
> house, where there groweth a fig tree, on the which
> many citizens have hanged themselves; and because
> I mean to make some building on the place, I thought
> good to let you all understand it that, before the fig
> tree be cut down, if any of you be desperate, you
> may there in time go hang yourselves." '
>
>   (*Shakespeare's Plutarch*, edited by
>   T. J. B. Spencer (1964), page 265)

203 *close* enclosure, ground about a house

204 *use* need

206 *in the sequence of degree* in the proper order of precedence

207–8 *that whoso please | To stop affliction, let him take his haste.*
  There is a mixture of two different grammatical con-
  structions here, of a kind fairly common in Shakespeare, resulting from a change of thought in mid-
  stream. But the sense is clear enough.
  whoso please | To stop affliction whoever may feel like
  putting an end to his miseries

208   *take his haste* hurry up (opposite of 'take his time')

210   *do my greeting* give the message with my kind regards

211   *still* always

213   *everlasting mansion* (grave)

214   *beachèd verge* beach that is the verge, shore

215   *Who* whom, and him (Timon). William Painter, in the account of Timon that he includes in his *The Palace of Pleasure* (1566), writes: 'By his last will, he ordained himself to be interred upon the sea-shore, that the waves and surges might beat and vex his dead carcass' (*Narrative and Dramatic Sources of Shakespeare*, edited by Geoffrey Bullough, Volume 6 (1966), page 294).

      embossèd foaming, full of foam. The word 'embossed' was normally used about a hunted animal foaming at the mouth with exhaustion.

218   *let four words go by, and language end* let a few final words pass, and then let speech cease. There are many instances in Shakespeare and other Elizabethan writers of 'four' being used for an indefinite number.

219   *What is amiss, plague and infection mend!* may plague and infection put right that which is wrong!

221   (stage direction) *Exit*. The Folio has '*Exit Timon*'. As a stage direction, this is unique in Shakespeare's work, for Timon is the only tragic hero – if he is a tragic hero – who leaves the stage for the last time by walking off it, instead of being carried from it.

222–3   *His discontents are unremovably | Coupled to nature* his bitter thoughts are part and parcel of his nature

226   *dear* extreme, grievous

      swift foot haste, speedy action

V.2   It is here that the action of the play moves into its final phase. The last three scenes are necessary, in order to explain what has happened to Timon and to bring the story of Alcibiades to a conclusion, but, since Timon himself is no longer present, they cannot help but appear somewhat anticlimactic. Moreover, the presentation of the Athenians in the earlier part of the play works strongly against the development of any real concern for them or their fate now.

1 THIRD SENATOR. The Folio has the speech heading '1' here, and '2' at line 5. The Senators have been renumbered in this edition in order to avoid confusion between them and the two who return from their embassy to Timon at line 13.

painfully discovered done some painstaking reconnoitring

1–2 *Are his files | As full* are his ranks as full, are the numbers of his men as great

2 *spoke the least* stated the lowest estimate

3–4 *his expedition promises | Present approach* the speed of his advance makes an immediate attack likely

5 *stand much hazard* face great danger

6 *courier* messenger sent in haste

one mine ancient friend a former friend of mine

7 *Whom* on whom

in general part in public affairs, in matters of general concern

8 *made a particular force* exerted a strong personal effect

11 *imported* expressed a request for

12 *fellowship* participation

i'th'cause in the movement

13 *moved* set on foot, initiated

14 FIRST SENATOR. The Folio has '3'; but the character is clearly the First Senator of the previous scene.

15 *scouring* violent aggressive movement by the enemy

16 *In* let us go in

17 *Ours is the fall, I fear; our foe's the snare* our role, I fear, is to fall into the trap; our enemy's to set it for us. The form *foe's* is demanded by the antithesis, though the Folio 'Foes' could mean either 'foe's' or 'foes'.

248

V.3   (stage direction) *a Soldier.* This soldier must be the *courier* referred to at V.2.6.

3–4   *Timon is dead . . . live a man.* There is nothing in the Folio to indicate that these two lines are an inscription, beyond the fact that both the sentiments and the style of them are Timon's, but it is hard to see what else they can be. The problem raised by the Soldier's reading out these lines and then failing to read what is written on the tomb, can be got over if it is assumed that this passage is in his own language – English – whereas the words on the tomb are in Latin, the usual language for epitaphs on the great in Shakespeare's England. In any case Shakespeare never seems to have made up his mind as to exactly what was to be written on Timon's tomb (see note to V.4.70–73).

    outstretched his span measured out his short span of life to its end

4   *there does not live a man* there is not a real man left alive to read it

6   *The character I'll take with wax* I'll make a waxen impression of the lettering

7   *hath in every figure skill* is adept at deciphering every kind of writing

8   *aged* experienced

9   *Before proud Athens he's set down by this* by this time he has already laid siege to proud Athens. To 'set down before' a place was the technical term for besieging it.

10   *Whose fall* the fall of which
    mark goal

V.4   This final scene brings about that restoration of order and peaceful living which is the normal conclusion of a Shakespeare tragedy, and, at the same time, establishes the moderation of Alcibiades, in contrast to the extremism of Timon which has been the main theme.
    (stage direction) *Powers* armed forces, army

1   *Sound* proclaim by a blast on the trumpets
        coward cowardly
2   *terrible* terrifying
        (stage direction) *upon the walls.* The upper stage or
        balcony of the Elizabethan theatre was frequently used
        to represent the walls of a town. A close parallel to the
        staging of this scene is to be found in *Coriolanus*, I.4.
4   *With all licentious measure* with every degree of licence
5   *The scope of justice* the equivalent of justice, the limits
        within which justice operated
6   *stepped.* The Folio has 'slept', which has been interpreted as 'lived'; but *stepped*, conveying the sense of an
        unguarded movement, fits Alcibiades's case far better,
        and the confusion of 'stept' and 'slept' would be an
        easy one for the compositor to make. There may also
        be a suggestion of the victim stepping within the magic
        circle drawn by a malevolent conjurer.
7   *traversed arms* arms folded (a sign of dejection)
7–8   *breathed | Our sufferance vainly* complained in vain
        about our sufferings
8   *flush* full to the brim, ripe for action
9   *crouching marrow in the bearer strong* the hitherto submissive spirit of the strong man
10   *of itself* spontaneously, of its own accord
        breathless wrong (abstract 'breathless injustice' for
        concrete 'your unjust senators out of breath through
        fear')
12   *pursy* (1) fat and short-winded; (2) purse-proud
        insolence the tyrants (abstract for concrete)
        break his wind gasp for breath
14   *griefs* grievances
        conceit fancy, idea
16   *sent to thee* sent messages to you
        balm a lenitive, a soothing ointment
18   *Above their quantity* greater in quantity than they were.
        The antecedent of *their* is not clear; it could be Alcibiades's *griefs* or his *rages.*

20   *promised means* the promise of wealth (referring back to the *heaps and sums of love and wealth* at V.1.150)

22   *The common stroke of war* the indiscriminate punishment war inflicts on all alike

23   *their hands* the hands of those men

24   *grief* cause of grievance
     they (those men)

25   *trophies* monuments

26   *private* personal, individual

27   *motives that you first went out* instigators of your original banishment

28-9 *Shame, that they wanted cunning, in excess | Hath broke their hearts* the unbearable shame they felt for their lack of cunning has broken their hearts. In the Folio this passage reads: '(Shame that they wanted, cunning in excesse) | Hath broke their hearts'; but it seems essential that *in excess* should go with *Shame*, since it was thought that an extremity of passion could cause the heart literally to burst. The senators who banished Alcibiades *wanted cunning* because they did it in such a way as to leave him with both the justification and the means to organize a revolt.

31   *tithèd death* the death of one in every ten. This phrase is an English equivalent of the learned word *decimation*. Shakespeare rather likes to follow a Latinate word with what is in effect a native English translation of it; compare *Macbeth*, II.2.61-3:

> No, this my hand will rather
> The multitudinous seas incarnadine,
> Making the green one red.

32-3 *that food | Which nature loathes* (human bodies). The imagery of food and eating, which is so characteristic of the play, is given an unexpected twist here.

34   *spotted die* dice that has spots on it

35   *the spotted* the guilty. The task of deciding who the

guilty are is to be left to the gods, who will control the way the dice turn up.

36 *were* were alive and are now dead
square right, just

37 *are* are alive now
revenges. The Folio has 'Reuenge', which is unmetrical; and it is *revenges* that are mentioned at line 32.

37–8 *Crimes like lands | Are not inherited* crimes are not inherited like lands. In modern English we should say 'unlike lands'.

39 *ranks* troops
without outside

40 *thy Athenian cradle* Athens your birthplace

41 *in the bluster of thy wrath* if your wrath storms on its way without restraint. A *bluster* is a 'wild storm' or 'tempest'.

43 *cull th'infected forth* identify and bring out the tainted

44 *What thou wilt* whatever it is you want

46 *hew to't* hew your way to it
Set but merely set, only set

47 *rampired gates* gates fortified against attack by having earth piled up behind them
ope open

48 *So* provided that
thou wilt send thy gentle heart before you will give us assurance of your kind intentions first

49 *friendly* in a friendly manner

50 *any token of thine honour else* any other token pledging your honour

52 *confusion* ruin, destruction
powers military forces

53 *make their harbour* find safe lodging

54 *sealed thy full desire* formally ratified all your demands

55 *uncharged ports* unassailed gates

57 *set out for reproof* pick out for punishment

58 *Fall* let them fall

58–9 *to atone your fears | With my more noble meaning* to

252

appease your fears with a statement of my intentions
which are nobler than you think

60   *pass his quarter* go outside the area allotted to his unit

60–61 *offend the stream | Of regular justice* commit an offence
that violates the drift of established laws

62   *But shall be* without being

     remanded sent back, handed over. The Folio reads
'remedied', which has been interpreted to mean
'handed over for remedy (or punishment)', though it is
hard to find a parallel for this use of 'remedy'. Most
editors emend to 'rendered'; but *remanded* has the
advantage of being a legal word, which the context
demands, and it is at least as plausible from the
graphical point of view.

63   *At heaviest answer* to pay the utmost penalty the law
exacts

64   (stage direction) *Soldier*. The Folio has '*a Messenger*';
but, from what he says, it is clear that he is the soldier
of V.3.

66   *hem* edge, shore

67   *insculpture* carved inscription

69   *Interprets* serves as interpreter (probably pronounced as
four syllables)

70–73 *Here lies . . . thy gait.* These two couplets contradict
each other. The first says *Seek not my name*; the second
Here lie I Timon. Both occur in Plutarch's *Life* of
Antony, except that there the *caitiffs* of line 71 reads
'wretches'. According to Plutarch, the first couplet was
the work of Timon himself, while the second was
'made by the poet Callimachus' (*Shakespeare's Plutarch*, pages 265–6). What seems to have happened is
that Shakespeare copied down both epitaphs, intending to delete one of them when he had decided which
suited his purpose better, but that he never got round
to doing so.

70   *corse* corpse

71   *caitiffs* villains, wretches

73   *stay not here thy gait* don't check your course here

74   *These* these words

        latter spirits more recent sentiments

76   *brains' flow* tears wrung from our brains

        droplets little tears (in contrast to the perpetual ebb and flow of the sea)

77   *niggard nature* parsimonious human nature

        rich conceit your bounteous imagination

78   *Neptune* (god of the sea in classical mythology)

        for aye for ever

82   *use the olive with my sword* combine peace with war, be merciful while exercising power

83   *stint* put an end to, check

84   *leech* physician. The idea that peace cures war is common enough, but the Elizabethans also thought that prolonged peace could lead to idleness and faction for which the only cure was war. Shakespeare's contemporary Thomas Nashe, in his *Pierce Penilesse* (1592), writes: 'There is a certain waste of the people for whom there is no use, but war: and these men must have some employment still to cut them off. . . . If they have no service abroad, they will make mutinies at home' (*The Works of Thomas Nashe*, edited by R. B. McKerrow (1904–10), Volume I, page 211). Hamlet gives utterance to a similar idea when he comments on the expedition of Fortinbras:

> This is th'imposthume of much wealth and peace,
> That inward breaks, and shows no cause without
> Why the man dies.   (*Hamlet*, IV.4.27–9)

AN ACCOUNT OF THE TEXT

Timon of Athens was printed for the first time in the Folio of 1623, where it appears as one of the Tragedies. Since no manuscript copy of the play has survived, the Folio is, therefore, the sole authority for the text.

It is not known whether those responsible for bringing together the material included in the Folio originally intended this play to be part of it or not. What is certain is that it was not meant to occupy the place that it does, following *Romeo and Juliet* and preceding *Julius Caesar*. This position should have been filled by *Troilus and Cressida*, for some copies of the Folio contain a cancelled leaf, bearing on one side of it the last page of the text of *Romeo and Juliet* and on the other the first page of the text of *Troilus and Cressida*. It is thus clear that as soon as *Romeo and Juliet* had been completed the printers went on to *Troilus and Cressida*. What then seems to have happened is that Jaggard, the printer of the Folio, found that he had run into copyright troubles over the text of *Troilus and Cressida*, which had been published in quarto form in 1609. He therefore suspended the printing of this play until he could reach an agreement with the owner of the copyright on it, and carried on with the printing of *Julius Caesar*, leaving an estimated space for the text of *Troilus and Cressida* when it should become available. The negotiations over the text of *Troilus and Cressida* must, however, have been difficult and protracted, because the Folio had been completed before anything could be done about it, and eventually it had to be wedged in between the Histories and the Tragedies. In the meantime Jaggard, in despair, had decided to fill the empty space with *Timon of Athens*. But this play is much shorter than *Troilus and Cressida*, and, as a result, there is a gap in the pagination of the Folio. The text of *Timon of Athens* ends on page 98; the next page, which is unnumbered, contains a very rough and inaccurate list of the *dramatis personae*; the following page, also unnumbered, is blank; and the text of *Julius Caesar* begins on the next page, which is numbered 109. The original estimate had, in fact, been a good one; the missing pages would have been required to cope with the text of *Troilus and Cressida*, had that play become available in time to take the space reserved for it.

Since *Timon of Athens* had not been published before, the Folio text must have been set from manuscript; but it is plain that the manuscript in question can never have been used in the playhouse, as it is quite unsuitable for production purposes. In the first place, it contains a cue that is not a cue. At IV.3.353 Apemantus, who is engaged in a dialogue with Timon that has already occupied 150 lines, suddenly says: 'Yonder comes a poet and a painter. . . . When I know not what else to do, I'll see thee again'. On hearing that, one naturally expects him to leave, and to see his place taken by the two characters he has just mentioned. But nothing of the kind happens. The dialogue between him and Timon is resumed for another fifty lines; he is then replaced by the Bandits; they, in turn, give way to Flavius; and the long-awaited Poet and Painter eventually appear nearly two hundred lines after their approach has been announced. Shakespeare clearly changed his mind in the process of writing, but forgot to cancel the misleading words. They would, of course, have been eliminated from any text prepared for stage use.

Secondly, many of the entrances are much too imprecise to be of practical service. The one with which the play opens is a case in point. It reads '*Enter Poet, Painter, Ieweller, Merchant, and Mercer, at seuerall doores*'; but it is evident from what the Poet and the Painter say at I.1.7–8 that only two other characters are on stage with them, and that those two are the Merchant and the Jeweller. The Mercer is a ghost character, the vestige of some idea that Shakespeare had but then discarded. Another misleading direction is to be found at I.2.111. It reads: '*Sound Tucket. Enter the Maskers of Amazons, with Lutes in their hands, dauncing and playing*'. The only words in this direction that are strictly relevant to the point at which they occur are '*Sound*

Tucket', since the Ladies do not enter till line 128. In fact, the greater part of this direction is not a direction at all in the proper sense of the word, but rather jottings for the plot in which the author sketches out what he intends to do next. In this particular case more detailed arrangements for the conduct of the action follow, with '*Enter Seruant*' at line 112 and '*Enter Cupid with the Maske of Ladies*' at line 119. But even this last direction is wrong, since it is plain from the text that Cupid enters alone, makes his speech, and then goes out again, though there is no direction for his exit, before he finally returns with the Ladies at line 128. Moreover, some of the entrances are too indefinite for production purposes. For example, '*Enter Steward with two or three Seruants*' (IV.2.0) is not very helpful to a producer, nor is '*Enter the Bandetti*' (IV.3.399), since the number of actors needed is left unspecified.

On top of all these inexactitudes – and the play is full of them – there is much looseness about the designation of the characters. It seems clear that the '*diuers Friends*', who enter at the opening of III.6 and who are then referred to in the speech headings as '1', '2', '3', and '4', are to be identified with Lucullus, Lucius, Sempronius, and Ventidius. But are the 'two Lords', who come in at I.1.259, Lucullus and Lucius, or not? It would economize in actors and tighten up the whole structure of the play if they were, but there is no clear indication that they are. Similarly, all four of Timon's friends must be present at the banquet in I.2, yet the only one actually named in that scene is Ventidius, apart from the fact that a speech of one line (I.2.128) is headed '*Luc.*', which could signify either Lucullus or Lucius.

All this evidence, together with that presented in the second section of the Introduction (pages 13–18), indicates beyond doubt that the manuscript used in setting up the Folio text was a rough draft which had never been thoroughly revised and prepared for use in the theatre, as do the two contradictory epitaphs on Timon's grave (V.4.70–73), one of which would, presumably, have been cancelled in the final version.

There is, however, one scene at least which suggests that Shakespeare may have begun to revise. In III.2 the Second Stranger tells Lucius that one of Timon's men 'was with the

Lord Lucullus to borrow so many talents' (lines 11–12). The words 'so many' make no sense in this context; a precise number is required, and we know, from the orders Timon gave at II.2.198, that the number should be 'fifty'. The repetition of 'so many' by Lucius at line 24 is possible; but the statement by Servilius that Timon has sent him to Lucius for 'so many talents' (line 37) obviously will not do; Servilius must ask for a definite sum. The reason why 'so many' occurs can only be that Shakespeare had come to realize that he did not know what a talent was worth – it was a very large sum indeed, amounting, even in Elizabethan terms, to something between £100 and £180 – and therefore used these indefinite words as a stop-gap, intending to replace them with a precise number when he had found out what the appropriate figure would be. But the reply of Lucius to the request is a very curious one; he says:

> I know his Lordship is but merry with me;
> He cannot want fifty fiue hundred Talents.
>
> III.2.38–9

Now, it may well be that, as T. J. B. Spencer thinks, the odd phrase 'fifty fiue hundred Talents' is Shakespeare's indication for '*either* fifty *or* five hundred', and that one number or the other would have been deleted later when he had found out what a talent was worth. But the use of the number 'fifty' here in Lucius's would-be jocular reply does suggest that there was a stage in the composition of the scene when Servilius actually asked for 'fifty talents', not for 'so many'. The revision, if revision it is, must have been of a very piecemeal nature, however, for the figure of 'fifty talents' was left standing at II.2.198, at III.1.20, and exceptionally, in a scene where Shakespeare moves on to safer ground by using 'crowns' instead of 'talents', at III.4.94. Moreover the fantastic sum of 'A thousand talents', which Timon tells Flavius to bid the Senate send to him 'o'th'instant' at II.2.204, remains unaltered.

The most difficult question relating to the manuscript used by the printer is whether it was entirely in Shakespeare's hand, as one would expect a rough draft of this kind to be, or whether parts of it at any rate were in another hand. The main evidence in this connexion is spellings. It is now known – thanks to the work of Charlton Hinman – that, as has been thought for some time, the text of *Timon of Athens* was set in type by one man, Compositor B as he is called, the less reliable of the two compositors who were largely responsible for the printing of the Folio. This means that spelling inconsistencies in the text cannot be ascribed to the different spelling habits of two or more compositors, but must go back to the manuscript itself. Yet such inconsistencies do exist, the most striking of them being the variant spellings of the name 'Apemantus'. It is in this form that his name appears when he is first mentioned at I.1.61; but the direction for his entry at I.1.177 is '*Enter Apermantus*', and five lines later Timon greets him as '*Apermantus*'. This happens at the foot of a page where the catchword is given as '*Aper.*'; but, on turning the leaf, one finds the speech prefix '*Ape.*', which is used for the rest of the scene, as is the form '*Apemantus*' in the text itself. He is still '*Apemantus*' in the stage direction at the opening of I.2, but for the rest of this scene he is always '*Apermantus*', and his speech prefix is '*Aper.*'. When he next appears, at II.2.49, it is as '*Apemantus*', and '*Apemantus*' he continues to be, with one lapse into '*Apermantus*' (II.2.78), for the rest of the play.

Rather similar is the case of Ventidius. He is '*Ventidius*' when we first hear of him (I.1.103), but when he enters, at the beginning of I.2, it is as '*Ventigius*', and it is thus that Timon addresses him at line 8. At II.2.225, however, he has become '*Ventiddius*', and at III.3.3 and 9 Sempronius refers to him as '*Ventidgius*'. The mistresses of Alcibiades are '*Phrynia and Timandra*' when they enter the play at IV.3.48, and for the time that they are on stage, but they are transmuted into '*Phrynica and Timandylo*' when the Painter mentions them at V.1.5–6. Finally, there is the rather different matter of Flavius. It is by this name that Timon summons him at I.2.154, and '*Flauius*' he remains, with the speech prefix '*Fla.*', for the rest of the scene. But on his next appearance, at the opening of II.2, he is called '*Steward*', and this is his designation thereafter.

How are these variants, which must go back to the manuscript, to be accounted for? One possibility is that Shakespeare had a collaborator, but this seems unlikely in view of the consistency of the play's imagery. The scene in which there is the highest incidence of anomalous forms, I.2, is closely linked to the rest of the work by its stress on the idea of Timon's friends eating him, and by Apemantus's description of him as 'a setting sun' (line 142) which initiates a train of imagery that runs right through the play to Timon's last speech. The second possibility is that a scribe was employed to produce a fair copy, from which a printer could work, of the rougher parts of Shakespeare's draft, and that the variant spellings may be his. This seems much more probable, but the evidence is so fine-grained that it is far from easy to be sure.

The third and, in the view of the present editor, the most satisfactory solution to the problem, since it fits in with the literary characteristics of the play, is the idea that *Timon of Athens* was written irregularly; that is to say, Shakespeare did not start at the beginning and write straight on until he reached the end, but worked in terms of scenes, roughing out one here, and then turning to another in a different part of the play. In fact, this tragedy has all the appearance of something that was not written, as Ben Jonson's *Volpone*, quite exceptionally for him, was, in five weeks. It lacks unity of inspiration. It will move forward confidently for a time, and then slide off into the tangential, as it does, for example, with the Fool and the Page in II.2. It gives the impression of something that was tinkered about with, probably over a period of time, because it was recalcitrant and refused 'to come out'. Some of the stage directions look suspiciously like the playwright's reminders to himself about who is who. III.3, for example, opens with the words: '*Enter a third seruant with Sempronius, another of Timons Friends*'. The description of Sempronius is quite unnecessary for stage purposes, but it would serve very well as an indication to the author of what he had planned to do in this scene. Even more remarkable, since it comes so early in the play, is the direction with which I.2 begins: '*Hoboyes Playing lowd Musicke. A great Banquet seru'd in: and then, Enter Lord Timon, the States, the Athenian Lords, Ventigius which Timon redeem'd from prison. Then comes dropping after all Apemantus discon-*

tentedly like himselfe.' The statement about Timon's having redeemed Ventidius from prison is irrelevant to the staging of the scene, but it is an excellent guide to what Shakespeare does in the first twenty lines of it. Had I.2 been written immediately after the completion of I.1, however, it would have been unnecessary, because fewer than 180 lines have elapsed since Timon took the steps to free Ventidius. Similarly the words about Apemantus in this direction suggest that before starting on the writing of I.2 Shakespeare found it desirable to jot down what kind of character he had made, or intended to make, of him. The indications that the scene was written out of sequence are strong.

If the idea that *Timon of Athens* was composed in an irregular manner is accepted, many of the puzzles disappear. It is easy to imagine Shakespeare going off to Stratford, for example, and leaving the completed portions of the play behind him in London. But it is still nagging at him, and eventually he sees how one of the missing scenes should go. He therefore sets to work, writing on loose sheets of paper which will later be fitted into place. He remembers the name Apemantus, but he is unsure of the spelling, because, while North gives it as 'Apemantus', it appears as 'Apermantus' in Thomas Lodge's *Wits Miserie* (1596). He therefore uses whichever form comes into his head. In much the same way, when he came to write III.6, he knew that Timon had four flattering friends who must be present at the mock-banquet, but he could not recall the precise names he had given them. Consequently, he labelled them '1', '2', '3', and '4', intending to insert the appropriate names later in the course of revision after the manuscript had been assembled. But, though the revision may have been begun, it was never completed.

When the nature of the material that the compositor must have been dealing with is taken into account, it has to be said that he did well with it. Most of the more obvious errors are of the sort that one expects to find in a Shakespeare text; and the punctuation is a good deal better than that of, for example, *Coriolanus*. A number of passages of verse are set as prose, and some of the prose is set as verse, but this is hardly surprising in

a play which contains speeches such as that of Apemantus at
I.2.37–51. It begins as prose, turns into verse for three lines,
goes back to prose, and concludes with a couplet. Only the final
couplet, which he printed as prose, defeated the compositor.

COLLATIONS

I

Below are listed the substantial departures of this text of *Timon
of Athens* from that of the first Folio (F). The reading of this
edition is to the left of the bracket, and that of the Folio to the
right of it. Folio readings are unmodernized, except that 'long
s' (ſ) is printed as 's'. Obvious minor misprints are not noted,
nor are changes in lineation and punctuation unless they are of
special significance. Some of these alterations were made in one
of the seventeenth-century reprints of the Folio (F2, F3, and
F4); these are indicated. Most of them were first made by
editors during the eighteenth century. Emendations due to
modern editors are gratefully acknowledged. In the following
instances the emendation is the work of the present editor:
I.1.39, III.4.40, III.5.117, IV.3.74–5, IV.3.117, IV.3.252, and
V.4.62.

THE CHARACTERS IN THE PLAY] *not in* F

I.1. 19–20 You are rapt . . . great lord] *prose in* F
21 gum which oozes] Gowne, which vses
25 chafes] chases
39 touches livelier] toutches, liuelier
41 Athens – happy man!] Athens, happy men.
48 tax] wax
75 conceived to scope.] conceyu'd, to scope
90 hands] (F2); hand
fall] (*C. J. Sisson, 1954*); sit
103 Noble Ventidius! Well,] Noble *Ventidius* well:
170 satiety] saciety
181 We'll bear, with] Wee'l beare with

182 Apemantus] *Apermantus*
215 cost] (F3); cast
227 feigned] (F2; *spelt* 'feign'd'); fegin'd
251–5 So, so . . . monkey] *prose in* F
251–2 So, so, there! | Aches] So, so; their Aches
263 more] most
272–5 No, I will . . . thee hence] *verse in* F
278 Come] (F2); Comes

I.2.   8 Ventidius] (F4); *Ventigius*
21 Hanged] (F2); Handg'd
22 Apemantus] (F3); *Apermantus*
28 ever] verie
41 up to't] vp too
44 their meat] (F2); there meate
50–51 Lest they . . . throats] *prose in* F
97 their] there
105 faults, I] Faults. I
114–15 Please you . . . admittance] *verse in* F
120–23 Hail to thee . . . bosom] *prose in* F
123–4 Th'ear, | Taste, touch, smell, all pleased] There tast, touch all, pleas'd
126–7 They're welcome . . . their welcome] *prose in* F
235–8 What a coil's . . . for 'em] *prose in* F

II.2.   4 resumes] resume
42 of broken bonds] of debt, broken Bonds
76 mistress' page] Masters Page
78 Apemantus] *Apermantus*
91–8 E'en so . . . served thief] *irregular verse in* F
96 Ay. Would] I would
104 my mistress' house] my Masters house
133 proposed] (F2); propose
140 found] (F2); sound
147–8 My loved lord – | Though you hear now too late, yet now's a time –] (*J. C. Maxwell, 1957*); my lou'd Lord, | Though you heare now (too late) yet nowes a time,
160 of falsehood] or Falshood
191 Flaminius] *Flauius*

263

II.2.   210   treasure] (F2); Treature
          225, 227 Ventidius] *Ventiddius*
III.1.   57   Unto this hour] vnto his Honor
III.2.   67   spirit] sport
III.3.   3, 9 Ventidius] *Ventidgius*
           13   Thrice] Thriue
           22   and I 'mongst lords] and 'mong'st Lords
           35   Of such ... love] *prose in* F
III.4.   13–14 recoverable. | I fear] recouerable, I feare:
         15–17 'Tis deepest ... Find little] *prose in* F
           40   that; he knows. You are] that, he knowes you are
           59   If 'twill] (F4); If't 'twill
           78   for an answer] for answer
         104–5 They have ... Devils!] *prose in* F
          111   fitly!] fitly?
          112   Sempronius – all.] *Sempronius Vllorxa:* All
         113–16 O my lord ... table] *prose in* F
          115   There is] there's
III.5.   4   bruise him] bruise 'em
           17   An honour] And Honour
         41–2   favour – pardon me, | If I speak like a captain –]
                fauour, pardon me, | If I speake like a Captaine.
           64   Why, I say] (F2); Why say
           68   with 'em] (F2); with him
          109   interest, I myself] interest. I my selfe
          117   worst lands] most Lands
III.6.   19   man here's so] (F4); man heares so
           91   with your] you with
IV.1.   6–7   steads. To general filths | Convert] steeds, to
                generall Filthes. | Conuert
          8–9   hold fast; | Rather than render back,] hold fast |
                Rather then render backe;
           13   Son] (F2); Some
IV.2.   41   does] (F4); do
IV.3.   9   deject] deny't
           10   senator] Senators
           12   pasture] Pastour
                wether's] Brothers

13 lean] (F2); leaue

15 say] (F2); fay

23 fang] phang

74-6 If thou wilt . . . a man] *prose in* F

74 wilt promise] wilt not promise

75 dost not perform] do'st performe

84-8 Be a whore . . . diet] *prose in* F

88 tub-fast] Fubfast

117 That, through the window, bared, bore] That through the window Barne bore

122 thy throat] the throat

130 gold yet? I'll] Gold yet, Ile

157 scolds] scold'st

168-71 More counsel . . . thee again] *prose in* F

186 thy human sons doth hate] the humane Sonnes do hate

196 unctuous] Vnctious

205 fortune] future

244 Outlives incertain] Out-liues: incertaine

252-3 never clasped. But, bred a dog, | Hadst thou] neuer claspt: but bred a Dogge. | Had'st thou

255 drudges] drugges

256 command] command'st

285 my company] thy company

306, 309, 311 medlar . . . medlar . . . meddlers] medler . . . Medler . . . Medlers

322 Women nearest. But men – men] Women neerest, but men: men

348-50 If thou . . . beasts] *irregular verse in* F

353-9 Yonder . . . Apemantus] *irregular verse in* F

365 thee.] thee,

371-2 Away, thou . . . by thee] *prose in* F

384 son and sire] Sunne and fire

399 abhor them] abhorre then

413 He.] He?

416 Both two – and] Both too, and

436 villainy] Villaine
do't,] (F3); doo't.

265

IV.3.   452   'Has] Has

          455   us, not] vs not

     456–7   I'll believe . . . trade] *verse in* F

     472–4   'Has caught . . . master] *prose in* F

          472   'Has] Has

          477   grantest] grunt'st

  480–81   me, I. | All] me, I all

          495   mild] wilde

   511–12   subtle-covetous, | A usuring kindness] subtle, couetous, | If not a Vsuring kindnesse

          528   Ha' sent] Ha's sent

V.1.   3–37   What's to . . . gold for thee] *irregular verse in* F

       5–6   Phrynia and Timandra] *Phrinica* and *Timandylo*

        50   worship; and thy saints for aye] worshipt, and thy Saints for aye:

        65   Let it go naked, men] Let it go, | Naked men

        68   travelled] trauail'd

        69   men] (F2); man

      108   reside] recide

      114   It is in vain] (F3); It is vaine

      124   chance] (F3); chanc'd

      142   general-gross] generall grosse

      145   sense] since

      146   fault] fall

      180   reverend'st] reuerends

      193   through] thorow

V.2.   15   enemy's] Enemies

        17   foe's] Foes

V.3.   2   Who's] (F3); Whose

V.4.   6   stepped] (*F. C. Danchin, 1944*); slept

        28   Shame, that they wanted cunning, in excess] (Shame that they wanted, cunning in excesse)

   30–31   spread. | By decimation and a tithèd death –] spred, | By decimation and a tythed death;

       37   revenges] Reuenge

       44   all together] altogether

       55   Descend] (F2); Defend

       62   remanded] remedied

2

The following lists contain the substantial alterations and addi-
tions that have been made in the present edition to the stage
directions and the speech headings of the Folio text. The
directions in round brackets, such as '(*aside*)', which occur in
this edition, are, with one exception (V.4.70), editorial and are
not included in this list.

Stage directions

I.1.   0 *Enter Poet and Painter, Jeweller and Merchant*]
           Enter Poet, Painter, Ieweller, Merchant, and
           Mercer

      39 *and pass over the stage*] *not in* F

      97 *a Messenger from Ventidius talking with him;*
           Lucilius and other servants following] *not in* F

    155 *Exeunt Lucilius and Old Athenian*] *Exit*

    177 *Apemantus*] *Apermantus*

    247 *Exeunt some attendants*] *not in* F

    259 *Exeunt all but Apemantus*] *Exeunt*

    276 *Exit*] *not in* F

I.2.   0 *Flavius and others attending*] *not in* F
           Alcibiades] *not in* F
           Ventidius] *Ventigius*

      19 *They sit*] *not in* F

      70 *He eats and drinks*] *not in* F

    111 *Sound tucket*] *Sound Tucket. Enter the Maskers of*
           Amazons, with Lutes in their hands, dauncing and
           playing

    119 *Enter Cupid*] *Enter Cupid with the Maske of Ladies*

    126 *Exit Cupid*] *not in* F

    128 *Music. Enter Cupid with a Masque of Ladies as*
           Amazons, with lutes in their hands, dancing and
           playing] (*The directions for the masque appear at*
           lines 111 *and* 119 *in* F.)

    154 *Exeunt Cupid and Ladies*] *Exeunt*

    164 *Enter Flavius, with the casket*] *not in* F

I.2. 174 *Exit Servant] Enter Flauius*
 184 *Exit Servant] not in* F
 190 *Exit Servant] not in* F
 235 *Exeunt all but Apemantus and Timon] Exeunt Lords*
II.1. 35 *He gives the bond to Caphis] not in* F
II.2. 0 *Enter Flavius, Timon's steward] Enter Steward*
 9 *Enter Caphis, with the Servants of Isidore and Varro] Enter Caphis, Isidore, and Varro*
 16 *train, with Alcibiades] Traine.*
 40 *Exeunt Alcibiades and Lords] not in* F
 49 *Exit] (after 'entertained') not in* F
 124 *Flavius] Steward*
 127 *Exeunt Apemantus and Fool] not in* F
 128 *Exeunt Servants] Exeunt*
 191 *Enter Flaminius, Servilius, and another Servant] Enter three Seruants*
 199 *Exeunt Servants] not in* F
III.1. 0 *with Lucullus] with a Lord*
 9 *Exit Servant] not in* F
 38 *Exit Servant] not in* F
 48 *He throws the money back at Lucullus] not in* F
III.2. 61 *Exit Servilius] placed after line 60 in* F
III.3. 0 *a Third Servant of Timon] a third seruant*
III.4. 0 *Enter two Servants of Varro, and the Servant of Lucius, meeting Titus, Hortensius, and other Servants of Timon's creditors, waiting for his coming out] Enter Varro's man, meeting others. All Timons Creditors to wait for his comming out. Then enter Lucius and Hortensius*
 41 *Exit] not in* F
  Flavius] Steward
 60 *Exit] not in* F
 103 *and Flavius] not in* F
III.5. 104 *Exeunt Senators] Exeunt*
III.6. 0 *Music. Servants attending. Enter Lucullus and Lucius, Sempronius and Ventidius, at several doors, senators and lords] Enter diuers Friends at seuerall doores*

24 *Enter Timon and attendants*] *placed after 'Here he comes' in F*

47 *The banquet is brought in*] *placed after line 41 in F*

85 *The dishes are uncovered and seen to be full of warm water and stones*] *not in F*

93 *He throws the water in their faces*] *not in F*

101 *He throws the stones at them, and drives them out*] *not in F*

IV.2. 0 *Flavius*] *Steward*

27 *He gives them money*] *not in F*

29 *Flavius and the Servants embrace each other. Exeunt Servants*] *Embrace and part seuerall wayes*

IV.3. 23 *He digs*] *not in F*

48 *He keeps some of the gold, and buries the rest*] *not in F*

176 *Drum beats*] *not in F*
Exeunt all but Timon] *Exeunt*

178 *he digs*] *not in F*

284 *He eats a root*] *not in F*
He offers Timon food] *not in F*

372 *He throws a stone at Apemantus*] *not in F*

382 *He addresses the gold*] *not in F*

398 *Enter the Bandits*] *Enter the Bandetti ; placed after line 399 in F*

459 *Exeunt Bandits*] *Exit Theeues*
Enter Flavius] *Enter the Steward to Timon*

540 *Exit Flavius ; Timon retires to his cave at the rear of the stage*] *Exit*

V.1. 52 *He comes forward*] *not in F*

113 *He beats them off the stage, and retires to his cave*] *Exeunt*
Flavius] *Steward*

V.2. 13 *Enter the two other Senators, from Timon*] *Enter the other Senators*

V.3. 2 *He reads*] *not in F*

V.4. 2 *The Trumpeter sounds a parley*] *Sounds a Parly*

64 *The Senators descend*] *not in F*
Enter Soldier] *Enter a Messenger*

Speech headings

I.1.	9	MERCHANT] *Mer. (and throughout the scene)*
	114–50	OLD ATHENIAN] *Oldm.*
	260	FIRST LORD] *1. Lord*
	262	FIRST LORD] *1 (and subsequently)*
	264	SECOND LORD] *2 (and subsequently)*
	288	FIRST LORD] *line assigned to '2' in F*
I.2.	1	VENTIDIUS] *Ventig.*
	21	APEMANTUS] *Aper. (and throughout the scene)*
	128	FIRST LORD] *Luc.*
	149	FIRST LADY] *1 Lord.*
	213	THIRD LORD] *1. L.*
II.2.	1	FLAVIUS] *Stew. (and for the rest of the play)*
	11	VARRO'S SERVANT] *Var. (and throughout the scene)*
	13	ISIDORE'S SERVANT] *Isid. (and throughout the scene)*
	81	PAGE] *Boy.*
III.2.	3	FIRST STRANGER] *1 (and throughout the scene)*
	10	SECOND STRANGER] *2 (and throughout the scene)*
	27	LUCIUS] *Lucil.*
	78	THIRD STRANGER] *3*
III.4.	1	FIRST VARRO'S SERVANT] *Var. man.*
	3	LUCIUS'S SERVANT] *Luci. (and throughout the scene)*
	30, 32	FIRST VARRO'S SERVANT] *Varro.*
	45	SECOND VARRO'S SERVANT] *2. Varro. (and throughout the scene)*
	61	FIRST VARRO'S SERVANT] *1. Varro. (and for the rest of the scene)*
	88	HORTENSIUS] *1. Var.*
	89	BOTH VARRO'S SERVANTS] *2. Var.*
III.5.	4, 68, 91	SECOND SENATOR] *2*
	6, 63	FIRST SENATOR] *1 (and for the rest of the scene)*
	92	THIRD SENATOR] *3*
III.6.	1	LUCULLUS] *1 (and throughout the scene)*
	2–107	LUCIUS] *2*

51–108 SEMPRONIUS] 3

    55 LUCULLUS *and* LUCIUS] *Both.*

    86 SOME] *Some speake.*

    87 OTHERS] *Some other.*

    109 VENTIDIUS] 4

    113 SEMPRONIUS] 2

    114 LUCIUS] 3

IV.2.   1, 5 FIRST SERVANT] 1

    8 SECOND SERVANT] 2

    17 THIRD SERVANT] 3

IV.3. 133, 150, 168 PHRYNIA *and* TIMANDRA] *Both.*

    400 FIRST BANDIT] 1 (*and throughout the scene*)

    404 SECOND BANDIT] 2 (*and throughout the scene*)

    405 THIRD BANDIT] 3

    411 THIRD BANDIT] *All.*

    413 THIRD BANDIT] 3

V.1.   73 POET *and* PAINTER] *Both.* (*and throughout the scene*)

    117 FIRST SENATOR] 1 (*and for the rest of the scene*)

    119 SECOND SENATOR] 2 (*and for the rest of the scene*)

V.2.   1, 13 THIRD SENATOR] 1

    5 FOURTH SENATOR] 2

    14 FIRST SENATOR] 3

V.4.   18 SECOND SENATOR] 2 (*and for the rest of the scene*)

    22 FIRST SENATOR] 1 (*and for the rest of the scene*)

    65 SOLDIER] *Mes.*

3

Below are listed instances where the present edition substantially preserves readings of the first Folio that have often, with some plausibility, been emended, or introduces an emendation that is different from the one normally accepted. Emendations frequently found in modern editions of the play are given after the square bracket.

I.1.   90 fall] (F1: sit); slip

    105 must need] (F1: must neede); most needs (F3)

I.2.   103 O, joy's] (F1: Oh ioyes); O joy

II.1.	13	sound] found
	34	I go, sir?] *omitted by some editors*
	35	in. Come.] in compt
II.2.	42	of broken bonds] (F1: of debt, broken Bonds); of date-broke bonds
	75	Good,] Good!
III.3.	5	Owes] Owe (F2)
III.5.	14	his fate] this fault
	22	behove] (F1: behooue); behave
	51	fellow] felon
III.6.	80	*leg*] (F1: *legge*); lag
IV.1.	21	yet] let
IV.3.	12	wether's] (F1: Brothers); rother's
	18	All's obliquy] (F1: All's obliquie); All is oblique
	39	wappened] (F1: wappen'd); wappered
	117	window, bared] (F1: window Barne); window-bars
	224	moist] (F1: moyst); mossed
	226	when] where
	435	rob. Take] (F1: Rob: Take); rob, takes
	528	Ha' sent] (F1: Ha's sent); Have sent
V.1.	131	cantherizing] cauterizing
	146	fault] (F1: fall); fail
V.2.	8	made] had
V.4.	24	grief] (F1: greefe); griefs
	62	remanded] (F1: remedied); rendered